Teach Yourself VISUAL
Python

by Guy Hart-Davis and
Ted Hart-Davis

Visual
A Wiley Brand

Teach Yourself VISUALLY™ Python®

Copyright © 2022 by John Wiley & Sons, Inc. All rights reserved.

Published by John Wiley & Sons, Inc., Hoboken, New Jersey.

Published simultaneously in Canada and the United Kingdom.

978-1-119-86025-9

978-1-119-86026-6 (ebk.)

978-1-119-86027-3 (ebk.)

For general information on our other products and services or for technical support, please contact our Customer Care Department within the United States at (800) 762-2974, outside the United States at (317) 572-3993 or fax (317) 572-4002.

If you believe you've found a mistake in this book, please bring it to our attention by emailing our reader support team at wileysupport@ wiley.com with the subject line "Possible Book Errata Submission."

Wiley also publishes its books in a variety of electronic formats. Some content that appears in print may not be available in electronic formats. For more information about Wiley products, visit our web site at www.wiley.com.

Library of Congress Control Number: 2022937470

Cover images: © Misha Shutkevych/Getty Images; Screenshot Courtesy of Guy Hart-Davis and Ted Hart-Davis

Cover design: Wiley

SKY10067910_022124

About the Authors

Guy Hart-Davis is the author of more than 175 computer books, including *Teach Yourself VISUALLY MacBook Pro and MacBook Air*; *Teach Yourself VISUALLY iPhone 12, 12 Pro, and 12 Pro Max*; *Teach Yourself VISUALLY iPad*; *Teach Yourself VISUALLY Google Workspace*; *Teach Yourself VISUALLY Chromebook*; and *Teach Yourself VISUALLY Word 2019*.

Ted Hart-Davis is the coauthor of *Samsung Galaxy Note 10 Photography* and is a programmer, photographer, and folk musician. He is a maintainer and administrator of the historic Minecraft server MinecraftOnline.com and studies cybersecurity and forensics at Edinburgh Napier University.

Authors' Acknowledgments

Our thanks go to the many people who turned this manuscript into the highly graphical book you are holding. In particular, we thank Devon Lewis for asking us to write the book; Lynn Northrup for keeping us on track; Kim Wimpsett for skillfully editing the text; Doug Holland for reviewing the book for technical accuracy and contributing helpful suggestions; Straive for laying out the book; and Debbye Butler for proofreading the pages.

How to Use This Book

Who This Book Is For

This book is for the reader who has never used this particular technology or software application. It is also for readers who want to expand their knowledge.

The Conventions in This Book

❶ Steps

This book uses a step-by-step format to guide you easily through each task. **Numbered steps** are actions you must do; **bulleted steps** clarify a point, step, or optional feature; and **indented steps** give you the result.

❷ Notes

Notes give additional information — special conditions that may occur during an operation, a situation that you want to avoid, or a cross-reference to a related area of the book.

❸ Icons and Buttons

Icons and buttons show you exactly what you need to click to perform a step.

❹ Tips

Tips offer additional information, including warnings and shortcuts.

❺ Bold

Bold type shows command names, options, and text or numbers you must type.

❻ Italics

Italic type introduces and defines a new term.

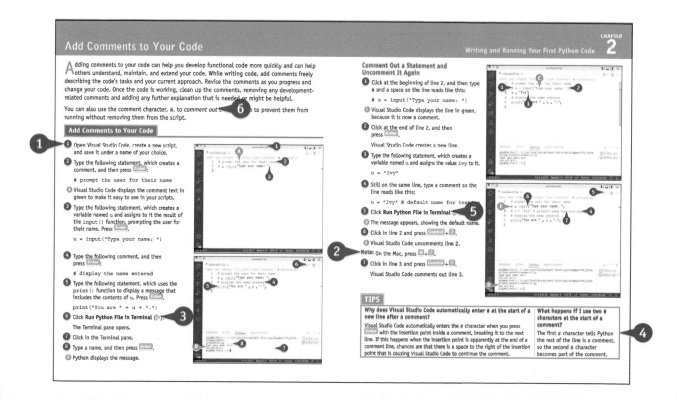

Table of Contents

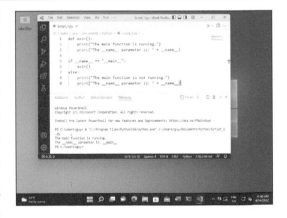

Chapter 3   Getting Started with Variables

Chapter 4   Working with Files and Directories

Table of Contents

| Chapter 6 | Making Decisions with `if` Statements |

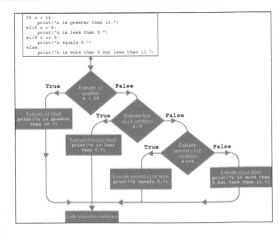

Chapter 7 Repeating Actions with Loops

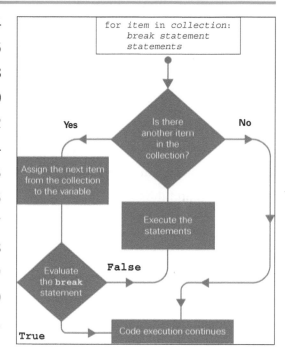

Chapter 8 Working with Functions

Table of Contents

```python
3    def make_title(sT):
4        rlist = []
5        rs = ""
6        for word in sT.split():
7            if not word.isupper() and word not in lwords:
8                word = word.title()
9            rlist.append(word)
10
11        if not rlist[0].isupper():
12            rlist[0] = rlist[0].title()
13        if not rlist[-1].isupper():
14            rlist[-1] = rlist[-1].title()
15
16        for word in rlist:
17            rs += " " + word
18
19        rs = rs.strip()
20        return rs
21
22   def main():
23       sT = input("Enter the title: ")
24       print(make_title(sT))
25
26   if __name__ == "__main__":
27       main()
```

```python
1    adrFile = "addresses.csv"
2    adrs=[]
3    try:
4        f = open(adrFile,'r')
5        try:
6            for line in f.readlines():
7                currAdr=[]
8                for field in line.strip('\n').split(','):
9                    currAdr.append(field)
10               adrs.append(currAdr)
11       except:
12           print("An error occurred in the inner try... except block.")
13   except FileNotFoundError:
14       print(f"The file '{adrFile}' was not found.")
15   except:
16       print("An error occurred in the outer try... except block.")
17   else:
18       f.close()
19       print(adrs)
```

```
sam@vubuntu: ~
sam@vubuntu:~$ python3
Python 3.8.10 (default, Nov 26 2021, 20:14:08)
[GCC 9.3.0] on linux
Type "help", "copyright", "credits" or "license" for more information.
>>> n1 = ["Sam", "George"]
>>> print(n1)
['Sam', 'George']
>>> n2 = ["Antonia", "Brett"]
>>> print(n2)
['Antonia', 'Brett']
>>> n1.insert(1, "Helen")
>>> print(n1)
['Sam', 'Helen', 'George']
>>> n1.extend(n2)
>>> print(n1)
['Sam', 'Helen', 'George', 'Antonia', 'Brett']
>>> n1.append("Sia")
>>> print(n1)
['Sam', 'Helen', 'George', 'Antonia', 'Brett', 'Sia']
>>> quit()
sam@vubuntu:~$
```

```
                                        class6
class6  2 ×
Users › guy › Dropbox › TYV_Python › Code › Classes › class6 › BranchOffice › cm2cf
  1   class BranchOffice():
  2       company = "CheeseWheat Associates"
  3       sector = "food science"
  4       @classmethod
  5       def showClassInfo(self):
  6           ci = self.company + ", a "
  7           ci = ci + self.sector + " trendsetter"
  8           return ci
  9       def __init__(self, city, street, state, zip, manager):
 10           self.city = city
 11           self.street = street
 12           self.state = state
 13           self.zip = zip
 14           self.manager = manager
 15       def getInfo(self):
 16           br = (
 17               f"{self.city} Office\n\n"
 18               f"Manager: {self.manager}\n\n"
 19               f"{self.street}\n"
 20               f"{self.city}, {self.state}  {self.zip}"
 21           )
 22           return br
 23       @staticmethod
 24       def cm2cf(n3):
 25
 26       a = BranchOffice("Arcata", "442 Front", "CA", "95221-1111", "Aurora
       Smith")
```

## CHAPTER 1

Getting Ready to Work with Python

In this chapter, you learn what Python is and get ready to work with it. You choose the version of Python that suits your needs and then install that version if your computer does not already have it. You also install and configure your main tool for working with Python, a powerful code editor/integrated development environment called Visual Studio Code.

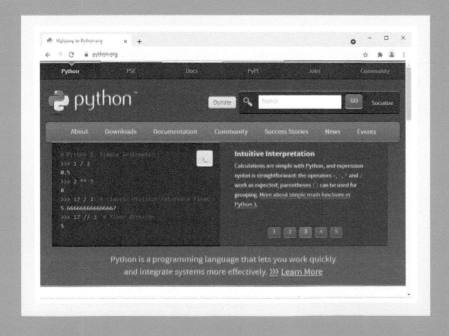

Understanding What Python Is and Does

Python is a programming language that is used both widely and for many different purposes. Python enables you to write applications that work on many different computing platforms, including Microsoft Windows, Apple's macOS, and Linux. Python is especially useful for automating routine tasks, thus enabling yourself and your colleagues to get more work done in less time.

A Dutch programmer named Guido van Rossum began work on Python in the late 1980s, eventually releasing the first version as Python 0.9.0 in 1991. Since 2001, Python has been run by a U.S.-based nonprofit organization called the Python Software Foundation.

Understanding What Python Is

A *programming language* is a type of computer language that is used to implement *algorithms*, which are instructions for performing particular actions — in other words, to make the computer do what the programmer wants it to do.

Python is a general-purpose programming language rather than a domain-specific programming language. As you might guess, a *general-purpose programming language* is a programming language designed for general programming use rather than for use in a specific area of computing. By contrast, a *domain-specific programming language* is a programming language designed for use in a specific area of computing. For example, Wolfram Mathematica is a programming language designed for symbolic mathematics; it is not designed for, and is not suitable for, general programming use, so it is domain specific.

Understanding Cross-Platform Programming

Python enables you to write applications that work on many different computing platforms. A *computing platform* means the hardware and operating system that together constitute a functional computer.

This book covers three widely used computing platforms:

- **PC hardware running Microsoft's Windows operating system.** This book uses Windows 10 and Windows 11 for examples.
- **Apple Macintosh hardware running Apple's macOS operating system.** This book uses macOS version 12, also known as macOS Monterey, for examples.
- **PC hardware running the Linux operating system.** Linux comes in many different versions, called *distributions*. This book uses the popular Ubuntu distribution for Linux examples.

Python fully supports the Windows, Mac, and Linux platforms, but it also supports many other platforms. These platforms range from those for personal devices, such as Apple's iOS operating system and iPhones, all the way up to "big-iron" platforms for minicomputers and mainframes, such as IBM's AIX and HP's HP-UX. Python versions for some platforms come from third-party vendors.

Understanding Who Uses Python

Many different types of programmers use Python. Here are two examples:

- Web developers use Python to create web services that provide custom information in response to requests they receive. For example, when you visit a web forum, Python may be generating some or all parts of the page that the server sends to your browser.
- Scientists, mathematicians, and engineers across many fields use Python to perform data analysis, because Python provides powerful and convenient tools for processing and applying complex equations to statistical data.

Know Where You Can Get Python

You can download Python for free from the Python Software Foundation's website, www.python.org. However, you may not need to download Python, because it may already be installed on your computer.

Windows typically does not include Python; see the section "Install Python on Windows," later in this chapter, for instructions on installing Python.

macOS includes Python 2. See the section "Install Python on the Mac," later in this chapter, for instructions on seeing which version a Mac contains and updating Python if necessary.

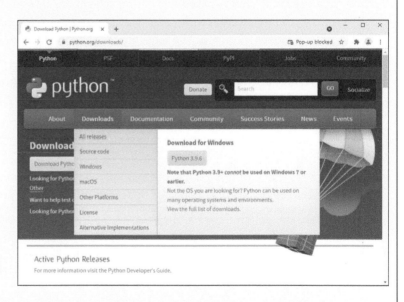

Many Linux distributions include one or more versions of Python. As of this writing, more distributions include Python 2 than include Python 3, but some distributions include both versions; see the following section, "Choose the Right Version of Python." See the section "Install Python on Linux If Necessary," later in this chapter, for instructions on checking the version and updating if necessary.

To find versions of Python for iOS or iPadOS, open the App Store app on the iPhone or iPad and search for **python**. Pythonista is a popular app, but there are plenty of other choices. Similarly, to find versions of Python for Android, open the Play Store app on your Android device and search for **python**.

Choose the Right Version of Python

As of this writing, two major versions of Python are in use: Python 2 and Python 3. Before you download and install Python on your computer, you should determine which version of Python will be best for your needs. This will most likely be Python 3, because Python 2 is out of date and the Python Software Foundation no longer supports it.

This section explains what you need to know about Python 2 and Python 3. It also explains the two types of Python builds that are available — stable builds and development builds — and advises you which build type to get.

Understanding Python 2 and Python 3

Two major versions of Python are currently in wide use: Python 2, released in 2000, and Python 3, released in 2008.

Each version uses a sequence-based numbering scheme for intermediate releases. For example, "Python 2.7.1" means Python 2, the seventh minor version, and the first update to that minor version. Similarly, "Python 3.10.0" means Python 3, the tenth minor version, and the initial release of that minor version.

The Python Software Foundation officially discontinued, or "sunset," Python 2 on January 1, 2020. *Sunsetting* means that the Python Software Foundation will not develop Python 2 any further, even if researchers discover serious security issues in it. Because Python 2 has been sunset, the Python Software Foundation recommends that all users upgrade to Python 3 as soon as possible. The final version of Python 2 was 2.7.18.

With most software, such as business productivity apps or multimedia apps, upgrading to a newer version is a straightforward and painless procedure: You upgrade to the new version, and everything still works, even if the user interface has changed and the new version of the app provides extra features.

Python 3 offers compelling new features that Python 2 does not have; even better, Python 3 typically runs faster than Python 2. However, Python 3 is not fully compatible with Python 2, and some Python 2 code may not run successfully in Python 3. This is why many companies and organizations still have not upgraded from Python 2 to Python 3. The more Python 2 code a company or organization has built up, the more time, effort, and expense it will take to upgrade to Python 3.

Which Version of Python Do You Need?

You almost certainly need Python 3 unless your workplace uses Python 2 and is not migrating to Python 3. For example, your employer may have developed substantial amounts of Python 2 code that is not fully compatible with Python 3 and may therefore be sticking with Python 2.

If you are planning to start developing code from scratch, you should definitely choose Python 3 rather than Python 2.

You can install both Python 2 and Python 3 alongside each other and use each version when you need it.

macOS and many Linux distributions include Python 2 because they require Python 2 to run some software packages included with the operating system or distribution. Because of this requirement, you should not uninstall Python 2, even if you do not need it. Instead, simply leave Python 2 alone, install Python 3, and use Python 3 for development.

Windows does not need Python 2, so normally, you should install Python 2 on Windows only if you need it.

What Are the Two Build Types of Python?

Python.org makes available two types of builds of Python, stable builds and development builds:

Stable build. A *stable build* is a build that has been fully tested and approved for distribution.

Development build. A *development build* is an experimental build used for testing and compatibility. Development testers provide feedback on changes and new features before they are finalized and added to stable builds.

You may also see Python builds described as "release candidates." A *release candidate* is a near-final development build made available — usually to a wide audience — for final testing. A release candidate is stable in theory but not always so in practice.

Which Build Type Should You Get?

You will almost always want to get a stable build of Python rather than a development build. Normally, you will want to get the latest stable build of Python so that you have access to the latest features. However, if your company, organization, or school is using an older stable build of Python, it will likely want you to use that build for compatibility.

When Will Python 4 Be Released?

The Python Software Foundation has not announced a release date for Python 4. In fact, Guido van Rossum has cast doubt on whether there will ever be Python 4, given how difficult and protracted the move from Python 2 to Python 3 turned out to be. Instead, the Python Software Foundation is continuing to develop Python 3.

As of this writing, the current stable version of Python is 3.10.4. Future versions of Python 3 are likely to use numbering such as 3.11.*x*, 3.12.*x*, and so on.

Install Python on Windows

Windows has no version of Python installed by default, so you will need to install Python unless you have already installed it or an administrator has installed it for you.

You can install Python either by using the Microsoft Store app or by downloading and running the Python installer from the Python Software Foundation. Microsoft recommends using the Microsoft Store app, but we recommend downloading the Python installer, because this enables you to make the latest version of Python available to the Visual Studio Code editor app, which you will meet later in this chapter.

Install Python on Windows

Download and Install Python on Windows

1 Open a browser window and go to the Python Software Foundation website, www.python.org.

2 Hold the pointer over Downloads.

A A pop-up window appears.

B The web page selects the Windows tab, because it detects your computer is running Windows.

3 Click the Python button under the Download for Windows heading.

This button shows the Python version, such as **Python 3.10.0** in the example.

The browser downloads the file.

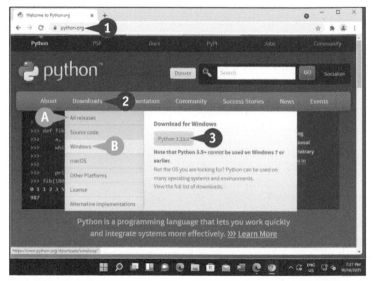

4 Open the downloaded file from the browser. For example, in Chrome, click **Actions** (∧ changes to ∨) to open the pop-up menu, and then click **Open** to open the file.

Note: In Microsoft Edge, click **Downloads** (⤓) to display the Downloads panel, locate the Python file you downloaded, and then click **Open file** beneath its name.

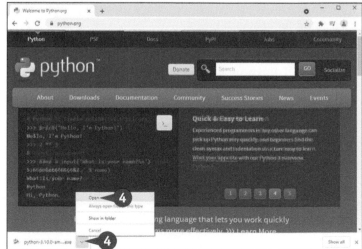

8

The Python Setup Wizard opens and displays the Install Python screen.

5 Select **Install launcher for all users** (☑) to install the Python launcher for all users of this computer. This is usually helpful.

Note: If an earlier version of Python is installed on the PC, the Upgrade Now button appears. See the subsection "Upgrade Python on Windows," later in this section.

6 Select **Add Python to PATH** (☑) to add the location of the Python executable file to your Windows PATH statement. Doing so enables Windows to find Python and is usually helpful.

C You can click **Install Now** to install Python and all its components for yourself, not for other users.

7 Click **Customize installation**.

The Optional Features screen appears.

8 Deselect the check box for any feature you do not want to install. For example, deselect **tcl/tk and IDLE** (☐) if you do not want to install the IDLE development environment.

9 Click **Next**.

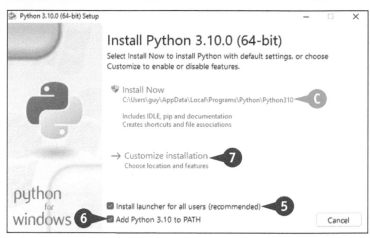

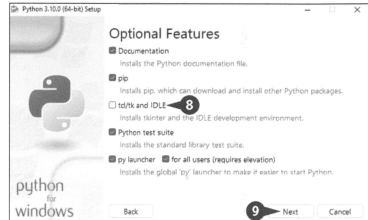

TIP

Which apps does the Python installation include?
The Python installation installs an app called Python — for example, Python 3.10 — and an app called IDLE, an integrated development environment for Python. The IDLE app's name includes the version of Python, such as IDLE (Python 3.10).

You can use the IDLE integrated development environment to create and test Python code, but we recommend you use Visual Studio Code instead, because it provides more features and is widely used. See the section "Download and Install Visual Studio Code," later in this chapter, for information on getting Visual Studio Code.

continued ▶

Whenever installing Python, you can choose to install the Python launcher component for just yourself or for all users. Separately, you can choose to install the main Python app and other components either for just yourself or for all users of your computer. You can also add the Python program location to your Windows PATH, which enables Windows to find Python without you having to specify the path explicitly.

After installing Python, you can update it to the latest version by downloading the latest installer from the Python Software Foundation website, running the installer, and clicking **Upgrade**.

Install Python on Windows (continued)

Download and Install Python on Windows (continued)

The Advanced Options screen appears.

Note: By default, the Python Setup Wizard installs Python and the components you choose only for you, not for all users of your computer.

Ⓓ The default install location is within the AppData folder in your user account. This location is available only to you.

⑩ Click **Install for all users** (☐ changes to ☑).

Ⓔ The install location changes to a Python folder within your computer's Program Files folder. This location is available to all users.

Ⓕ You can click **Browse** and select a different install location if necessary. Normally, the default location works well.

⑪ Click **Install**.

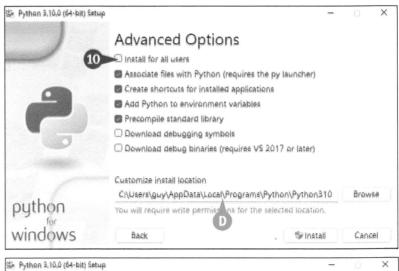

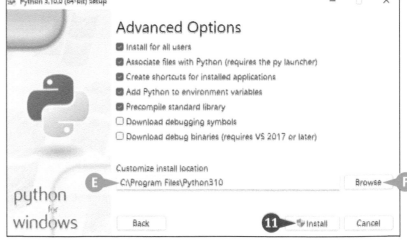

Note: If the User Account Control dialog box opens, prompting you to decide whether to allow the Python Setup Wizard to make changes to your computer, click **Yes**.

The Python Setup Wizard installs the components you chose.

The Setup Was Successful screen appears.

12 If you want to disable the path length limit, click **Disable path length limit**, and then click **Yes** in the User Account Control dialog box that appears.

13 Click **Close**.

The Python Setup Wizard closes.

Upgrade Python on Windows

1 Follow steps **1** to **4** in the previous subsection to download the Windows installer for the latest version of Python from the Python Software Foundation website, www.python.org, and open the installer file.

The Python Setup Wizard screen appears.

2 Click **Upgrade Now** to upgrade Python but retain all your settings.

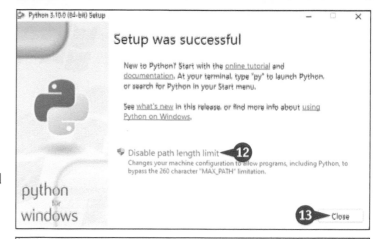

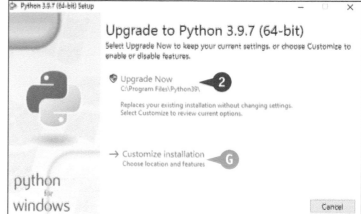

G If you want to change your settings, click **Customize installation**, and then make your choices on the Options screen and the Advanced Options screen.

TIP

What is the path length limit, and should I disable it?
The Windows path is a text variable that tells Windows where to find important items. For example, `PATH=C:\Windows;C:\Program Files` tells Windows where to find the Windows folder and the Program Files folder. Selecting **Add Python to PATH** (☑) adds Python's folder to the path, so Windows can find Python without you having to specify the folder.

The PATH variable has a length limit of 260 characters for backward compatibility with older versions of Windows. However, this limit may cause errors when compiling and running Python code that uses long paths. Normally, you should click **Disable path length limit** on the Setup Was Successful screen to disable the path length limit.

Install Python on the Mac

Whether it has an Intel CPU or an Apple Silicon CPU, your Mac almost certainly has a version of Python installed — but it is most likely to have only Python 2. If so, you will want to install Python 3, probably the latest stable version of it.

In this section, you use the Terminal app in macOS to check whether Python is installed and, if so, which version. Then, if needed, you can download and install a newer version of Python.

Install Python on the Mac

Check Which Version of Python Is Installed on Your Mac

1 Click **Launchpad** (⊞).

Launchpad opens.

2 Start typing **terminal**.

Launchpad narrows the selection to the apps that include what you have typed.

3 Click **Terminal** (▣).

A Terminal window opens.

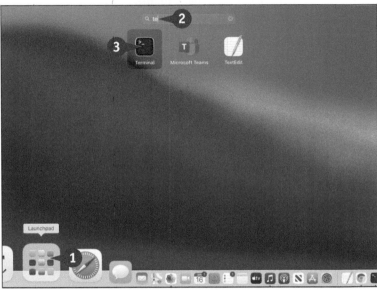

4 Type **python3** and press Return.

Note: If Terminal displays the version of Python, as shown in the final screen of this section, go to step **8**. Python 3 is already installed on your Mac.

A A dialog box opens, prompting you to install the command-line developer tools.

5 Click **Install**.

The Downloading Software dialog box opens, showing a progress readout.

When the installation completes, a The Software Was Installed dialog box opens.

6 Click **Done**.

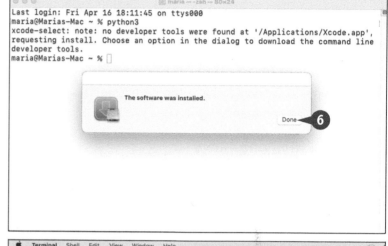

The dialog box closes.

The Terminal window becomes active again.

7 Type **python3** and press Return.

B The version of Python appears.

8 Type **quit()** or press Ctrl + D.

The Python app quits.

9 Press ⌘ + Q.

The Terminal app quits, and the Terminal window closes.

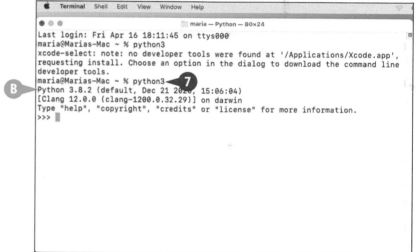

How can I update the version of Python on my Mac?

The easiest way to update the version of Python on your Mac is to download the latest Python installer file for macOS from the Python Software Foundation website, www.python.org; run the installer; and click **Upgrade Now**.

On a Mac that you administer yourself, another option is to install the Homebrew package manager, which you can download for free from the Homebrew website, https://brew.sh. After installing Homebrew, you can quickly update Python by opening the Terminal app and running the appropriate command.

Install Python on Linux If Necessary

Many Linux distributions include a version of Python, so you may not need to install Python on Linux. In this section, you check whether Python is already installed on your Linux box and install it if it is not. If Python is already installed but is out of date, you update it to the latest version available for your Linux distribution.

This section uses Ubuntu Linux as the example and provides brief notes on other widely used Linux distributions. You need to have the permission to run commands as superuser — as the root user — using the `sudo` command.

Install Python on Linux If Necessary

Verify That Python Is Installed on Linux

1 Open a Terminal window. For example, on Ubuntu:

Ⓐ Click **Show Applications** (▦).

The Activities screen appears.

Ⓑ Type **terminal**.

Matching search results appear.

Ⓒ Click **Terminal** (▣ or similar).

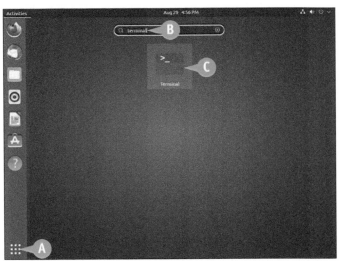

A Terminal window opens.

2 Type **python3** and press Enter.

Ⓓ If Terminal displays details of the Python version, such as Python 3.9.5, Python is installed.

Ⓔ You can quit Python by typing **quit()** and pressing Enter. Alternatively, press Ctrl + D.

Note: If you see a message saying that Python was not found, you need to install Python. In the Terminal window, type **sudo apt install python3** and press Enter. If Terminal prompts you for your password, type it and press Enter. Linux then downloads and installs Python.

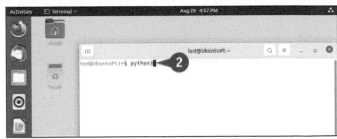

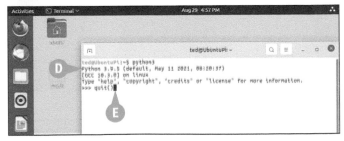

Update Python on Linux

1 Open a Terminal window. For example, on Ubuntu, click **Show Applications** (▦), type **terminal**, and then click **Terminal** (▣).

2 Type the `sudo apt update` command and press Enter.

Linux prompts you for your password.

3 Type your password and press Enter.

Linux downloads the latest list of software packages available.

F Terminal displays information about available upgrades.

4 Type the `sudo apt upgrade` command and press Enter.

Note: If Terminal displays information about the amount of additional disk space that will be used and prompts you to decide whether to continue, type **y** and press Enter.

Linux downloads and installs the updates.

G When the upgrade finishes, the prompt reappears.

You can then type **python3** and press Enter to see the Python version that has been installed.

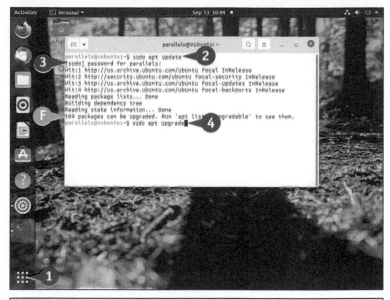

TIP

How do I install Python on other Linux distributions?

Generally, you would install Python from your distribution's application repository.

Here are the commands for other popular distributions:

- Fedora: `sudo dnf install python3`
- Arch: `sudo pacman -S python3`
- SUSE: `sudo rpm install python3`
- Other Debian-based distributions: `sudo apt install python3`

Learn About Development Tools for Python

Python code consists of plain text with structured layout, so you can create the code in any app that can output plain text. For example, you can create Python code in the Notepad text editor on Windows or in the TextEdit text editor on macOS.

But unless you like doing things the hard way, you will be better off using an app that is designed for creating code and that provides features to help you create code that is both correct and correctly formatted. This app can be either a code editor or an integrated development environment, IDE for short.

What Is a Code Editor?

A *code editor* is an app that is designed and built to make the writing of programming code easier, faster, and more efficient. While you can write code using any text editor or word processor, these apps do not provide the programming-specific features that a code editor gives you.

A code editor typically includes features such as the following:

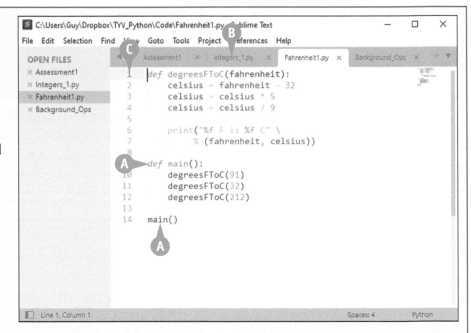

- **Syntax evaluation and highlighting.** As you program, the editor determines the code's different elements and highlights them in different colors and font styles (A) to help you identify them visually.
- **Automatic completion of code.** When you start typing a keyword or another known element, the code editor displays suggestions for completing it. By accepting these suggestions, you can work faster.
- **Multifile interface.** Whereas most word processors keep each document in a separate window, many code editors use a tabbed interface (B) that enables you to open multiple files in the same window and switch quickly from one file to another by clicking the appropriate tab. Many text editors likewise use a tabbed interface.
- **Line numbers.** The code editor automatically displays line numbers (C) so that you can easily navigate through your code.

16

What Is an Integrated Development Environment?

An *integrated development environment*, or IDE, is an application designed for developing code. The development environment is integrated because you can both write the code in the environment and run the code to make sure it works correctly.

An IDE typically provides similar features to those in a code editor, such as syntax evaluation and highlighting, automatic code completion,

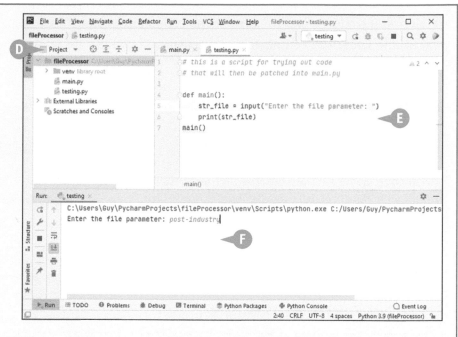

and the ability to switch easily among multiple files. To these features the IDE adds tools for testing and debugging your code.

For example, the figure shows the PyCharm IDE. In the upper-left corner is the Project pane (D), which enables you to navigate among the files in your current project; gives you access to external libraries, repositories containing code you can add; and provides a scratch window for quick work and notes, and consoles for running code outside the IDE. In the upper-right corner is the Code pane (E), where you write your code. And across the bottom is the Run window (F), in which the output from your running code appears.

Should I Use a Code Editor, an IDE, or Both?

Which coding tools you use for Python is very much a personal preference. That said, you will almost certainly want to use an IDE for debugging your Python code. The question then becomes whether you want to use a code editor as well as an IDE.

You may want to use both a code editor and an IDE for different aspects of your work developing code in Python. Experiment with different tools to discover which tool or combination of tools works best for you.

continued ▶

When it comes to development tools for Python, there are a lot of choices. Many Python-capable code editors and IDEs are available, offering various combinations of features likely to appeal to different developers. Most of these code editors and IDEs work for multiple — or many — programming languages, but you can find IDEs built to work only with Python.

This section introduces you to some of the code editors and IDEs you may want to explore, including Visual Studio Code, the coding tool we recommend you use for working with Python.

Which IDEs Can I Use for Creating Python Code?

You can use a bewildering variety of IDEs for creating Python code. Some IDEs are designed for use only with Python, whereas other IDEs are designed for use with various programming languages. Some IDEs are much fuller featured than others and provide more help as you work. Extra help may be welcome while you are starting to use Python but may become annoying as you gain more experience.

Here are three examples of IDEs for Python:

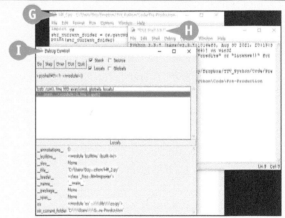

- **IDLE.** IDLE is a minimalist IDE that is included in the Python packages you can download from the Python Software Foundation website, www.python.org. IDLE, shown in the figure, uses multiple separate windows for the Editor (G), the Shell (H), and features such as Debug Control (I) rather than displaying multiple panes inside a single window.
- **PyCharm.** PyCharm (www.jetbrains.com/pycharm) is a full-featured IDE that comes in two editions. Normally, you would want the Community Edition, which is free and works only with Python. The other edition, Professional, is a paid version that has a free trial and works with HTML, JavaScript, and SQL, as well as Python.
- **Thonny.** Thonny (https://thonny.org) is a lightweight IDE designed to help beginners come to grips with Python coding. Thonny offers three modes for different levels of experience: Simple Mode for beginners, Regular Mode for those who need greater control, and Expert Mode for advanced users. The accompanying figure shows Regular Mode.

Which Code Editors Can I Use for Python?

You have a wide choice of code editors suitable for programming Python. Here are three examples of code editors well worth your consideration:

- **Sublime Text.** Sublime Text, shown in the "What Is a Code Editor?" sub-section earlier in this section, is a powerful text editor with a minimal-ist interface that provides as much space as possible for displaying your code files. Sublime Text supports more than 40 other programming languages as well as Python. You can download an evaluation version of the app from the Sublime Text website, www.sublimetext.com; the app then costs $99 for a 3-year subscription.

- **Atom.** Atom, shown on this page, is a highly customizable code editor that makes working with multiple files easy. As of this writing, Atom seems to place greater demands on the computer running it than the other code editors listed here; as a result, Atom tends to run more slowly. Atom is free to download from the Atom website, https://atom.io.

- **Visual Studio Code.** Visual Studio Code is a powerful code editor developed by Microsoft. It is separate from Microsoft's Visual Studio IDE and runs on Windows, macOS, and Linux. See the following section for more information.

Which Code Editor or IDE Does This Book Recommend for Python?

This book recommends that you use Visual Studio Code as your main coding tool for working with Python, at least while using this book. Visual Studio Code is free, provides powerful coding features, and is widely used for various programming languages from C++ and C# to PHP and PowerShell.

While Visual Studio Code is generally described as a code editor, it also provides full-scale debugging features, so it is effectively also an IDE.

The following section, "Download and Install Visual Studio Code," shows you how to get the app on your Windows PC, Mac, or Linux box. Subsequent sections show you how to set Visual Studio Code's look by applying a theme, install Python-related extensions to provide extra functionality, and configure some essential settings.

Download and Install Visual Studio Code

In this section, you download and install the Visual Studio Code app. Visual Studio Code is the code editor and IDE we recommend you use for creating Python code. Visual Studio Code runs on Windows, macOS, and Linux; this section shows Windows and provides notes and tips on the differences in macOS and Linux.

On Windows, you can add an Open with Code command to the context menus for files and for directories. This command enables you to easily open a file or a folder in Visual Studio Code from File Explorer, which is usually helpful.

Download and Install Visual Studio Code

1 Open your web browser and go to https://code.visualstudio.com.

The home page of the Visual Studio Code website appears.

2 Click the Download link for your computer's operating system.

A The Download button shows the operating system your computer is using.

B To download Visual Studio Code for another operating system, click the drop-down arrow (∨), and then click **Download** (↓) in the Stable column for the operating system.

The Documentation for Visual Studio Code screen appears, and the download starts.

3 Launch the Setup Wizard. For example, in the Chrome browser, click ∧ (∧ changes to ■), and then click **Open** on the pop-up menu.

The Setup Wizard's License Agreement screen appears.

4 Read the license agreement.

5 If you want to continue, click **I accept the agreement** (○ changes to ◉).

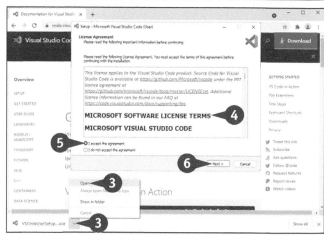

6 Click **Next**.

7 Click **Next** on the Select Destination Location screen.

8 Click **Next** on the Select Start Menu Folder screen.

The Select Additional Tasks screen appears.

9 Select **Create a desktop icon** (☑) if you want a Visual Studio Code icon on your desktop.

10 Select **Add "Open with Code" action to Windows Explorer file context menu** (☑), as needed.

11 Select **Add "Open with Code" action to Windows Explorer directory context menu** (☑), as needed.

12 Select **Register Code as an editor for supported file types** (☑) to associate Visual Studio Code with the file types it supports.

13 Select **Add to PATH** (☑) to add Visual Studio Code to your Windows path. This helps Windows locate Visual Studio Code.

14 Click **Next**.

The Ready to Install screen appears.

15 Verify that the summary shows the choices you intended to make.

C If you need to make changes, click **Back** until you reach the appropriate screen.

16 Click **Install**.

The Setup Wizard installs Visual Studio Code.

The Completing the Visual Studio Code Setup Wizard screen appears.

Note: If you want to use Visual Studio Code immediately, select **Launch Visual Studio Code** (☑) on the Completing the Visual Studio Code Setup Wizard screen.

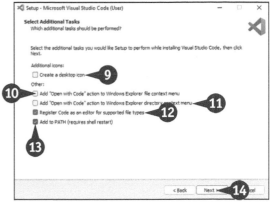

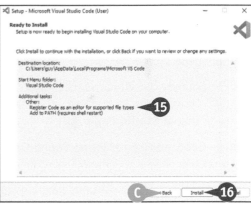

17 Click **Finish**.

The Setup Wizard closes.

Visual Studio Code opens.

You can now configure Visual Studio Code, as explained in the section "Configure Visual Studio Code for Working with Python," later in this chapter.

TIPS

How do I install Visual Studio Code on macOS?
Download the latest Mac Universal Stable Build from https://code.visualstudio.com. Double-click the downloaded zip file to extract its contents, the Visual Studio Code app. Drag this app to the Applications folder. You can then delete the downloaded zip file.

How do I install Visual Studio Code on Linux?
Go to https://code.visualstudio.com and download the appropriate installer package for your distribution — for example, the Debian installer package or the Red Hat Package Manager installer package. Open the file and follow the prompts.

Get Started with Visual Studio Code and Apply a Theme

The first time you run Visual Studio Code, the app displays the Get Started with Visual Studio Code screen, which walks you through some initial configuration steps. You can return to the Get Started with Visual Studio Code screen later if you like; alternatively, you can use the app's other means of accessing its settings to configure the app to work the way you prefer.

The first change you will likely want to make is to the theme, which controls the overall look of Visual Studio Code. The app includes various dark themes and various light themes; third-party themes are also available.

Get Started with Visual Studio Code and Apply a Theme

Launch Visual Studio Code

1 Launch Visual Studio Code in one of the standard ways for your computer's operating system.

For example, on Windows, click **Start** (⊞) to open the Start menu, and then click **Visual Studio Code** (✕).

A The Get Started with Visual Studio Code screen appears.

The list on the left contains headings for several initial configuration steps.

2 Click **Choose the look you want**.

B Controls under the heading section appear.

C A preview appears.

3 Click **Browse Color Themes**.

The Theme drop-down list opens.

D The highlight shows the current theme.

E The Light Themes section at the top contains themes based on light colors.

F The Dark Themes section contains themes based on dark colors.

4 Press ⬆ or ⬇ to move the highlight to the theme you want to preview.

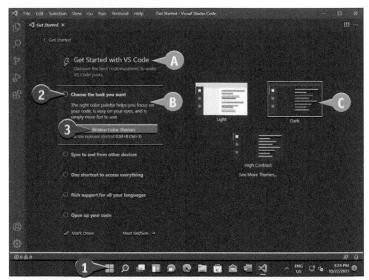

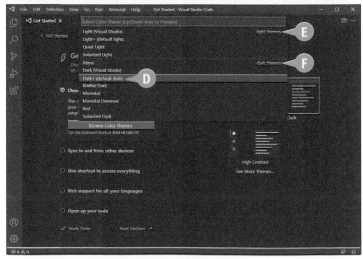

Visual Studio Code displays a preview of the theme.

5 Click the theme you want to apply.

Note: You can also press `Enter` to apply the currently selected theme.

The Get Started screen appears fully again.

6 Click the next heading whose settings you want to explore.

G The settings for the heading appear, and you can work with them.

H When you finish working through the list, you can click **Mark Done** (✍) to tell Visual Studio Code you finish using this list.

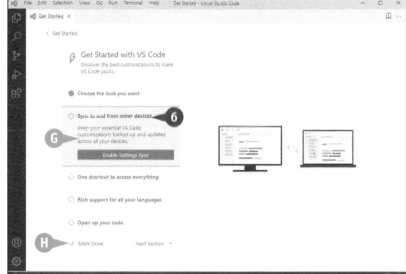

TIPS

How do I go back to the Getting Started screen?

Click **Help** to open the Help menu, and then click **Getting Started**. On the screen that appears, click **Get Started with Visual Studio Code** in the Getting Started list on the right.

Why does Visual Studio Code have so many dark themes?

Dark-hued themes tend to be easier on the eye, especially when you are coding for a long time in a dimly lit room. By contrast, this book uses a light-hued theme to increase readability on both the printed page and the screen.

Install Visual Studio Code Extensions for Python

Visual Studio Code comes with powerful built-in features, but it also enables you to add further functionality by installing extensions. An *extension* is an add-on unit of code that you can install or uninstall separately. Many extensions are available from third-party developers, providing a wide range of supplementary functionality for Visual Studio Code.

For working with Python, you should install the Python extension, as explained in this section. The Python extension includes the Pylance server language extension and the Jupiter Notebook Renderers extension, so you effectively install three extensions in a single move.

Install Visual Studio Code Extensions for Python

1 Launch Visual Studio Code in one of the ways your computer's operating system offers.

For example, on macOS, click **Launchpad** ( ) to display the Launchpad screen, and then click **Visual Studio Code** ( ).

Visual Studio Code opens.

2 Click **Extensions** ( ).

The Extensions screen appears.

A You can click **Search Extensions in Marketplace** and type a search term to search by name.

However, the Python extension often appears toward the top of the Popular list, which is sorted by number of downloads, so you may not need to search.

3 Click **Python**.

The information screen for the Python extension appears.

B You can read detailed information about the extension.

4 Click **Install**.

Visual Studio Code downloads the Python extension and installs it.

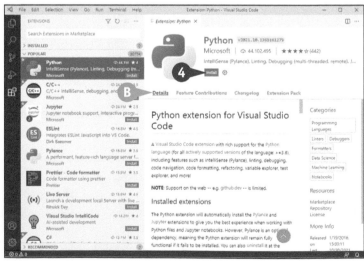

C You can click **Disable** if you need to disable the extension temporarily without uninstalling it.

D You can click **Uninstall** if you decide you want to uninstall the extension.

5 Click **Installed**.

The Installed list expands.

E You can see all the extensions you have installed.

F You can click **Settings** (⚙) to configure settings for an extension.

6 Click **Close** (✕).

The pane showing information about the Python extension closes.

7 Click **Extensions** (▦).

The Extensions pane closes.

TIP

What other extensions can I use for Python in Visual Studio Code?

A wide range of Visual Studio Code extensions is available for working with Python; you can get a list by entering **python** in the Search Extensions in Marketplace box in the Extensions pane in Visual Studio Code. In particular, you may want to try the Python Indent extension, which automatically controls indentation on new lines of code, and the Python Snippets extension, which can save you typing by providing built-in code snippets. Look also at the Kite AutoComplete AI Code extension, which provides automatic completion for both Python and other major programming languages.

Configure Visual Studio Code for Working with Python

Visual Studio Code is highly customizable, so you should spend a few minutes configuring the code editor suitably for your work in Python. This section shows you how to access Visual Studio Code's configuration preferences and explains the preferences you are most likely to benefit from setting. These preferences include the "Files: Auto Save" setting, which controls whether Visual Studio Code automatically saves unsaved changes as you work; the font size and font family in which Visual Studio Code displays your code; and whether Visual Studio Code automatically inserts a closing bracket to match each opening bracket you type.

Configure Visual Studio Code for Working with Python

1 Launch Visual Studio Code.

For example, on Windows, click **Start** (⊞) to open the Start menu, and then click **Visual Studio Code** (◁).

2 Click **File**.

The File menu opens.

3 Click or highlight **Preferences**.

The Preferences submenu opens.

4 Click **Settings**.

Note: On Windows and Linux, you can press Ctrl + , to display the Settings screen. On macOS, press ⌘ + , . Alternatively, click **Manage** (⚙) in the lower-left corner, and then click **Settings** on the menu that opens.

The Settings screen appears.

A The Commonly Used settings category appears at first.

Note: If the Commonly Used category does not appear, click **Commonly Used**.

5 Click **Files: Auto Save** (∨), and then click the Auto Save option you want. See the first tip for advice.

6 Click **Editor: Font Size** and type the font size you want to use in the editor.

B You can click **Editor: Font Family** and type the font family you want to use in the editor.

7 Click **Text Editor**.

The Text Editor settings category appears.

8 Click **Auto Closing Brackets** (∨), and then click **always**, **languageDefined**, **beforeWhitespace**, or **never**, as needed.

Note: Auto Closing Brackets controls whether Visual Studio Code automatically enters a closing bracket when you type an opening bracket. Auto Closing Delete controls whether Visual Studio Code automatically deletes adjacent closing quotes or brackets during deletion.

9 Click **Auto Closing Delete** (∨), and then click **always**, **auto**, or **never**, as needed.

10 Click **Features**.

The Features settings category appears.

11 Click **Auto Reveal** (∨), and then click **true**, **false**, or **focusNoScroll**, as needed.

12 Select **Confirm Delete** (☑) to make the explorer confirm your file deletions.

13 Select **Confirm Drag And Drop** (☑) to make the explorer confirm your file drag-and-drop actions.

14 When you finish configuring settings, click **Close** (✕).

The Settings tab closes.

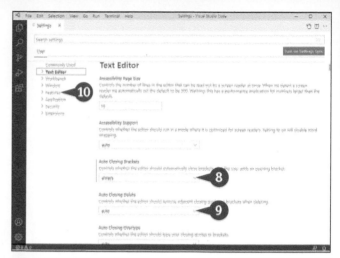

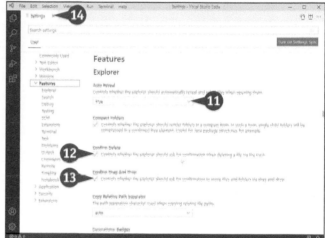

TIPS

What are the Files: Auto Save options?
Click **off** to disable automatic saving. Click **onFocusChange** to save changes when you move the focus from the file that contains changes. Click **onWindowChange** to save changes when you activate another app. Click **afterDelay** to have Visual Studio Code automatically save changes after a delay. The default delay is 1000 microseconds — 1 second. To change the delay, click **Text Editor** and change the value in the File: Auto Save Delay box.

How do I update Visual Studio Code?
By default, Visual Studio Code automatically checks for updates and notifies you when one is available. If Visual Studio Code displays the Restart Visual Studio Code to Apply the Latest Update dialog box, click **Update Now** to start the update.

## CHAPTER 2

Writing and Running Your First Python Code

In this chapter, you start writing code in Python using the Visual Studio Code editor and the terminal window. You learn about Python's `main()` function and create a simple function. You also learn how to run code either in Visual Studio Code or in a terminal window, add comments to your code, and import and use Python modules and objects.

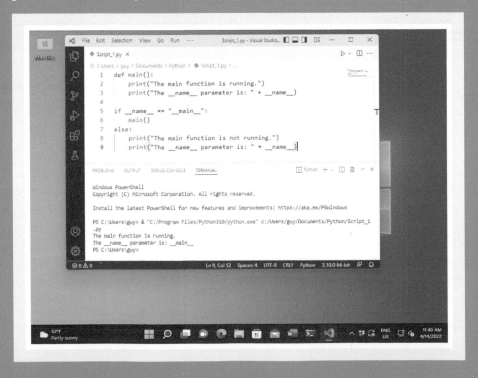

Understanding the `main()` Function

You can create a Python script that simply uses commands and does not define any functions; you do this extensively later in this book. But many Python scripts include a function called `main()` that contains the main set of actions the script performs. In this section, you learn the purpose of the `main()` function and when and how to create one.

You also learn about the two ways to run code using the Python interpreter. How you run a script affects how Python sets the built-in `__name__` parameter, which you can use to control whether the `main()` function runs.

What Is the `main()` Function?

As its name suggests, the `main()` function typically forms the core part of a Python script. You would normally use the `main()` function in conjunction with an `if` statement that checks the value of the `__name__` parameter. Doing so enables your script to determine whether it was launched from the command line or whether it was imported into the interpreter or into another script or module.

Here is pseudocode showing a `main()` function and its `if` statement, with italics indicating a placeholder:

```
def main():
    statements

if __name__ == "__main__":
    main()
```

Here is how this works:

- `def`. This keyword starts the definition of the function.

- `main():`. This is the name of the function, followed by a colon to end the line. This line is called the *function header*.

- `statements`. This is where you place statements that specify the actions the `main()` function is to take. The statements are indented by four spaces to indicate that they belong to the function's block of code.

- `if`. This keyword begins the condition, which compares the value of the `__name__` parameter to the string `"__main__"`. Two equal signs, `==`, denote equality. The double quotes, `"`, mark the beginning and end of a literal string of text. The colon ends the line.

- `main()`. This statement tells Python to execute the `main()` function if the condition evaluates to `True`. This statement is indented by four spaces to show it belongs to the `if` statement's block of code.

When Should You Create a `main()` Function?

Create a `main()` function in any script that you want to have execute in a different way when it is run from the command line than when it has been imported into the interactive interpreter or into another script or module.

Understanding the Two Ways to Run Python Code

You can run a Python script either by launching it from the command line or by importing it into the interactive interpreter or another Python file.

Launch a Script via the Command Line

The first way to launch a script is by using the command line. You start by opening a terminal window, such as a Command Prompt window on Windows or a window in the Terminal app on macOS or Linux. You then navigate to the appropriate folder, type the Python app's name and the script's name, and press 🔲.

For example, to run the script called `my_script.py` from the current folder, you might use this command on Windows:

```
python myscript.py
```

Or you could use this command on macOS or Linux:

```
python3 my_script.py
```

When you launch a script from the command line, Python sets the script's __name__ parameter to __main__.

Import a Script into the Interactive Interpreter or into Another Script or Module

To import a script, you use the `import` keyword followed by the script's name without its extension. For example, if the script's name is `acme_calcs.py`, you can import it using the following statement:

```
import acme_calcs
```

When you import a script into the interactive interpreter, into another script, or into another module, Python sets the script's __name__ parameter to the script's name without the extension. Continuing the previous example of importing, Python sets the __name__ parameter to `acme_calcs`.

Create and Save a New Script in Visual Studio Code

In this section, you run the Visual Studio Code app, create a new script, and specify that you want to use the Python language for the script. You then save the script under a name of your choice in a suitable location, creating a new folder if necessary. Saving the script file gets you ready for creating code in it, which you do in the following section, "Write and Run Code in Visual Studio Code."

Create and Save a New Script in Visual Studio Code

① Open Visual Studio Code if it is not already running.

For example, on Windows, click **Start** (⊞), and then click **Visual Studio Code** (⬡). On macOS, click **Launchpad** (⠿), and then click **Visual Studio Code** (⬡).

Note: If Visual Studio Code is already running or does not start a new script by default, start a new script manually by pressing `Control`+`N` on Windows or Linux or `⌘`+`N` on the Mac.

The Select a Language to Get Started prompt appears.

② Click **Select a language to get started**.

Ⓐ The Select Language Mode pop-up menu opens.

③ Type **p**.

The P section of the pop-up menu appears.

④ Click **Python (python)**.

Ⓑ Visual Studio Code sets the language to Python.

⑤ Click **File**.

The File menu opens.

⑥ Click **Save**.

Note: On Windows and Linux, you can press `Control`+`S` to give the Save command. On macOS, press `⌘`+`S`.

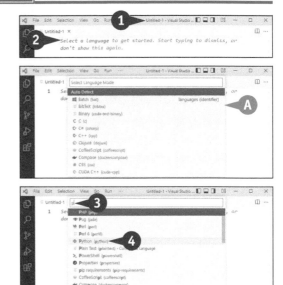

The Save As dialog box opens.

7 Navigate to the folder in which you want to store your script.

8 If you need to create a new folder for your Python code, click **New folder**. If not, go to step **11**.

C The app creates a new folder.

9 Type the name for the new folder, and then press **Enter**.

10 Double-click the new folder.

The folder opens.

11 Type the filename for the script.

12 Verify that Python is selected in the Save As Type drop-down list.

13 Click **Save**.

The Save As dialog closes.

Visual Studio Code saves the script.

You can now enter the code for the script. See the next section, "Write and Run Code in Visual Studio Code," for an introductory example.

TIP

Should I use the Auto Save feature in Visual Studio Code?
You decide. You can toggle Auto Save on or off by clicking **File** to open the File menu and then clicking **Auto Save** to display or remove the check mark next to it. To configure Auto Save, click **File**, click or highlight **Preferences**, and then click **Settings** to display the Settings screen. In the left pane, click **Commonly Used** to display the Commonly Used list. Click **Files: Auto Save** (⌄) and then click **afterDelay** to save after a short delay, **onFocusChange** to save after you move the focus in the code window, or **onWindowChange** to save after you activate another window.

Write and Run Code in Visual Studio Code

After creating a new script file in Visual Studio Code, as explained in the previous section, "Create and Save a New Script in Visual Studio Code," you can write code in the script and then run it. In this section, you create a short script that demonstrates how the script's __name__ property varies depending on how you run the script. The script uses the print() function to display output and includes an if... else statement, a decision-making tool you will meet in detail in Chapter 6, "Making Decisions with if Statements."

Write and Run Code in Visual Studio Code

Write Code in Visual Studio Code

1 Open Visual Studio Code, and then open the new script file you created and saved in the previous section.

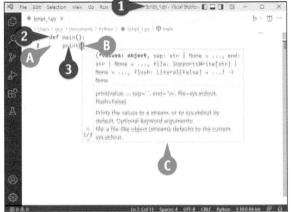

2 On line 1, type the following statement, which uses the def keyword to create a function named main(). Press **Enter**.

```
def main():
```

A Visual Studio Code automatically indents the next line, making it part of the code block for the main() function.

3 Type the following partial statement:

```
print(
```

B Visual Studio Code automatically enters the closing parenthesis,), for you to the right of the insertion point.

C A ScreenTip containing help for the print() function appears.

4 Type ".

Visual Studio Code enters the closing quotes for you, again to the right of the insertion point.

D Visual Studio Code highlights the parentheses to indicate that they are a matching pair.

5 Inside the quotes, type the following string of text, carrying the closing quotes along to the right:

```
The main function is running.
```

6 Press ➡ to move the insertion point past the closing quotes, and then press **Enter**. The complete line of code looks like this:

```
print("The main function is running.")
```

Visual Studio Code retains the indent on the next line.

⑦ Type the following partial statement, which uses the `print()` function to display information about the `__name__` parameter, moving the closing parenthesis along to the right.

```
print("The __name__ parameter
is: " + __na
```

Note: When you type the closing quotes, ", Visual Studio Code moves the insertion point to the right of the " character that your typing has been carrying along. You can also press ➡ to move the insertion point past the " character.

Ⓔ When you type `__na`, Python displays an AutoComplete list of matching items.

⑧ Click `__name__`.

Visual Studio Code enters the `__name__` item, so the statement looks like this:

```
print("The __name__ parameter
is: " + __name__)
```

⑨ Type) to move the insertion point past the closing parenthesis, and then press **Enter**.

⑩ Press **Backspace** to delete the indent, ending the `main()` function's block, and then press **Enter** again.

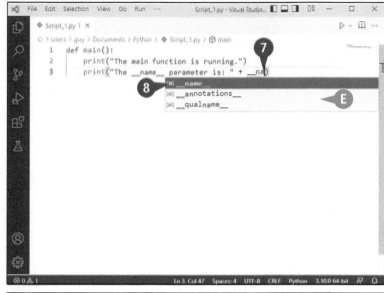

TIP

How else can I navigate the AutoComplete list?
Instead of clicking the item you want to insert in your code, you can press ⬆ or ⬇ to move the highlight to the item and then press **Tab** or **Enter** to enter it. You can also "type down" to highlight the name — simply continue typing the remaining characters of the name until Visual Studio Code highlights the name.

continued ▶

Normally, the if __name__ == "__main__" statement does not have an else statement, as the if statement is all that is needed to control whether the main() function runs. In this example, however, you add an else statement to demonstrate how the value of __name__ changes when you run the script by importing it. The else statement runs when __name__ is not __main__; it displays a message including the value of __name__.

If you have turned off Visual Studio Code's Auto Save feature, save your work manually whenever you have made changes you would rather not have to make again.

Write and Run Code in Visual Studio Code (continued)

Visual Studio Code creates a blank line.

11 Type the following if statement, which compares the value of __name__ to the string __main__, and then press **Enter**:

```
if __name__ == "__main__":
```

F Python indents the next line, making it part of the if block.

12 Type the following statement, which runs the main() function, and then press **Enter**:

```
main()
```

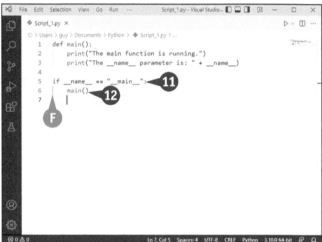

13 Press **Backspace** to delete the indent, and then type the else keyword and a colon. Press **Enter**.

```
else:
```

Visual Studio Code indents the next line, making it part of the else block.

14 Type the following print() statement, and then press **Enter**:

```
print("The main function is not
running.")
```

15 Type the following statement, which is the same as that in line 3:

```
print("The __name__ parameter is:
" + __name__)
```

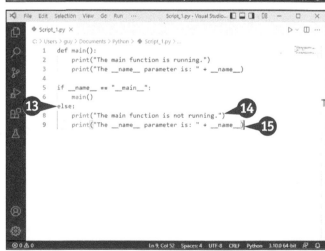

Run Your Script in Visual Studio Code

1 Click **Run Python File in Terminal** (▷).

The Terminal pane appears in the lower part of the Visual Studio Code window.

G The script's path and name appear here.

H The script's output appears, indicating that the `main()` function is running and that the value of the `__name__` parameter is `__main__`.

2 Click **Kill Terminal** (🗑).

Visual Studio Code kills the Terminal.

Visual Studio Code closes the Terminal pane.

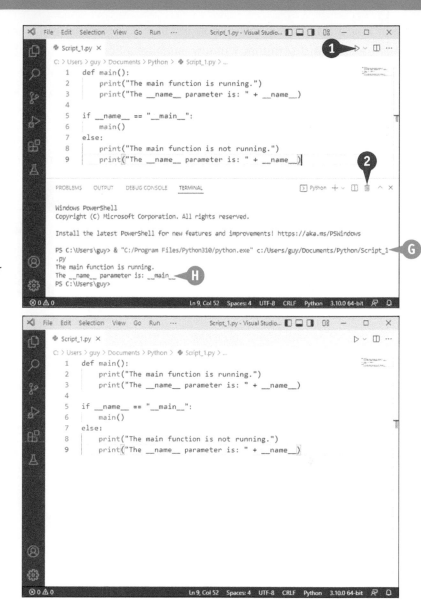

How can I save time when creating repetitive code in Visual Studio Code?

You can use the Copy and Paste commands. For example, instead of typing a line of code again, select a previous instance, and then give a Copy command, such as clicking **Edit** and then **Copy**; click in line 8, and then give a Paste command, such as clicking **Edit** and then **Paste**. If you prefer, you can use the standard keyboard shortcuts: Press Control+C for Copy, Control+V for Paste, or Control+X for Cut. On the Mac, press ⌘+C, ⌘+V, and ⌘+X, respectively.

Execute Python Commands in a Terminal Window

The Python interactive interpreter enables you to execute commands in a terminal window. You open a standard terminal window, such as a Command Prompt window on Windows or a Terminal app window on macOS or Linux; and then launch the interactive interpreter using the `python` command on Windows or the `python3` command on macOS or Linux. You can then type Python commands and get an immediate response.

Working in the interactive interpreter is great for learning, and you will use this approach extensively in this book. This section provides an introduction to the interactive interpreter.

Execute Python Commands in a Terminal Window

1 Open a terminal window.

For example, on Windows, click **Start** (⊞), type **com**, and then click **Command Prompt** (■).

2 Type **python** and press Enter.

Note: On macOS and Linux, type **python3** and press Enter.

The interactive interpreter launches.

A The Python prompt, >>>, appears.

3 Type the following statement, which creates a variable named u and assigns to it the result of the `input()` function prompting you to type your name. Press Enter.

```
u = input("Type your name: ")
```

Python displays the prompt:

```
Type your name:
```

4 Type whatever you like, and then press Enter.

Python accepts your input.

5 Type the following statement, which uses the `print()` function to display a short message including what you typed. Press Enter.

```
print("You are " + u)
```

Python displays the message, such as this:

```
You are Ann
```

6 Type the following statement, which gives the `quit()` command, and then press Enter.

```
quit()
```

The Python interpreter quits.

The terminal window's standard prompt appears again.

Note: Use the `quit()` command when you want to quit Python. For concision, terminal window tasks from here on do not show this command.

Run a Python Script in a Terminal Window

After creating a Python script, you can execute it by running it in a terminal window. In this section, you open a terminal window and run the script you created earlier in this chapter, which shows you whether the main() function is running and what the value of the __name__ parameter is.

You then launch Python and import the script. By doing so, you can see the different way in which Python handles the main() function for a script you import.

Run a Python Script in a Terminal Window

1 Open a terminal window.

For example, on macOS, click **Launchpad** (:::), and then click **Terminal** (▣).

2 Change the directory to the one in which you saved the script. The following macOS example uses the cd command to change to the ~/Dropbox/TYV_Python/Code directory, starting from the user's home directory, which is represented by ~.

cd Dropbox/TYV_Python/Code

3 On Windows, type **python**; on macOS or Linux, type **python3**.

4 On the same line, type a space, and then type the name of the script. For example, on macOS, the following command runs the script Script_1.py:

python3 Script_1.py

A The script's output appears, indicating that the main() function is running.

5 Type **python** on Windows, or **python3** on macOS or Linux, and then press Enter. For example, on macOS, type this:

python3

Python launches.

B The Python prompt appears.

6 Type the following statement, which uses the import statement to import the script as a module:

import Script_1

C The script's output appears, indicating that the main() function is not running and giving the value of the __name__ parameter as Script_1.

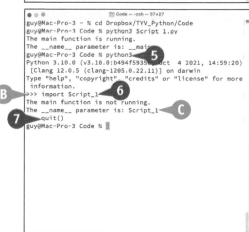

7 Type the quit() command, and then press Enter.

quit()

Python quits.

Understanding Comments in Python

Like most programming languages, Python enables you to add comments to your code. A *comment* is text that appears in a script but that is marked as not to be executed. You can add comments to your code at any point. For example, as you develop a script, you might use comments to describe the tasks the code needs to perform and possible approaches for them. After finishing the script's commands, you might rework the comments so that they explain what the script does. Such comments will help others understand and maintain the code.

Formally, Python supports only single-line comments, but you can also use multiline strings to create informal multiline comments.

Create Formal Comments Using the # Character

Python uses the # character to mark the start of a single-line comment. You can place the # character at the start of the line to make the entire line into a comment, as in the following example:

```
# display the value of y
print(y)
```

Alternatively, you can place the # character after some code, as in the following example. This method works better for short comments and for comments you intend to remove once you get the code working.

```
t = "Placeholder 1" # replace this placeholder text
```

You cannot use the continuation character, \, to continue a single-line comment to the next line. Instead, type # at the beginning of the next line if you need to continue the comment, as in the following example:

```
# prompt the user for the company name
# compare the company name to an approved list
```

Using Multiline Strings to Create Informal Comments

Another way to create a multiline comment in a script is to create a multiline string but not assign it to a variable. To create a multiline string, you place three double quotes at the beginning and at the end, or three single quotes at the beginning and at the end. The following example uses three double quotes:

```
"""
Run an external check with the chem_verify() method
to confirm the formula is correct.
Log the formula in the standard file.
"""
```

This method of creating informal comments works but has no real advantage over using the # character on each line. You should know about this method not because you should use it in your own code but because you may encounter it in other people's code.

Using Comments to Prevent Code from Executing

Apart from adding textual commentary to your code, comments have a secondary use: You can use the # character to prevent a specific line of code from executing. This is called *commenting out* the code — turning a statement into a comment prevents the code from running without you having to remove it from the script, but you can restore the code by removing the comment character.

For example, the # character comments out the first of the following statements:

```
# u = input("Type your name: ")
u = "Bob" # default name for testing
print("You are " + u + ".")
```

Enter Comments in a Terminal Window

You can enter comments when working interactively in a terminal window. Doing so is sometimes useful, such as when you are working in multiple terminal windows and want to make sure you do not lose your train of thought. Generally, though, comments are more widely useful when you are creating a script.

Enter Comments in a Code Editor or an IDE

When you are working in a code editor or an IDE, you can create a comment manually by typing the # character before the comment text. But most code editors and IDEs also provide commands for commenting out text and uncommenting it again.

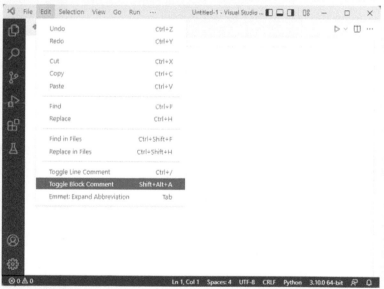

For example, in Visual Studio Code, you can toggle commenting on or off for the current line or selected lines by pressing **Control**+**** on Windows or Linux or **⌘**+**** on the Mac. From the menu bar, you can click **Edit** and then click **Toggle Line Comment**.

Visual Studio Code's Edit menu also offers the Toggle Block Comment, which places three double quotes before and after the selected text, making it into an informal comment. You can give this command from the keyboard by pressing **Control**+**Shift**+**A** on Windows or Linux or **Option**+**Shift**+**A** on the Mac.

Add Comments to Your Code

Adding comments to your code can help you develop functional code more quickly and can help others understand, maintain, and extend your code. While writing code, add comments freely describing the code's tasks and your current approach. Revise the comments as you progress and change your code. Once the code is working, clean up the comments, removing any development-related comments and adding any further explanation that is needed or might be helpful.

You can also use the comment character, #, to *comment out* lines of code to prevent them from running without removing them from the script.

Add Comments to Your Code

1 Open Visual Studio Code, create a new script, and save it under a name of your choice.

2 Type the following statement, which creates a comment, and then press **Enter**:

```
# prompt the user for their name
```

A Visual Studio Code displays the comment text in green to make it easy to see in your scripts.

3 Type the following statement, which creates a variable named u and assigns to it the result of the input() function, prompting the user for their name. Press **Enter**.

```
u = input("Type your name: ")
```

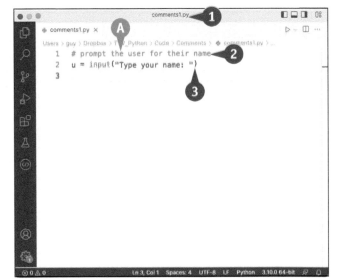

4 Type the following comment, and then press **Enter**:

```
# display the name entered
```

5 Type the following statement, which uses the print() function to display a message that includes the contents of u. Press **Enter**.

```
print("You are " + u + ".")
```

6 Click **Run Python File in Terminal** (▷).

The Terminal pane opens.

7 Click in the Terminal pane.

8 Type a name, and then press **Enter**.

B Python displays the message.

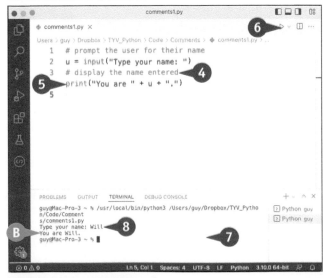

Comment Out a Statement and Uncomment It Again

1 Click at the beginning of line 2, and then type # and a space so the line reads like this:

```
# u = input("Type your name: ")
```

C Visual Studio Code displays the line in green, because it is now a comment.

2 Click at the end of line 2, and then press Enter.

Visual Studio Code creates a new line.

3 Type the following statement, which creates a variable named u and assigns the value Ivy to it.

```
u = "Ivy"
```

4 Still on the same line, type a comment so the line reads like this:

```
u = "Ivy" # default name for testing
```

5 Click **Run Python File in Terminal** (▷).

D The message appears, showing the default name.

6 Click in line 2 and press Control+/.

E Visual Studio Code uncomments line 2.

Note: On the Mac, press ⌘+/.

7 Click in line 3 and press Control+/.

Visual Studio Code comments out line 3.

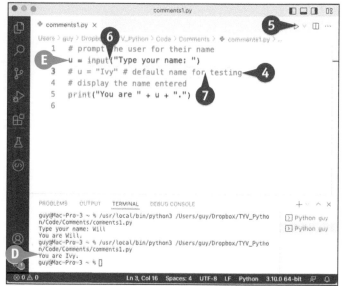

TIPS

Why does Visual Studio Code automatically enter # at the start of a new line after a comment?

Visual Studio Code automatically enters the # character when you press Enter with the insertion point inside a comment, breaking it to the next line. If this happens when the insertion point is apparently at the end of a comment line, chances are that there is a space to the right of the insertion point that is causing Visual Studio Code to continue the comment.

What happens if I use two # characters at the start of a comment?

The first # character tells Python the rest of the line is a comment, so the second # character becomes part of the comment.

Grasp Importing Modules and Objects

When you load Python using the `python` or `python3` command, depending on the operating system, Python loads its core modules, which provide essential functionality. When you need further functionality, you can import one or more additional *modules*, files containing Python code. For example, when you need to work with directories, such as creating or deleting them, you can import the `os` module, which contains methods for interacting with the operating system.

You can either import an entire module by using an `import` statement or import an individual object from a package by using a `from... import` statement.

Understanding What Modules Are and Why Python Uses Them

In Python, a module is a stand-alone file that contains code. Python breaks down code into modules so as to have multiple smaller files rather than one gargantuan file. These smaller files have various advantages, such as helping the organization of code by functionality, streamlining the updating of code, and making code run better on less-powerful systems by avoiding loading items that are not needed.

The main disadvantage of having code in separate modules is that your code must load any modules it needs. But as you will see, loading the modules is quick and easy.

Import a Module

To import a module, use the `import` keyword and specify the module name. For example, the following statement imports Python's `os` module, which provides operating system–related commands:

```
import os
```

Similarly, if you have created a custom module named `acme_calculations.py`, you can import it by using the following command:

```
import acme_calculations
```

Note that you omit the `.py` file extension from the custom module's filename in the `import` statement.

When you import a module of your own like this, navigate to the directory that contains the module first, and then launch Python from there. Alternatively, you can import the module from a subdirectory of the directory from which you launched Python. For example, if the `acme_calculations` module is stored in the `final` subdirectory, specify the subdirectory like this:

```
from final import acme_calculations
```

Access the Contents of an Imported Module

When you import a module like this, you specify the module's name to access its contents. For example, the os module's contents include the path module, which provides methods for working with file-system path names. After importing the os module, you access the path module like this:

```
os.path
```

Similarly, if you have imported the acme_calculations module, and it contains a method named ave_product, you access it through the module like this:

```
acme_calculations.ave_product()
```

Import an Object from a Module

Instead of importing an entire module, you can import a single object from a module. You might do this if that object is the only part of the module you will need and you want to be able to refer directly to the object rather than having to refer to it via the module. Counterintuitively, importing only an object does not reduce resource usage, as Python imports the whole module into its mapping table; the difference is in how you refer to the object.

To import an object from a module, begin the statement with the from keyword; then supply the module name, then the import keyword, and finally the object name. For example, the following statement imports the path module from the os module:

```
from os import path
```

After importing a single object like this, you refer to it by its unqualified name, such as path in this case, rather than via its parent module, such as os.path. Here is an example:

```
print(path)
```

If the object you import contains other objects or methods, you can access those objects or methods by using the name of the imported object followed by a period and the name of the item you want to use. For example, the path object contains many methods, including os.path.basename(), which returns the base name of the specified path. After importing the path object, you can access the basename() method via the path object like this:

```
path.basename()
```

You can also import a nested object on its own. For example, the following statement imports basename() from os.path:

```
from os.path import basename
```

continued ▶

The standard way of importing a module or an object adds it to Python's mapping table, but Python also enables you to import a module or object under an alias of your choice. Using an alias can make your code more compact and easier to read.

Because you have not imported the module, you cannot refer to the object via the module. So if you have imported only the `path` object from the `os` module, you cannot use `os.path` to refer to it; you must use the unqualified `path` instead.

Import a Module or Object Under an Alias

When you import a module or an object from a module, you can create an alias for the object. For example, the following statement imports the module `acme_quants_derivatives` and assigns the alias `aqd`:

```
import acme_quants_derivatives as aqd
```

You can then use the alias to refer to the module or object. For example, the following statement uses the `aqd` alias to refer to the `ohlc()` method in the `acme_quants_derivatives` module, assigning it to the variable `n`:

```
n = aqd.ohlc()
```

Similarly, you can use the `from` syntax to import an object from a module under an alias. The following example imports the `version` method from the `platform` module under the alias `pv`:

```
from platform import version as os_version
```

Likewise, you can then use the alias in your code. For example, the following statement uses the `print()` function to display the value of the method aliased as `os_version`:

```
print(os_version())
```

This statement returns information such as the following on a Mac:

```
Darwin Kernel Version 20.6.0: Mon Aug 30 06:12:21 PDT 2021;
root:xnu-7195.141.6~3/RELEASE_X86_64
```

Using an alias can be useful when you import multiple modules or objects that have the same name or names similar enough to be confusing. Using a shorter alias can also tighten and streamline your code.

List the Methods and Variables in a Module or Object

After importing a module or object, you can use Python's `dir()` function to list the methods and variables it contains. For example, if you have imported `acme_quants_derivatives` and assigned the alias `aqd`, you can list the contents of `aqd` like this:

```
dir(aqd)
```

Python returns a list of the contents, such as the following:

```
['__builtins__', '__cached__', '__doc__', '__file__', '__init__', '__loader__',
'__name__', '__package__', '__spec__', 'export_weekly_stats', 'five_minute_
chart', 'import_daily_stats', 'ohlc', 'statbank', 'two_minute_chart']
```

The items whose names start and end with two underscores are built-in Python methods. These are called *dunder methods* after the double underscore characters that precede and follow their names.

The items whose names do not use the double underscores, such as `import_daily_stats` and `ohlc`, are the methods and variables in the module or object.

You access the methods and variables through the alias of the imported object. For example, the following statement creates a variable named `my_two_minute_chart` and assigns to it the result of the `two_minute_chart()` method, which it accesses via the `aqd` alias:

```
my_two_minute_chart = aqd.two_minute_chart()
```

Reload a Module

Normally, you do not need to reload a module, because the Python interpreter does not unload modules. This means the only reason to reload a module is if it has changed since you first loaded it. While possible, such change in a loaded module is relatively rare.

To reload a module, first use the `import` command to import the `importlib` package:

```
import importlib
```

You can then use the `reload()` method of `importlib` to reload the module. For example, the following statement reloads the module named `cust1`:

```
importlib.reload(cust1)
```

Import Modules and Use Their Methods

I n this section, you import two Python modules and use the methods they contain. The modules you import are called `os` and `sys`, two of Python's utility modules. The `os` module lets you work with the computer's operating system, while the `sys` module enables you to manipulate the Python runtime environment. You also import objects from `platform`, another utility module.

To use commands in an imported library, you specify the library's name followed by the command's name. For example, to use the `getcwd()` method in the `os` module, you use `os.getcwd()`.

Import Modules and Use Their Methods

① Open a terminal window and launch Python.

For example, on Ubuntu, click **Show Applications** (▦), type **term**, and then click **Terminal** (▤).

Ⓐ The Python prompt appears.

② Type the following statement, which uses the `import` command to import the `os` module. Press **Enter**.

```
import os
```

③ Type the following statement, which uses the `getcwd()` method of the `os` module to return the current working directory. Press **Enter**.

```
os.getcwd()
```

Ⓑ Python returns the directory, such as `'/Users/guy'`.

Note: See Chapter 4, "Working with Files and Folders," for more information about the `os` module.

④ Type the following statement, which uses the `import` command with the `as` keyword to import the `sys` module under the alias `rt`. Press **Enter**.

```
import sys as rt
```

⑤ Type the following statement, which uses the `print()` function to display the result of returning the `version` property of the object aliases as `rt`. Press **Enter**.

```
print(rt.version)
```

Ⓒ Python displays the version information, as in the following example, with the headline number at the beginning:

```
3.10.0 (v3.10.0:b494f5935c, Oct  4 2021,
14:59:20) [Clang 12.0.5 (clang-1205.0.22.11)]
```

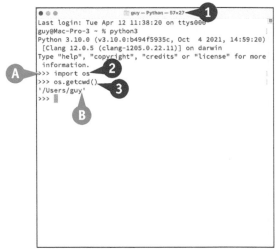

```
●  ●  ●              guy — Python — 57×27              1
Last login: Tue Apr 12 11:38:20 on ttys000
guy@Mac-Pro-3 ~ % python3
Python 3.10.0 (v3.10.0:b494f5935c, Oct  4 2021, 14:59:20)
  [Clang 12.0.5 (clang-1205.0.22.11)] on darwin
Type "help", "copyright", "credits" or "license" for more
  information.
>>> import os                  2
>>> os.getcwd()
'/Users/guy'                   3
>>>
                          B
```

```
●  ●  ●              guy — Python — 57×27
guy@Mac-Pro-3 ~ % python3
Python 3.10.0 (v3.10.0:b494f5935c, Oct  4 2021, 14:59:20)
  [Clang 12.0.5 (clang-1205.0.22.11)] on darwin
Type "help", "copyright", "credits" or "license" for more
  information.
>>> import os
>>> os.getcwd()
'/Users/guy'
>>> import sys as rt           4
    print(rt.version)
5
3.10.0 (v3.10.0:b494f5935c, Oct  4 2021, 14:59:20) [Clang
  12.0.5 (clang-1205.0.22.11)]
>>>
                          C
```

6 Type the following statement, which uses the `from` keyword with the `import` command to import the `system()` method from the `platform` module. Press Enter.

```
from platform import system
```

7 Type the following statement, which uses the `print()` function to display the result of the `system()` method. Press Enter.

```
print(system())
```

D Python displays a term indicating the operating system: `Windows` for Windows, `Darwin` for macOS, or `Linux` for Linux.

```
● ● ●                    guy — Python — 57×27
guy@Mac-Pro-3 ~ % python3
Python 3.10.0 (v3.10.0:b494f5935c, Oct  4 2021, 14:59:20)
 [Clang 12.0.5 (clang-1205.0.22.11)] on darwin
Type "help", "copyright", "credits" or "license" for more
 information.
>>> import os
>>> os.getcwd()
'/Users/guy'
>>> import sys as rt
>>> print(rt.version)
3.10.0 (v3.10.0:b494f5935c, Oct  4 2021, 14:59:20) [Clang
 12.0.5 (clang-1205.0.22.11)]
>>> from platform import system              6
>>> print(system())              7
Darwin
>>>
```

8 Type the following statement, which uses the `from` keyword with the `import` command and the `as` keyword to import the `processor()` method from the `platform` module under the alias `cpu`. Press Enter.

```
from platform import processor as cpu
```

9 Type the following statement, which uses the `print()` function to display the result of the `cpu()` method. Press Enter.

```
print(cpu())
```

E Python returns the processor type, such as `i386` for an Intel processor or `amdk6` for an AMD processor.

```
● ● ●                    guy — Python — 57×27
guy@Mac-Pro-3 ~ % python3
Python 3.10.0 (v3.10.0:b494f5935c, Oct  4 2021, 14:59:20)
 [Clang 12.0.5 (clang-1205.0.22.11)] on darwin
Type "help", "copyright", "credits" or "license" for more
 information.
>>> import os
>>> os.getcwd()
'/Users/guy'
>>> import sys as rt
>>> print(rt.version)
3.10.0 (v3.10.0:b494f5935c, Oct  4 2021, 14:59:20) [Clang
 12.0.5 (clang-1205.0.22.11)]
>>> from platform import system
>>> print(system())
Darwin
>>> from platform import processor as cpu              8
>>> print(cpu())              9
i386
>>>
```

TIP

How do I unimport a module or an object?
You do not normally need to unimport a module or an object. Once you have imported a module or an object, Python retains access to it until you quit Python.

CHAPTER 3

Getting Started with Variables

In this chapter, you learn to work with variables, named areas of memory that you can use to store data as your apps run. You explore the different data types Python uses and learn how to use each data type effectively. Along the way, you create variables by assigning data to them, retrieve data from variables, change the contents of variables, and determine the data type of the values assigned to variables.

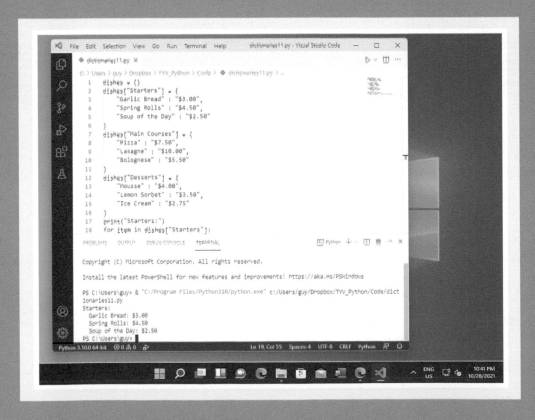

Understanding Variables and Their Usage

In this section, you learn the essentials of variables, which are named areas of memory that you can create for storing data while your Python code runs.

Python supports various different data types, such as integers for whole-number values, Booleans for True/False values, and strings for words or other sequences of text characters. After creating a variable, you can assign any type of data to it that Python uses. See the following section, "Understanding Python's Data Types," for details on Python's data types.

What Is a Variable?

A *variable* is an area of memory in which you can store data. When you create a variable, you give it a name that enables you to access it to retrieve or change its contents. When your code runs, Python allocates a space in memory for each variable.

Variable Name		Variable Name		Variable Name	
name ◂A		age ◂B		isOnProbation ◂C	
Contents		Contents		Contents	
Anna Connor		27		True	
Current Data Type		Current Data Type		Current Data Type	
str		int		bool	

For example, you might create a variable called `name` to store an employee's name (A). The name would normally be a string of text characters, such as `Anna Connor` or `Bill Ramirez`, so the value would receive the `str` data type, which Python uses for strings. Similarly, you might create a variable called `age` to store the employee's age in years as a whole number (B). That value would be an integer, so Python would assign the value the `int` data type that it uses for integers. Or you might create a variable called `isOnProbation` to store the employee's probation status (C). This variable would store the value `True` or the value `False`, and Python would assign the value the `bool` data type that it uses for Boolean values.

A Variable Does Not Have a Data Type, But Its Value Does

In Python, variables themselves do not have data types, so you do not specify the data type when you create a variable. Instead, the value assigned to the variable has a type. So instead of, say, creating a variable and giving it the `int` data type, which is for integers, you would create a variable and assign data of the `int` data type to it.

This treatment of variables is called *dynamic typing* and is different from various other programming languages that enable — or require — you to give each variable a specific data type, a practice called *static typing*. For example, Microsoft's Visual Basic programming language encourages you to declare each variable explicitly and assign a data type. For instance, `Dim intAge As Integer` "dimensions" — creates — a variable called `intAge` that has the Integer data type and will accept only integer data. Such explicit declarations prevent you from putting the wrong type of data in a variable — trying to do so causes an error — and from overwriting the variable unintentionally by using the same name later in your code.

Creating a Variable and Assigning Data to It

In Python, you create a variable and assign data to it in a single statement. For example, consider the following line:

```
price = 125
```

This line (A) declares a variable called `price` and initializes it by assigning the value `125` to it. This value is an integer, a number with no decimal component, so Python gives it the `int` data type.

You can then change the value if needed, as in the following line:

```
price = 250
```

This line (B) assigns the value `250` to the `price` variable.

You can also assign data of a different data type to the `price` variable. For example, the following line (C) assigns a string value:

```
price = "moderate"
```

Because the `price` variable does not have a static data type, it accepts the string value without comment.

However, some IDEs display a warning when your code contains this kind of change, because it could represent an error, as a programmer would not normally change the data type contained in a variable.

Seeing What Data and Data Type a Variable Contains

To see what data a variable contains, you can use the `print` command to display the contents to the console. For example, the following line (A) displays the contents of the `price` variable:

```
print(price)
```

The `print` command works fine for values that are text or can easily be interpreted as text, but trying to print a variable containing binary data — for example, an image — will usually cause problems.

To see what data type the value assigned to a variable has, you can use the `type` command with the variable's name. For example, the following line (B) displays the data type of the value assigned to the `price` variable:

```
type(price)
```

This command returns the value's class, such as `<class 'int'>` for the `int` data type or `<class 'str'>` for the `str` data type.

Understanding Python's Data Types

Python includes various built-in data types designed for handling different types of data efficiently. For example, Python's `bool` data type is designed for storing Boolean data, data that can be either True or False but no other possible value. Similarly, Python's `str` data type is designed for storing strings of text.

Python's built-in data types mostly fall into six categories: numerics for numbers; sequences for data such as lists; mappings for dictionaries, where one item maps to another; classes for creating custom objects; instances for the objects created with those classes; and exceptions for handling errors.

Understanding How Python Builds on the C Programming Language

The Python programming language is primarily implemented using C, a long-standing and robust programming language that is still widely used across many industries. C is called a *low-level* programming language, which means that it can interface directly with hardware features, lending itself to software and operating-system development. C is relatively easy to understand but extremely hard to master.

Python is a high-level programming language and includes many built-in features that C does not natively support, giving you an easier way to harness some of the power of C to develop solutions rather than using C directly. Python's extensive feature set and capability to run well on many platforms contributes to its great versatility.

Because Python is built on C, Python's data types are constructed using combinations of C's data types. For example, Python includes a data type called `set` that enables you to store multiple pieces of information in a single variable — a capability that C itself does not directly provide. Furthermore, some of Python's more complex data types are constructed using simpler Python data types.

Understanding the Numeric Data Types

Python provides three main numeric types for handling different kinds of numeric data:

- `int`. This data type is used for storing integer numbers — numbers that do not have a decimal component. For example, 0, 3, 42, and 4817 are all integers. The following section, "Work with Integers," provides examples of working with the `int` data type in Python. Technically, the `bool` data type for storing Boolean values is a subtype of `int`.
- `float`. This data type is used for storing floating-point numbers, those that have a decimal component. For example, 9876.54321 is a floating-point number. The section "Work with Floating-Point Values," later in this chapter, gives you examples of working with the `float` data type in Python.

Understanding the Numeric Data Types (continued)

- `complex`. This data type is used for storing complex numbers — numbers that consist of a real component and an imaginary component. Complex numbers have mostly specialized uses beyond the scope of this book.

Understanding the Sequence Data Types

In Python, a sequence is a set of data that is *ordered* — in other words, it has a specific order. Some sequence data types are *immutable*, or unchangeable, whereas others are *mutable*, or changeable.

The following list explains the main data types in the sequence category:

- `list`. This data type contains a sequence of similar items — for example, a list of integers might contain 1, 2, and 3, or a list of strings might contain `dog`, `cat`, and `snake`. Lists are mutable, so you can change their contents, their order, or both. See the section "Start Working with Lists," later in this chapter, for more about this data type.
- `tuple`. This data type is used to store an ordered sequence of values. The values do not need to be unique, so a tuple can contain multiple instances of the same value. A tuple is immutable, so you cannot change its contents or its order once you have created it. See the section "Work with Tuples," later in this chapter, for more about this data type.
- `range`. This data type is used to contain an immutable sequence of integer values — for example, from 1 to 10. Ranges are often used to control the number of iterations in `for` loops.
- `str`. This data type is used for storing strings of text. Python considers a string to be an immutable — unchangeable — sequence of characters. The section "Start Working with Strings," later in this chapter, gets you started with the `str` data type, while Chapter 9, "Working with Text," shows you the most useful moves with strings.

continued ▶

Understanding Python's Data Types (continued)

In addition to the sequence data types — `list`, `tuple`, `range`, and `str` — discussed so far in this section, Python provides a `set` data type for storing sets of data. A `set` is not a sequence because it does not have a specific order.

Python also provides a single mapping data type, `dict`, which is used for creating dictionaries. A dictionary in Python is not a dictionary in the everyday sense, although there are some similarities between the two: A key in the dictionary maps to a particular value, enabling you to look up that value.

Understanding the Set Data Type

In Python, the `set` data type enables you to store multiple values in a single variable. The `set` data type has the following characteristics:

- **It contains elements.** The elements, also called members, are the discrete objects that make up the set.
- **Each element is unique.** A set cannot have duplicate elements. By contrast, a list or a tuple can have duplicate elements.
- **It is unordered.** The elements in a set have no specific order. This means you cannot refer to an element in a set by its index or position.
- **It is immutable.** Once you have created a set, you cannot change its existing items, but you can add further items to the set if you need to.

The section "Work with Sets," later in this chapter, gives you an example of creating and manipulating a set.

Understanding the Mapping Data Type

Python's mapping category contains a single data type, `dict`, which is used for dictionaries. A dictionary consists of key/value pairs, with the key in each pair giving you access to set, retrieve, or modify the associated collection of information in the value.

A dictionary is unordered; you access the data by supplying the appropriate key rather than an index value. A dictionary is mutable, so you can change its contents after creating it.

The section "Start Working with Dictionaries," later in this chapter, introduces working with dictionaries. Chapter 11, "Working with Lists and Dictionaries," goes into dictionaries in depth.

Understanding Python's Classes

In Python, a *class* is a kind of template you use for creating a new object of a particular type. You can create a class object to organize the functions and other code in a particular project.

That sounds nebulous, but if you work with office productivity software, you are likely used to a similar paradigm. For example, if you need to create many memos of the same type in Microsoft Word, you may create a custom memo template containing the layout and formatting for the memo, and perhaps some VBA code for automation. That memo template is analogous to a Python class.

Chapter 12, "Working with Classes," explains how classes work, tells you what classes are useful for, and shows you how to create a class and put it to use.

Understanding the Instance Data Type

In Python, an *instance* is an individual object created from a particular class. For example, say you create a class that contains the functions needed to run a particular data-aggregation and assessment task. When you want to work on that data, you create an instance of the class — or, to use the formal term, you *instantiate* the class.

Continuing the previous example, when you need to produce a memo, you create a new document based on your memo template rather than using the memo template itself. The document is analogous to an instance of the template class.

Chapter 12, "Working with Classes," covers how to create and use instances of your custom classes.

Understanding the Exception Data Type

In Python, an *exception* is an object representing an error that occurred during code. Chapter 10, "Handling Errors," shows you how to work with Python's built-in exceptions to handle errors when they occur. This chapter also explains how to create custom exceptions.

Work with Integers

Python provides the `int` data type for storing integer values. An integer is a whole number, one with no fractional component. For example, 1, 7, and 49 are integers, whereas 1½ and 7.25 are not.

In this section, you use the `input()` command twice to prompt the user to enter two integers. Each `input()` command returns a string that you convert to an integer by using the `int()` command. You then use the addition operator, `+`, to add the numbers; use the `str()` command to create a string from the result; and use the `print()` command to display that string.

Work with Integers

Create the Script

1 In Visual Studio Code, create a new script, and then save it.

For example, press Ctrl+N, click **Select a Language**, and then click **Python**. Press Ctrl+S, specify the filename and location, and then click **Save**.

2 Type the following statement, which uses the `input()` command to prompt the user to enter an integer and assigns the result to a variable named `strN1`:

```
strN1 = input("Enter an
integer: ")
```

3 Press Enter, and then type the following statement, which prompts the user to enter another integer and assigns it to a variable named `strN2`:

```
strN2 = input("Enter another
integer: ")
```

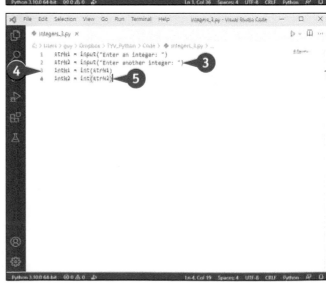

4 Press Enter, and then type the following statement, which uses the `int()` command to convert `strN1` to an integer and assigns it to a variable named `intN1`:

```
intN1 = int(strN1)
```

5 Press Enter, and then repeat step 4, but this time convert `strN2` to an integer and assign it to `intN2`:

```
intN2 = int(strN2)
```

6 Press **Enter**, and then type the following statement, which adds `intN1` and `intN2`, assigning the result to a variable named `intTotal`:

```
intTotal = intN1 + intN2
```

7 Press **Enter**, and then type the following statement, which uses the `str()` command to convert `intTotal` to a string:

```
strTotal = str(intTotal)
```

8 Press **Enter**, and then type the following statement, which uses the strings to display the calculation and its result:

```
print(strN1 + "+" + strN2 +
"=" + strTotal)
```

Run the Script

1 Click **Run Python File in Terminal** (▷).

A The Terminal pane opens.

B The Terminal pane displays the details of the code it is running.

The first prompt appears.

2 Type a value and press **Enter**.

The second prompt appears.

3 Type another value and press **Enter**.

C The calculation and its result appear.

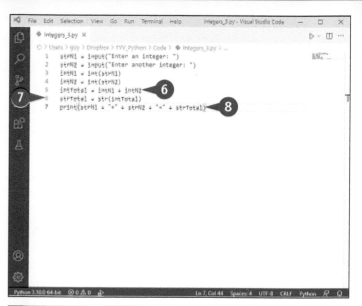

59

Work with Floating-Point Values

A *floating-point value* is a value that includes both an integer part and a decimal part, such as 6.155 or 0.1. In Python, floating-point values are often called *floats*.

A floating-point number's value is represented in binary using two components, a mantissa and an exponent. The *mantissa* stores the binary value for the number, whereas the *exponent* specifies the position of the decimal point in the mantissa. This means that, while a float is an efficient means of storing a number that includes a decimal point, its accuracy can vary.

Work with Floating-Point Values

1 In Visual Studio Code, create a new script, and then save it.

For example, press Ctrl+N, click **Select a Language**, and then click **Python**. Press Ctrl+S, specify the filename and location, and then click **Save**.

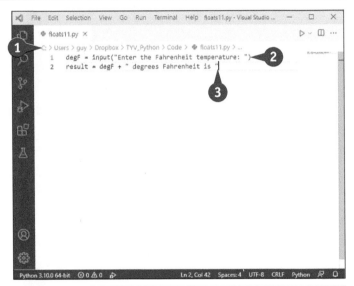

2 Type the following statement, which prompts the user to enter the Fahrenheit temperature, assigning the result to the variable degF:

```
degF = input("Enter the Fahrenheit temperature: ")
```

3 Press Enter and type the following statement, which assigns the input() command's string and explanatory text to a variable named result:

```
result = degF + "degrees Fahrenheit is "
```

4 Press Enter and type the following statement, which converts the input() command's string to a float data type:

```
degF = float(degF)
```

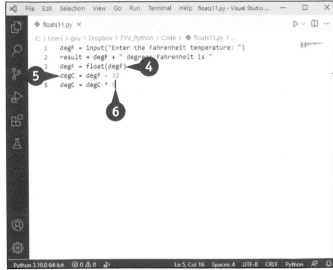

5 Press Enter and type the following statement, which subtracts 32 from the float value in degF and assigns the result to the variable named degC.

```
degC = degF - 32
```

6 Press Enter and type the following statement, which multiplies the value in degC by 5:

```
degC = degC * 5
```

7 Press **Enter** and type the following statement, which divides the value in degC by 9:

```
degC = degC / 9
```

8 Press **Enter** and type the following statement, which rounds the degC value down to one decimal place:

```
degC = round(degC,1)
```

9 Type the following statement, which derives a string from the degC value and adds that string and further explanatory text to the existing string in the result variable:

```
result = result + str(degC) + "
degrees Celsius."
```

10 Press **Enter** and type the following statement, which uses the print() command to display the contents of the result variable:

```
print(result)
```

11 Click **Run Python File in Terminal** (▷).

A The Terminal pane opens.

B The Terminal pane displays the details of the code it is running.

The first prompt appears.

The input() prompt appears.

12 Type a Fahrenheit temperature and press **Enter**.

C The result appears.

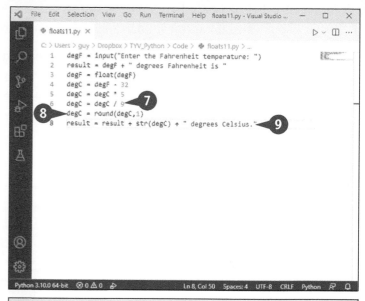

TIP

Can you write the calculation using fewer lines?

Yes — you can write the calculation in a single line, and doing so is more efficient. This example shows the calculation steps on separate lines for ease of reading.

A more condensed version of this calculation is `degC = (degF - 32) * 5 / 9.`

While condensing code is generally helpful, make sure your code is readable to anyone who will need to work on it. If in doubt whether your code is readable, document it by adding comments.

Work with Boolean Values

A Boolean value has only two possible states: `True` and `False`. The keywords `True` and `False` must use an initial capital followed by lowercase letters; other casing causes errors.

Boolean values are useful for checking status and making decisions in code. You can use the `bool()` function to determine whether a particular value is `True` or `False`. For example, if a particular value is `True`, the code takes certain actions; otherwise — since that value must be `False` — the code takes other specific actions. You can use the logical operators `and`, `or`, and `not` to create complex Boolean expressions.

Work with Boolean Values

1 Open a terminal window and launch Python.

Ⓐ The Python prompt appears.

2 Type the following statement, which creates a variable named `number1` and assigns the value `10` to it, and then press Enter:

```
number1 = 10
```

3 Type a similar statement to create a variable named `number2` and assign the value `10` to it too, again pressing Enter to complete the command:

```
number2 = 10
```

4 Type the following statement and press Enter to display the result of testing whether `number1` equals `number2`:

```
print(number1==number2)
```

Note: Python uses `==` to compare equality. It uses `=` for assigning values, as in step **3**.

Ⓑ Python returns `True`, the Boolean result for the comparison.

5 Type the following statement and press Enter to display the result of testing whether `number2` is greater than `number1`:

```
print(number2>number1)
```

Ⓒ Python returns `False`, the Boolean result for the comparison.

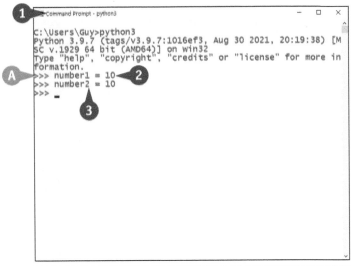

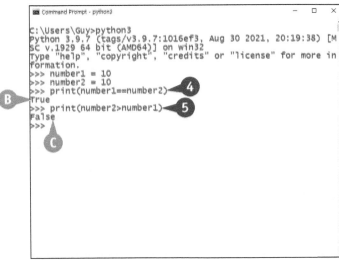

6 Type the following statement and press **Enter** to create a variable named `are_numbers_equal` and assign to it the result of testing whether `number1` equals `number2`:

```
are_numbers_equal = number1==number2
```

7 Type the following statement and press **Enter** to display the type of the `are_numbers_equal` variable:

```
type(are_numbers_equal)
```

D The type appears.

8 Type the following statement and press **Enter** to display the value of the `are_numbers_equal` variable:

```
print(are_numbers_equal)
```

E The value appears.

9 Type the following statement and press **Enter** to toggle the value of the `are_numbers_equal` variable:

```
are_numbers_equal = not are_numbers_
equal
```

10 Type the following statement and press **Enter** to display the value of the `are_numbers_equal` variable:

```
print(are_numbers_equal)
```

F The value appears.

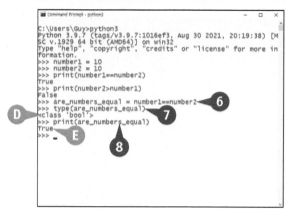

11 Type the following statement and press **Enter** to compare the `are_numbers_equal` variable to `False`; to quit Python if they match; and, if not, to display the value of `are_numbers_equal`:

```
quit() if are_numbers_equal == False
else print(are_numbers_equal)
```

Python quits.

G The terminal's standard prompt appears.

TIP

Which values evaluate to the Boolean `False`?

Python returns a Boolean `False` value for the following values:

- The value `False` or the value `None`
- The number zero, `0`
- An empty string, empty list, empty tuple, or empty dictionary

Python returns a Boolean `True` value for all other values. `True` has a numeric value of `1`.

Work with Tuples

Python provides several data types that are sequences, including tuples, lists, strings, and sets. A *tuple* is a variable that stores an ordered sequence of values. Unlike a list, whose contents and order you can change, a tuple is immutable, so you cannot change its contents or its order. Unlike a set, a tuple can contain multiple instances of the same value. Tuples are useful for grouping related information that you want to be able to use as a single item.

In this section, you use a terminal window to create and manipulate tuples.

Work with Tuples

1 Open a terminal window and launch Python.

A The Python prompt appears.

2 Type the following statement, which creates a variable named `offices` and assigns to it a tuple of five cities, and press Enter:

```
offices = ("Atlanta","Bridgeport",\
"Chicago","Chicago","Denver")
```

Note: You can create an empty tuple by placing a pair of parentheses with no contents after the tuple's name — for example, `myEmptyTuple = ()`.

3 Type the following statement, which displays the tuple's contents, and press Enter:

```
print(offices)
```

Note: When creating a tuple that contains only a single item, you must use a trailing comma, a comma placed after the item. For example, `mySingleTuple = (1,)` creates a tuple containing only the value 1.

B The tuple's contents appear.

④ Type the following statement, which displays the first item in the tuple, and press **Enter**:

```
print(offices[0])
```

ⓒ The first item appears.

⑤ Type the following statement, which uses the `len()` function to return the number of items in the tuple, and press **Enter**:

```
print(len(offices))
```

ⓓ The number of items, 5, appears.

⑥ Type the following statement, which displays the number of instances of the item `"Chicago"` in the tuple, and then press **Enter**:

```
print(offices.count("Chicago"))
```

ⓔ The number of instances of `"Chicago"`, 2, appears.

⑦ Type the following statement, which uses the `del` command to delete the tuple, and then press **Enter**:

```
del offices
```

⑧ To verify that the tuple is gone, type the following `print` command, and then press **Enter**:

```
print(offices)
```

ⓕ Python returns an error because the tuple no longer exists.

```
guy@Mac-Pro-3 ~ % python3
Python 3.9.6 (v3.9.6:db3ff76da1, Jun 28 2021, 11:49:53)
[Clang 6.0 (clang-600.0.57)] on darwin
Type "help", "copyright", "credits" or "license" for more information.
>>> offices = ("Atlanta","Bridgeport",\
... "Chicago","Chicago","Denver")
>>> print(offices)
('Atlanta', 'Bridgeport', 'Chicago', 'Chicago', 'Denver')
>>> print(offices[0])
Atlanta
>>> print(len(offices))
5
>>>
```

```
guy@Mac-Pro-3 ~ -zsh — 70×23
guy@Mac-Pro-3 ~ % python3
Python 3.9.6 (v3.9.6:db3ff76da1, Jun 28 2021, 11:49:53)
[Clang 6.0 (clang-600.0.57)] on darwin
Type "help", "copyright", "credits" or "license" for more information.
>>> offices = ("Atlanta","Bridgeport",\
... "Chicago","Chicago","Denver")
>>> print(offices)
('Atlanta', 'Bridgeport', 'Chicago', 'Chicago', 'Denver')
>>> print(offices[0])
Atlanta
>>> print(len(offices))
5
>>> print(offices.count("Chicago"))
2
>>> del offices
>>> print(offices)
Traceback (most recent call last):
  File "<stdin>", line 1, in <module>
NameError: name 'offices' is not defined
>>>
```

Can I add items to or remove items from a tuple?

Technically, no, because the tuple is immutable. However, you can achieve the same effect by converting the tuple to a list, adding or removing the items, and then converting the list back to a tuple.

Why would I create an empty tuple?

You might create an empty tuple to indicate that no data was available for a particular item or category. For example, if you were creating one tuple for each of 20 categories, having empty tuples where no data was available might be helpful. Otherwise, if you were creating only a single tuple, creating it with no data would be largely useless.

Work with Sets

Python's set data type enables you to store multiple values in a single variable. A *set* is a collection of objects, usually called *elements* or *members*. Each element must be unique in the set, without duplicates, unlike in a tuple, which can have duplicates. Also unlike a tuple, a set is *unordered* — that is, it has no specific order. A set is immutable: After creating a set, you cannot change its existing items, but you can add further items as needed. In this example, you use a set to remove duplicate values from a tuple.

Work with Sets

① In Visual Studio Code, create a new script, and then save it.

For example, press Ctrl+N, click **Select a Language**, and then click **Python**. Press Ctrl+S, specify the filename and location, and then click **Save**.

② Type the following statement to create a variable named mySet and assign an empty set to it:

```
mySet = set()
```

③ Press Enter, and then type the following statement to create a variable named myTuple and assign to it various numbers, including duplicates:

```
myTuple = (1,1,1,1,1,2,2,2,2,3,\
    3,3,3,4,4,4,4,5,5,5,6,6,7)
```

④ Press Enter, and then type the following statement, which uses the update method to add the unique values from myTuple to mySet:

```
mySet.update(myTuple)
```

⑤ Press Enter, and then type the following statement, which displays the text myTuple:, a space, and a string containing the contents of myTuple:

```
print("myTuple: " + str(myTuple))
```

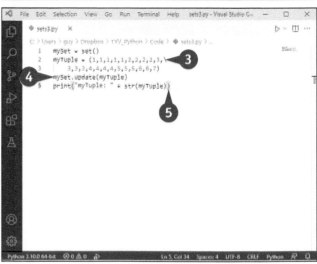

6 Press Enter, and then type the following statement, which displays a blank line in the output:

```
print()
```

7 Press Enter, and then type the following statement, which displays the text mySet:, a space, and a string containing the contents of mySet:

```
print("mySet: " + str(mySet))
```

Note: The print() statements for myTuple and mySet use the str() function to cast the contents of myTuple and mySet to strings because the first item printed is a string. Using print("mySet: " + mySet) causes an error from trying to concatenate a string and a set.

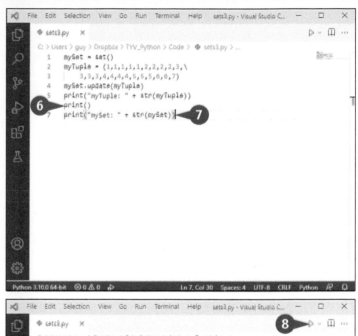

8 Click **Run Python File in Terminal** (▷).

Visual Studio Code runs the script.

Ⓐ The contents of myTuple appear.

Ⓑ The contents of mySet appear.

You can see that mySet contains only the unique elements from myTuple — all the duplicates are gone.

TIP

How do I create a set with contents?
You can create a set with contents in either of two ways. First, put the set's items inside braces, separated by commas — for example, fruitSet = {"apricot","berry","cucumber"}. Second, use the set() function, as in the main text, to create a set from a list or a tuple. For example, if you have a list called testMarks that contains duplicate values, you could create a variable named uniqueMarks and assign to it a set of the unique values from testMarks by using the command uniqueMarks = set(testMarks).

Start Working with Strings

To store and manipulate text in your scripts, you use strings. In Python, a string is an immutable sequence of characters, so once you have assigned a string to a value, you cannot change it. A string value has the `str` data type, and you can use the `str()` function to convert various other data types to strings.

Chapter 9, "Working with Text," shows you how to take widely useful actions with strings. This section provides an introduction to strings. In it, you create and manipulate strings using a terminal window.

Start Working with Strings

1 Open a terminal window and launch Python.

Ⓐ The Python prompt appears.

2 Type the following statement, which creates a variable named `str1` and assigns text to it, and then press Enter:

`str1 = "Industry"`

3 Type the following statement, and then press Enter, to display `str1`:

`print(str1)`

Ⓑ The string appears.

4 Type the following statement, and then press Enter, to create a second string:

`str2 = "Assessment"`

5 Type the following statement, and then press Enter, to display `str2`:

`print(str2)`

Ⓒ The string appears.

6 Type the following statement, which uses the + operator to concatenate, or join, `str1` and `str2`, adding a space between them and assigning the result to `str1`. Again, press Enter.

`str1 = str1 + " " + str2`

7 Type the following statement, and then press Enter, to display `str1`:

`print(str1)`

Ⓓ The string appears.

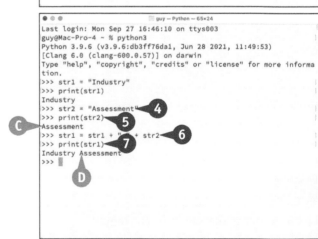

68

⑧ Type the following statement, which uses the `find` method to locate the position of the space in `str1`, assigning the result to a variable called `intSplit`. Press Enter.

```
intSplit = str1.find(" ")
```

⑨ Type the following statement, and then press Enter, to display the value of `intSplit`:

```
print(intSplit)
```

Ⓔ The value appears.

⑩ Type the following statement, and then press Enter, to create a variable named `strWord1` and assign to it the leftmost characters in `str1`, up to the space:

```
strWord1 = str1[0:intSplit]
```

⑪ Type the following statement, and then press Enter, to display the string in `strWord1`:

```
print(strWord1)
```

Ⓕ The string appears.

```
● ● ●                        🖳 guy — -zsh — 65×24
Last login: Mon Sep 27 16:46:10 on ttys003
guy@Mac-Pro-4 ~ % python3
Python 3.9.6 (v3.9.6:db3ff76da1, Jun 28 2021, 11:49:53)
[Clang 6.0 (clang-600.0.57)] on darwin
Type "help", "copyright", "credits" or "license" for more informa
tion.
>>> str1 = "Industry"
>>> print(str1)
Industry
>>> str2 = "Assessment"
>>> print(str2)
Assessment
>>> str1 = str1 + " " + str2
>>> print(str1)
Industry Assessment
>>> intSplit = str1.find(" ")        ⑧
>>> print(intSplit)        ⑨
Ⓔ 8
>>> strWord1 = str1[0:intSplit]        ⑩
>>>
```

```
● ● ●                        🖳 guy — -zsh — 65×24
Last login: Mon Sep 27 16:46:10 on ttys003
guy@Mac-Pro-4 ~ % python3
Python 3.9.6 (v3.9.6:db3ff76da1, Jun 28 2021, 11:49:53)
[Clang 6.0 (clang-600.0.57)] on darwin
Type "help", "copyright", "credits" or "license" for more informa
tion.
>>> str1 = "Industry"
>>> print(str1)
Industry
>>> str2 = "Assessment"
>>> print(str2)
Assessment
>>> str1 = str1 + " " + str2
>>> print(str1)
Industry Assessment
>>> intSplit = str1.find(" ")
>>> print(intSplit)
8
>>> strWord1 = str1[0:intSplit]
>>> print(strWord1)        ⑪
Ⓕ Industry
>>>
```

TIP

Do I use single quotes or double quotes around a string?
In Python, you can use either single quotes or double quotes to delimit a string. For example, you could assign text to the variable named `myString` by using either `myString = 'sample text'` or `myString = "sample text"`. Use single quotes if the string contains double quotes, such as `myString = 'Text with "double" quotes'`; use double quotes if the string contains single quotes, such as `myString = "Text with 'single' quotes"`. Otherwise, use whichever you prefer.

Start Working with Lists

A *list* is a variable that enables you to store multiple items of the same type or of different types. The list contains an index that enables you to set or retrieve the individual items. Technically, a list is a mutable sequence, so you can change the order of its items, add and remove items, sort the items, and so on.

Chapter 11, "Working with Lists and Dictionaries," shows you how to work with lists. This section gives you a preview in which you create a list, add items to it, and return items from it.

Start Working with Lists

1 In Visual Studio Code, create a new script, and then save it.

For example, press `Ctrl`+`N`, click **Select a Language**, and then click **Python**. Press `Ctrl`+`S`, specify the filename and location, and then click **Save**.

2 Type the following statement, which creates a variable called `names` and then assigns a list of four names to it:

```
names = ["Anna", "Bill", "Carly",
"Dennis"]
```

3 Type the following statement, which displays the first item in the list:

```
print(names[0])
```

4 Click **Run Python File in Terminal** (▷).

The Terminal pane opens.

Ⓐ The first list item appears. See the tip for information about the numbering.

5 Click **Kill Terminal** (🗑).

Visual Studio Code closes the Terminal pane.

6 Select the `print(names[0])` statement and type the following statement over it, using the `append` method to add an item to the `names` list:

```
names.append("Frank")
```

7 Press `Enter` and type the following statement, which displays the fifth item in the list:

```
print(names[4])
```

8 Click **Run Python File in Terminal** (▷).

The Terminal pane opens.

Ⓑ The fifth list item appears.

9 Click **Kill Terminal** (🗑).

Visual Studio Code closes the Terminal pane.

⑩ Click at the end of line 2 and press
`Enter` to start a new line, moving the
`print(names[4])` line down from line
3 to line 4.

⑪ On the empty line 3, type the following
statement, which uses the `insert` method
to insert an item at position `4` in the list:

`names.insert(4, "Emily")`

⑫ Click at the end of line 4 and press `Enter`
to start a new line.

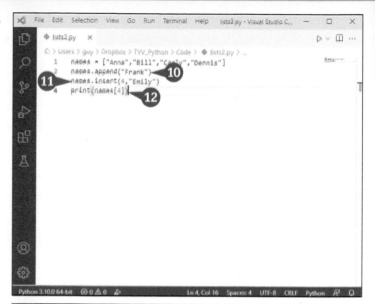

⑬ Type the following statement, which uses
the `remove` method to remove the name
`Bill` from the list:

`names.remove("Bill")`

⑭ Finally, press `Enter` and type another
`print(names[4])` statement:

`print(names[4])`

⑮ Click **Run Python File in Terminal** (▷).

The Terminal pane opens.

Ⓒ The first `print` statement displays the fifth
name, `Emily`.

Ⓓ The second `print` statement displays the
fifth name after removing the `Bill` item,
`Frank`.

TIP

Why is the first list item numbered 0?
Starting to count at 0 rather than 1 is a convention of computing; the technical name is *zero-based numbering*. So `names[0]` is the first item in the `names` list, `names[1]` is the second item, and so on.

Start Working with Dictionaries

In Python, a dictionary is a kind of super-list that allows you to assign collections of information to names called *keys*. You use a key to set, modify, or retrieve the associated collection of information.

Chapter 11, "Working with Lists and Dictionaries," shows you how to work with dictionaries. This section gives you an introduction to dictionaries. Here, you create a dictionary that contains information about the dishes offered by a restaurant. The dishes fall into three categories: Starters, Main Courses, and Desserts. You then display the category of dishes you want to see.

Start Working with Dictionaries

1 In Visual Studio Code, create a new script, and then save it.

For example, press `Ctrl`+`N`, click **Select a Language**, and then click **Python**. Press `Ctrl`+`S`, specify the filename and location, and then click **Save**.

2 Type the following statement, which declares a dictionary named `dishes`:

```
dishes = {}
```

3 Press `Enter` and type the following statements, which add the category called `Starters` and assign three items and their prices to it:

```
dishes["Starters"] = {
    "Garlic Bread" : "$3.00",
    "Spring Rolls" : "$4.50",
    "Soup of the Day" : "$2.50"
}
```

4 Press `Enter` and type the following statements, which add the category called `Main Courses` and assign three items and their prices to it:

```
dishes["Main Courses"] = {
        "Pizza" : "$7.50",
        "Lasagne" : "$10.00",
        "Bolognese" : "$5.50"
}
```

5 Press `Enter` and type the following statements, which add the `Desserts` category, again with three priced items:

```
dishes["Desserts"] = {
    "Mousse" : "$4.00",
    "Lemon Sorbet" : "$3.50",
    "Ice Cream" : "$2.75"
}
```

6 Press Enter and type the following statement, which displays the word `Starters` and a colon:

```
print("Starters:")
```

7 Press Enter and type the following statements, which use a `for` loop to list each dish in the `Starters` category:

```
for item in dishes["Starters"]:
    print("   " + item + ":",
dishes["Starters"][item])
```

Note: A `for` loop is a loop that repeats once for each item in a collection — in this case, once for each item in the `Starters` collection in the `dishes` dictionary. Chapter 7, "Repeating Actions with Loops," explains `for` loops in detail.

Run the Script

1 Click **Run Python File in Terminal** (▷).

The Terminal pane opens.

A The list of starters appears.

TIP

How do I change the code to display another collection?

In lines 17–19, replace `Starters` with `Main Courses` or `Desserts`, as appropriate. Here is an example:

```
print("Desserts")
for item in dishes["Desserts"]
    print "   " + item + ":", dishes["Desserts"][item]
```

Convert Data from One Type to Another

In your Python programming, you will often need to convert data from one data type to another so that you can use it the way you want. Python converts some data automatically and provides functions for converting data manually. For example, you can use the `str()` function to convert data to a string, use the `int()` function to convert numeric data to an integer, or use the `float()` function to convert numeric data to a float, as you have seen so far in this chapter.

This section summarizes the data-conversion functions Python provides and shows examples of using them.

Understanding Implicit Conversion and Explicit Conversion

Python performs two types of data conversion: implicit conversion and explicit conversion.

Implicit conversion occurs when Python automatically converts an existing value to a different data type to avoid losing data. For example, if you create a variable named `intTest` and assign the integer value 1, Python gives the value the `int` data type. But if you add a float, such as `3.19`, to `intTest`, Python changes the value's data type to `float` so as not to lose the data that could not be stored in the `int` data type.

Explicit conversion occurs when you use a data-conversion function to convert data to a different type, as explained in this section. Explicit data conversion is also called *type casting* or simply *casting*. For example, you might cast an integer to a float.

Understanding What Kinds of Data You Can Convert

Python's data-conversion functions are effective and easy to use, but they work only with suitable data. For example, if the variable `strQuantity` contains the string data `"20"` — including the double quotes, which delimit the string — you can use `int(strQuantity)` to convert the string `"20"` to the integer `20`. But if `strQuantity` contains `"Twenty"`, using `int(strQuantity)` returns an error.

Meet Python's Functions for Converting Data

Table 3-1 summarizes the functions that Python provides for converting data from one data type to another. You will notice that each function shares the name of the data type to which it converts data. For example, the `bool()` function converts data to the `bool` data type, the `int()` function converts data to the `int` data type, and the `tuple()` function converts data to the `tuple` data type.

Table 3-1 Python's Functions for Converting Data

Function	Converts	To
bool()	Any data type	A Boolean value, True or False
chr()	An integer	The corresponding ASCII character
complex()	A real number and an imaginary number	A complex number
dict()	Key/value pairs	A dictionary
float()	Any data type	A float
hex()	An integer	A hexadecimal string
int()	Any data type	An integer
list()	A sequence, collection, or iterator object	A list
oct()	An integer	An octal string
ord()	A character	The corresponding ASCII or Unicode code value
set()	A sequence, collection, or iterator object	A set
str()	Any data type	A string
tuple()	A sequence, collection, or iterator object	A tuple

Examples of Using Python's Data-Conversion Functions

Here are brief examples of using Python's data-conversion functions:

- chr(76) returns L, the ASCII character represented by 76; ord("L") returns 76, the ASCII character number.
- bool(1>2) returns False, because 1 is not greater than 2.
- complex(4,7) returns the complex number 4 + 7j.
- dict_Subjects = {1: "History", 2: "Geography", 3: "Math"} returns a dictionary with three subjects identified by integer keys.
- float(1 + 1.111) returns a float containing 2.111, rounded.
- hex(64000) returns 0xfa00, the hexadecimal value for 64000.
- int(47.2536) returns the integer 47.
- list(("death","sickness","taxes")) returns a list containing those three cheerless nouns.
- oct(64) returns 0o100, the octal value for 64.
- set(myTuple) returns a set containing the unique values from the myTuple collection.
- str(45 + 99) returns a string containing 144.
- tuple(("shoes", "boots", "waders", "sandals")) returns a tuple containing ill-assorted footwear.

## CHAPTER 4

Working with Files and Directories

In this chapter, you learn to use Python to work with files and directories. You start by learning the essentials and then move on to navigating between directories and working with them. You learn how to return information about the user and system and how to split a file path into its components. And you gain expertise in opening and closing text files, writing data to them, and reading their contents.

Understanding Working with Files and Directories

This section gives you an overview of how you work with files and directories in Python. To make sure you are clear on the essentials, we first cover what files and directories are and what directory paths and file paths consist of. We then introduce you to three key modules you will need to load at different points during this chapter, briefly discuss the basic structure of a file, and give you an executive overview of the process of working with text files.

Understanding What Files and Directories Are

A *file* is a named storage unit on a computer. For example, you might create a text file named `cats.txt` that contains textual information about different types of cats. The file has a base name, `cats`, and a file extension, `.txt`. The file extension typically identifies the type of file; `.txt` normally indicates a text-only file, as in this example.

A *directory*, also called a *folder*, is a special type of file that acts as a container for other files. Python commands refer to "directory" rather than "folder," and this discussion follows suit. If a directory contains other directories, that directory is a *parent directory*, and the directories it contains are *subdirectories* or *child directories*.

Most computer operating systems provide each user account with a "home" directory that is kept separate from each other user account's directories, such as a `C:\Users\Al` directory on Windows or a `/Users/Ann` directory on macOS. A user's home directory typically contains various subdirectories, such as a `Desktop` subdirectory and a `Pictures` subdirectory.

Understanding Directory Paths and File Paths

A *directory path* or *folder path* gives the location of a directory. For example, if you are the user Ann and your home directory on macOS contains a subdirectory called `Text`, the directory path is `/Users/Ann/Text`.

A *file path* consists of the directory path to a file plus the filename and file extension. For example, if you are still Ann and you store the file `cats.txt` in the `Text` subdirectory in your home directory, the file path is `/Users/Ann/Text/cats.txt`.

Understanding Three Key Modules for Working with Files and Directories

For working with files and directories, you will typically need to import one or more of the following Python modules:

- os. The Operating System module, os, includes commands for working with individual files and directories. For example, later in this chapter, you use os to create and delete individual directories and to return, slice, and dice file paths.
- glob. The Global module, glob, includes commands for searching for file paths that match the pattern you specify. For example, in this chapter, you import glob so that you can search using wildcards.
- shutil. The Shell Utility module, shutil, includes commands for taking broad-based actions with files and directories. For example, later in this chapter, you use shutil to create multiple directories in a single operation — and to remove a whole directory tree, likewise in a single operation.

To import these modules, you use the import command:

```
import os
import glob
import shutil
```

Understanding a File's Basic Structure

A file typically consists of three sections:

- **Header section.** This section contains metadata about the file, such as the filename and the file type.
- **Data section.** This section contains the file's actual contents, such as text for a text file or image data for a picture.
- **End-of-file marker.** The end-of-file marker, or EOF marker, is a special character that denotes the end of the file.

Understanding the Essentials of Working with Files

To access a file via Python, you open the file by using the open() function. Opening the file does not open it in the conventional sense, as you do not see the file's contents, if there are any; instead, opening the file returns a file object that enables you to manipulate the file.

Once the file is open, you can read its contents; write new data to the file, either preserving or overwriting its existing contents; or append new data to the file while preserving its existing contents.

When you finish working with a file, you use Python's close() command to close the file.

Load the os Module and List Files and Directories

In this section, you load the os module, which provides methods for working with the file system. You use the getcwd() method of the os module to return the current working directory. You then use the listdir() method of the os module to return a list of the files and directories in a specified directory.

You also import the glob module and use its glob() method to return a list of files and directories using wildcards. This way enables you to return a targeted list of files and directories.

Load the os Module and List Files and Directories

Load the os Module

1 Open a terminal window and launch Python.

A The Python prompt appears.

2 Type the following statement, which imports the os module, and then press Enter.

```
import os
```

Python loads the os module.

The Python prompt appears, but there is no other acknowledgment that Python has loaded the module.

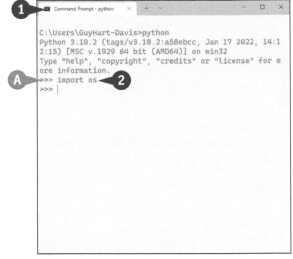

List Files and Directories

1 Type the following statement, which creates a variable named current and assigns to it the result of using the getcwd() method of the os module. Press Enter.

```
current = os.getcwd()
```

2 Type the following statement, which uses the print() command to display the contents of current, and then press Enter:

```
print(current)
```

Python returns the directory, such as 'C:\Users\Guy' on Windows or '/Users/guy' on macOS.

3 Type the following statement, which creates a variable named ff and assigns to it the result of using the listdir() method of the os module to list the files in current. Press Enter.

```
ff = os.listdir(current)
```

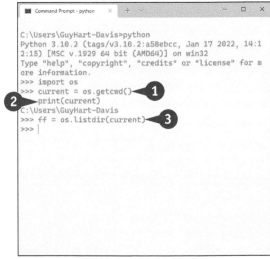

4 Type the following statement, which uses the `sort()` method to sort the contents of `ff` in ascending order. Press Enter.

```
ff.sort()
```

5 Type the following statement, which uses the `print()` function to display the contents of `ff`, and then press Enter:

```
print(ff)
```

Python displays a list of the directory's contents. The following example shows an abbreviated version of the list from a Windows PC.

```
['AppData', 'Application Data',
'Contacts', 'Cookies', 'Desktop',
'Documents', 'Downloads', 'Favorites',
. . .
'ntuser.dat.LOG1', 'ntuser.dat.LOG2',
'ntuser.ini']
```

6 Type the following statement, which imports the `glob` module, and then press Enter.

```
import glob
```

7 Type the following statement, which creates the variable `fg` and assigns to it the result of using the `glob()` method in the `glob` module to search for files and directories whose names begin with *D*.

```
fg = glob.glob("D*")
```

8 Type the following `print()` statement to display the contents of `fg`. Press Enter.

```
print(fg)
```

Python displays the list of items beginning with *D*, such as `['Desktop', 'Documents', 'Downloads']`.

TIPS

How can I determine which operating system Python is running on?

First, type the **import sys** command, and then press Enter, to import the `sys` module. Next, type **sys.platform**, and then press Enter, to display the value for the platform: `win32` for Windows, `darwin` for macOS, and `linux` for Linux.

How can I tell which version of Python is running my code?

The `sys` module can tell you the version of Python. Type **import sys**, and then press Enter, to import the `sys` module. Next, type **sys.version_info**, and then press Enter. Python returns information such as `sys.version_info(major=3, minor=10, micro=4, releaselevel='final', serial=0)`, which represent Python 3.10.4.

Navigate Among Directories

Python's `os` module provides the tools you need to navigate among the directories in the computer's file system. You can use the `expanduser()` method of the `path` object in the `os` module to return the path to the user's home directory and then use the `chdir()` method of the `os` module to switch to that directory. You can use the `isfile()` method of the `os` module to determine whether a particular directory is present; if it is, you can navigate to the directory and then navigate back up from it.

Navigate Among Directories

1 Open a terminal window and launch Python.

Ⓐ The Python prompt appears.

2 Type the following statement, which imports the `os` module, and then press **Enter**.

`import os`

3 Type the following statement, which creates a variable named `thisdir` and assigns to it the result of using the `getcwd()` method of the `os` module. Press **Enter**.

`thisdir = os.getcwd()`

4 Type the following statement, which uses the `print()` function to display the contents of `thisdir`. Press **Enter**.

`print(thisdir)`

Python displays the current directory.

5 Type the following statement, which creates a variable named `homedir` and assigns to it the result of using the `expanduser()` method of the `path` object in the `os` module. Press **Enter**.

`homedir = os.path.expanduser("~")`

Note: The `expanduser()` method here takes the argument ~, which represents the current user's home directory.

6 Type the following statement, which uses the `chdir()` method of the `os` module to change directory to `homedir`. Press **Enter**.

`os.chdir(homedir)`

```
guy — Python — 55×25                1
guy@Mac-Pro-2 ~ % python3
Python 3.10.0 (v3.10.0:b494f5935c, Oct  4 2021, 14:59:2
0) [Clang 12.0.5 (clang-1205.0.22.11)] on darwin
Type "help", "copyright", "credits" or "license" for mo
re information.
>>> import os          2
>>> thisdir = os.getcwd()     3
>>> 
```

```
guy — Python — 55×25
guy@Mac-Pro-2 ~ % python3
Python 3.10.0 (v3.10.0:b494f5935c, Oct  4 2021, 14:59:2
0) [Clang 12.0.5 (clang-1205.0.22.11)] on darwin
Type "help", "copyright", "credits" or "license" for mo
re information.
>>> import os
>>> thisdir = os.getcwd()
   print(thisdir)
/Users/guy/Music/Music/Music
>>> homedir = os.path.expanduser("~")     5
>>> os.chdir(homedir)
>>> 
            6
```

7 Type the following statement, which uses the `getcwd()` method of the `os` module, and then press Enter:

```
os.getcwd()
```

Python displays the current working directory, such as `'C:\\Users\\Ted'` on Windows or `'/Users/guy'` on macOS. See the tip for an explanation of the use of `\\`.

8 Type the following two-line `if` statement, which uses the `isdir()` method of the `path` object in the `os` module to determine whether the `Pictures` directory exists in the current directory and changes directory to it if it does. Press Enter at the end of each line, and then press Enter again to end the statement.

```
if os.path.isdir("Pictures"):
    os.chdir("Pictures")
```

Note: Indent the second line of the `if` statement by four spaces.

9 Type the following statement, which uses the `dirname()` method of the `path` object in the `os` module to return the parent directory of the current working directory, and the `chdir()` method of the `os` module to switch to it. Press Enter.

```
os.chdir(os.path.dirname(os.getcwd()))
```

10 Type the following statement to change to the original directory, and then press Enter:

```
os.chdir(thisdir)
```

11 Press ↑ five times to repeat the `os.getcwd()` statement, and then press Enter.

```
os.getcwd()
```

Python displays the directory from which you started.

```
guy@Mac-Pro-2 ~ % python3
Python 3.10.0 (v3.10.0:b494f5935c, Oct  4 2021, 14:59:2
0) [Clang 12.0.5 (clang-1205.0.22.11)] on darwin
Type "help", "copyright", "credits" or "license" for mo
re information.
>>> import os
>>> thisdir = os.getcwd()
>>> print(thisdir)
/Users/guy/Music/Music/Music
>>> homedir = os.path.expanduser("~")
>>> os.chdir(homedir)
>>> os.getcwd()           ⑦
'/Users/guy'
>>> if os.path.isdir("Pictures"):    ⑧
...     os.chdir("Pictures")
...
>>>
```

```
guy@Mac-Pro-2 ~ % python3
Python 3.10.0 (v3.10.0:b494f5935c, Oct  4 2021, 14:59:2
0) [Clang 12.0.5 (clang-1205.0.22.11)] on darwin
Type "help", "copyright", "credits" or "license" for mo
re information.
>>> import os
>>> thisdir = os.getcwd()
>>> print(thisdir)
/Users/guy/Music/Music/Music
>>> homedir = os.path.expanduser("~")
>>> os.chdir(homedir)
>>> os.getcwd()
'/Users/guy'
>>> if os.path.isdir("Pictures"):
...     os.chdir("Pictures")
...
>>> os.chdir(os.path.dirname(os.getcwd()))  ⑨
>>> os.chdir(thisdir)      ⑩
⑪  os.getcwd()
'/Users/guy/Music/Music/Music'
>>>
```

TIP

Why does Python show \\ instead of \ in Windows paths?
Python uses the backslash, `\`, as an *escape character*, a character that modifies the following character rather than being executed as itself. Here, `\\` represents a single "real" backslash in the path. So the path that Python shows as `C:\\Users\\Ted` is really `C:\Users\Ted`. You might think of `\\` as an escaped escape character.

Create and Delete Directories

In your code, you will likely need to create directories in which to store files. You may also need to delete directories that you no longer require.

Python's `os` module includes the `mkdir()` function for creating a single directory. The `os` module also provides the `makedirs()` method, which enables you to create multiple directories at once. For example, if you give the command `os.makedirs("/home/sam/Pictures/2022/Dec")` from the `/home/sam` directory, which already contains the `Pictures` directory, Python creates the `2022` subdirectory and the `Dec` subdirectory.

Create and Delete Directories

Create Directories

1 Open a terminal window and launch Python.

A The Python prompt appears.

2 Type the following statement, which imports the `os` module, and then press Enter.

```
import os
```

3 Type the following statement, which creates a variable named `thisdir` and assigns to it the result of using the `getcwd()` method of the `os` module. Press Enter.

```
thisdir = os.getcwd()
```

4 Type the following statement, which uses the `print()` function to display the contents of `thisdir`. Press Enter.

```
print(thisdir)
```

Python displays the current directory.

5 Type the following two-line `if` statement, which uses the `isdir()` method of the `path` object in the `os` module to check whether the `TYV_Python` directory exists and then uses the `mkdir()` method of the `os` module to create it if it does not. Press Enter at the end of each line, and press Enter once more to end the `if` statement.

```
if not os.path.isdir("TYV_Python"):
    os.mkdir("TYV_Python")
```

Note: Indent the second line of the `if` statement by four spaces.

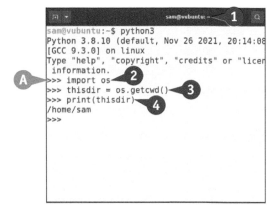

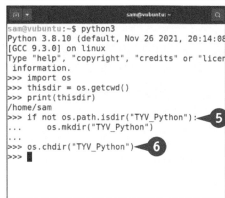

6 Type the following statement, which uses the `chdir()` method of the `os` module to change to the `TYV_Python` directory. Press Enter.

```
os.chdir("TYV_Python")
```

7 Type the following statement, which uses the `getcwd()` method of the `os` module to return the current working directory, and then press **Enter**:

```
os.getcwd()
```

Python displays the directory path, such as `'/home/sam/TYV_Python'`.

8 Type the following statement, which uses the `listdir()` method of the `os` module to display a list of the files and directories in the current working directory. Press **Enter**.

```
os.listdir()
```

Python displays a list of files and directories in brackets. If the directory is empty, as it will be if you just created it, Python displays `[]`, indicating an empty list.

9 Verify visually that the list of files and directories does not contain a file or directory called `Examples`.

10 Type the following statement, which uses the `mkdir()` method of the `os` module to create a directory named `Examples`. Press **Enter**.

```
os.mkdir("Examples")
```

Python creates the `Examples` directory but gives no confirmation that it has done so.

```
sam@vubuntu:~$ python3
Python 3.8.10 (default, Nov 26 2021, 20:14:08)
[GCC 9.3.0] on linux
Type "help", "copyright", "credits" or "license" for more
 information.
>>> import os
>>> thisdir = os.getcwd()
>>> print(thisdir)
/home/sam
>>> if not os.path.isdir("TYV_Python"):
...     os.mkdir("TYV_Python")
...
>>> os.chdir("TYV_Python")
>>> os.getcwd()           7
'/home/sam/TYV_Python'
>>> os.listdir()          8
[]
>>>
```

```
sam@vubuntu:~$ python3
Python 3.8.10 (default, Nov 26 2021, 20:14:08)
[GCC 9.3.0] on linux
Type "help", "copyright", "credits" or "license" for more
 information.
>>> import os
>>> thisdir = os.getcwd()
>>> print(thisdir)
/home/sam
>>> if not os.path.isdir("TYV_Python"):
...     os.mkdir("TYV_Python")
...
>>> os.chdir("TYV_Python")
>>> os.getcwd()
'/home/sam/TYV_Python'
>>> os.listdir()
[]                        9
>>> os.mkdir("Examples")  10
>>>
```

TIP

What happens if I try to create a directory that already exists?
Python throws a `FileExistsError` error, such as `FileExistsError: [Errno 17] File exists: 'Temp'`. You can write code to handle the error, but usually, it is better to use `os.path.isdir()` to check whether a directory exists before trying to create it.

continued ▶

Create and Delete Directories (continued)

Python's `os` module includes the `rmdir()` method for removing a single file or directory. When you need to remove multiple files or directories, you can use the `rmdir()` method in a loop.

Sometimes you may need to remove an entire directory tree — a directory and all its subdirectories — in a single move. To remove a directory tree, you can import the Shell Utility module, `shutil`, and then use its `rmtree()` method.

Create and Delete Directories (continued)

11 Type the following statement, which uses the `makedirs()` method of the `os` module to create a directory and its subdirectories, and then press Enter.

```
os.makedirs("Files/Final")
```

Python creates the directories but gives no confirmation.

12 Type the following statement, which uses the `listdir()` method of the `os` module to display the directory's contents, and then press Enter.

```
os.listdir()
```

Python returns the list of files and directories, such as `['Examples', 'Files']`.

13 Type the following statement, which uses the `chdir()` method of the `os` module to change to the `Files` directory. Press Enter.

```
os.chdir("Files")
```

14 Press ⬆ twice to repeat the `os.listdir()` command, and then press Enter:

```
os.listdir()
```

Python displays the list of contents of the `Files` directory: `['Final']`.

15 Type the following statement to change to the `Final` directory, again pressing Enter.

```
os.chdir("Final")
```

16 Press ⬆ twice to repeat the `os.listdir()` command, and then press Enter:

```
os.listdir()
```

Python displays the list of contents of the `Files` directory: `[]` — in other words, nothing.

```
sam@vubuntu:~$ python3
Python 3.8.10 (default, Nov 26 2021, 20:14:08)
[GCC 9.3.0] on linux
Type "help", "copyright", "credits" or "license" for more
 information.
>>> import os
>>> thisdir = os.getcwd()
>>> print(thisdir)
/home/sam
>>> if not os.path.isdir("TYV_Python"):
...     os.mkdir("TYV_Python")
...
>>> os.chdir("TYV_Python")
>>> os.getcwd()
'/home/sam/TYV_Python'
>>> os.listdir()
[]
>>> os.mkdir("Examples")
>>> os.makedirs("Files/Final")        11
>>> os.listdir()                       12
['Examples', 'Files']
>>> os.chdir("Files")                  13
>>>
```

```
[GCC 9.3.0] on linux
Type "help", "copyright", "credits" or "license" for more
 information.
>>> import os
>>> thisdir = os.getcwd()
>>> print(thisdir)
/home/sam
>>> if not os.path.isdir("TYV_Python"):
...     os.mkdir("TYV_Python")
...
>>> os.chdir("TYV_Python")
>>> os.getcwd()
'/home/sam/TYV_Python'
>>> os.listdir()
[]
>>> os.mkdir("Examples")
>>> os.makedirs("Files/Final")
>>> os.listdir()
['Examples', 'Files']
>>> os.chdir("Files")
>>> os.listdir()                       14
['Final']
>>> os.chdir("Final")                  15
>>> os.listdir()                       16
[]
>>>
```

Note: Use `os.chdir("..")` to move up one directory. Add `/..` for each additional directory level — for example, use `os.chdir("../../..")` to move up three levels.

17 Type the following statement, which uses the chdir() method with the argument ../.. to move up two directories. Press **Enter**.

```
os.chdir("../..")
```

18 Type the os.getcwd() command again, and then press **Enter**, to display the current directory:

```
os.getcwd()
```

Python displays the directory path.

19 Type the following statement, which displays the contents of the current directory, and then press **Enter**:

```
os.listdir()
```

Python displays the contents of the TYV_Python directory, ['Examples', 'Files'].

20 Type the following statement, which uses the rmdir() method to remove the Examples directory. Press **Enter**.

```
os.rmdir("Examples")
```

21 Type the following statement, which imports the shutil module, and then press **Enter**:

```
import shutil
```

22 Type the following statement, which uses the rmtree() method of shutil to remove the Files directory tree. Press **Enter**.

```
shutil.rmtree("Files")
```

23 Press ⬆ four times to repeat the os.listdir() command, and then press **Enter**:

```
os.listdir()
```

Python displays the directory's contents: [] — in other words, nothing.

```
>>> import os
>>> thisdir = os.getcwd()
>>> print(thisdir)
/home/sam
>>> if not os.path.isdir("TYV_Python"):
...     os.mkdir("TYV_Python")
...
>>> os.chdir("TYV_Python")
>>> os.getcwd()
'/home/sam/TYV_Python'
>>> os.listdir()
[]
>>> os.mkdir("Examples")
>>> os.makedirs("Files/Final")
>>> os.listdir()
['Examples', 'Files']
>>> os.chdir("Files")
>>> os.listdir()
['Final']
>>> os.chdir("Final")
>>> os.listdir()
[]
>>> os.chdir("../..")    ◄17
>>> os.getcwd()    ◄18
'/home/sam/TYV_Python'
>>>
```

```
>>> os.chdir("TYV_Python")
>>> os.getcwd()
'/home/sam/TYV_Python'
>>> os.listdir()
[]
>>> os.mkdir("Examples")
>>> os.makedirs("Files/Final")
>>> os.listdir()
['Examples', 'Files']
>>> os.chdir("Files")
>>> os.listdir()
['Final']
>>> os.chdir("Final")
>>> os.listdir()
[]
>>> os.chdir("../..")
>>> os.getcwd()
'/home/sam/TYV_Python'
>>> os.listdir()    ◄19
['Examples', 'Files']
>>> os.rmdir("Examples")    ◄20
>>> import shutil    ◄21
>>> shutil.rmtree("Files")    ◄22
>>> os.listdir()    ◄23
[]
>>>
```

TIP

Why do I need to use shutil.rmtree() to delete a directory tree?
Python's os.rmdir() method enables you to delete a directory only if it is empty. If the directory has contents, Python returns the error OSError: [Errno 66] Directory not empty. To delete the directory using os.rmdir(), you must first remove all its contents. By contrast, the shutil.rmtree() method can delete the directory and all its contents. The deletion is immediate and permanent, so use rmtree() with great care.

Rename, Move, and Copy Files and Directories

Python's `os` module and `shutil` module provide the commands you need to copy, move, and rename files and directories. The `rename()` method of the `os` module enables you not only to change the name of a file or directory, but also move it to different location by specifying the appropriate directory. The `remove()` method of the `os` module lets you delete a file, whereas the `rmdir()` method lets you delete a directory that has no contents.

Rename, Move, and Copy Files and Directories

1 Open a terminal window and launch Python.

A The Python prompt appears.

2 Type the following statement, which imports the `os` module, and then press Enter.

```
import os
```

3 Type the following statement, which creates the variable `tdir` and assigns to it the path to the user's home directory plus `temp1`. Press Enter.

```
tdir = os.path.expanduser("~") + "/
temp1"
```

Note: See the following section, "Get Information About the User and System," for information about the `expanduser()` method.

4 Type the following two-line `if` statement, which uses the `isdir()` method of the `path` object in the `os` module to check whether the `tdir` directory exists and then uses the `mkdir()` method of the `os` module to create it if it does not. Press Enter at the end of each line, and press Enter once more to end the `if` statement.

```
if not os.path.isdir(tdir):
    os.mkdir(tdir)
```

Note: Indent the second line of the `if` statement by four spaces.

5 Type the following statement, which uses the `chdir()` method of the `os` module to change to the `tdir` directory. Press Enter.

```
os.chdir(tdir)
```

```
guy@Mac-Pro-2 ~ % python3
Python 3.10.0 (v3.10.0:b494f5935c, Oct  4 2021, 14:59:20) [C
lang 12.0.5 (clang-1205.0.22.11)] on darwin
Type "help", "copyright", "credits" or "license" for more in
formation.
>>> import os
>>> tdir = os.path.expanduser("~") + "/temp1"
>>>
```

```
guy@Mac-Pro-2 ~ % python3
Python 3.10.0 (v3.10.0:b494f5935c, Oct  4 2021, 14:59:20) [C
lang 12.0.5 (clang-1205.0.22.11)] on darwin
Type "help", "copyright", "credits" or "license" for more in
formation.
>>> import os
>>> tdir = os.path.expanduser("~") + "/temp1"
>>> if not os.path.isdir(tdir):
...     os.mkdir(tdir)
...
>>> os.chdir(tdir)
>>>
```

6 Type the following statement, which uses the `getcwd()` method of the `os` module to return the current directory, and then press Enter.

```
os.getcwd()
```

Python returns the path, such as `'/Users/guy/temp1'`.

7 Type the following statement, which creates the variable `f1` and assigns to it a text file created in the current directory using the `open()` function. Press Enter.

```
f1 = open("myfile.txt", "w")
```

8 Type the following statement, which uses the `close()` method to close the `f1` file object. Press Enter.

```
f1.close()
```

9 Type the following statement, which uses the `os.listdir()` method to list the directory's contents, and then press Enter:

```
os.listdir()
```

Python displays the list, such as `['myfile.txt']`.

10 Type the following statement, which imports the `shutil` module, and then press Enter:

```
import shutil
```

11 Type the following statement, which uses the `copy()` method of the `shutil` module to copy `myfile.txt` to a file named `copy.txt` in the same directory. Press Enter.

```
shutil.copy("myfile.txt", "copy.txt")
```

Python returns `'copy.txt'`, indicating that `shutil` has copied the file.

```
guy@Mac-Pro-2 ~ % python3
Python 3.10.0 (v3.10.0:b494f5935c, Oct  4 2021, 14:59:20) [C
lang 12.0.5 (clang-1205.0.22.11)] on darwin
Type "help", "copyright", "credits" or "license" for more in
formation.
>>> import os
>>> tdir = os.path.expanduser("~") + "/temp1"
>>> if not os.path.isdir(tdir):
...     os.mkdir(tdir)
...
>>> os.chdir(tdir)
>>> os.getcwd()          6
'/Users/guy/temp1'
>>> f1 = open("myfile.txt", "w")   7
>>> f1.close()           8
>>>
```

```
guy@Mac-Pro-2 ~ % python3
Python 3.10.0 (v3.10.0:b494f5935c, Oct  4 2021, 14:59:20) [C
lang 12.0.5 (clang-1205.0.22.11)] on darwin
Type "help", "copyright", "credits" or "license" for more in
formation.
>>> import os
>>> tdir = os.path.expanduser("~") + "/temp1"
>>> if not os.path.isdir(tdir):
...     os.mkdir(tdir)
...
>>> os.chdir(tdir)
>>> os.getcwd()
'/Users/guy/temp1'
>>> f1 = open("myfile.txt", "w")
>>> f1.close()
>>> os.listdir()       9
['myfile.txt']
10  import shutil
>>> shutil.copy("myfile.txt", "copy.txt")   11
'copy.txt'
>>>
```

TIP

What is the difference between `shutil.copy()` and `shutil.copyfile()`?
The `shutil.copy()` method is the standard means of copying a file. It copies the source file to the specified destination and preserves the file's metadata in the copy. The `shutil.copyfile()` method likewise copies the source file to the destination directory, but does not preserve the file's metadata in the copy.

continued ▶

Rename, Move, and Copy Files and Directories
(continued)

There is some overlap between the file- and directory-management capabilities of the `os` module and those of the `shutil` module, but generally speaking, the `shutil` module's commands are wider ranging than those of the `os` module.

The `copy()` method of the `shutil` module lets you create a copy of a file, whereas the `copytree()` method of `shutil` enables you to copy a directory and all its contents. Similarly, the `move()` method of the `shutil` module enables you to move an entire directory tree from one directory to another.

Copy, Move, and Rename Files and Directories (continued)

12 Press ⬆ three times to repeat the `os.listdir()` command, and then press **Enter**:

```
os.listdir()
```

Python displays the list, such as `['copy.txt', 'myfile.txt']`.

13 Type the following statement, which uses the `rename()` method of the `os` module to rename the `copy.txt` file to `spare.txt`. Press **Enter**.

```
os.rename("copy.txt", "spare.txt")
```

14 Type the following statement, which uses the `remove()` method of the `os` module to remove `spare.txt`, and then press **Enter**.

```
os.remove("spare.txt")
```

15 Type the following statement, which uses the `mkdir()` method of the `os` module to create a subdirectory called `today` in the `temp1` directory. Press **Enter**.

```
os.mkdir("today")
```

16 Press ⬆ four times to repeat the `os.listdir()` command, and then press **Enter**:

```
os.listdir()
```

Python returns `['today', 'myfile.txt']`.

17 Type the following statement, which uses the `copy()` method of the `shutil` module to copy `myfile.txt` to the `today` directory, and then press **Enter**:

```
shutil.copy("myfile.txt", "today")
```

Python returns `'today/myfile.txt'`, indicating that `shutil` has copied the file.

```
guy — Python — 60×28
guy@Mac-Pro-2 ~ % python3
Python 3.10.0 (v3.10.0:b494f5935c, Oct  4 2021, 14:59:20) [C
lang 12.0.5 (clang-1205.0.22.11)] on darwin
Type "help", "copyright", "credits" or "license" for more in
formation.
>>> import os
>>> tdir = os.path.expanduser("~") + "/temp1"
>>> if not os.path.isdir(tdir):
...     os.mkdir(tdir)
...
>>> os.chdir(tdir)
>>> os.getcwd()
'/Users/guy/temp1'
>>> f1 = open("myfile.txt", "w")
>>> f1.close()
>>> os.listdir()
['myfile.txt']
>>> import shutil
>>> shutil.copy("myfile.txt", "copy.txt")
'copy.txt'
>>> os.listdir()
['copy.txt', 'myfile.txt']
>>> os.rename("copy.txt", "spare.txt")
>>> os.remove("spare.txt")
>>>
```
12 **13** **14**

```
guy — Python — 80×28
lang 12.0.5 (clang-1205.0.22.11)] on darwin
Type "help", "copyright", "credits" or "license" for more in
formation.
>>> import os
>>> tdir = os.path.expanduser("~") + "/temp1"
>>> if not os.path.isdir(tdir):
...     os.mkdir(tdir)
...
>>> os.chdir(tdir)
>>> os.getcwd()
'/Users/guy/temp1'
>>> f1 = open("myfile.txt", "w")
>>> f1.close()
>>> os.listdir()
['myfile.txt']
>>> import shutil
>>> shutil.copy("myfile.txt", "copy.txt")
'copy.txt'
>>> os.listdir()
['copy.txt', 'myfile.txt']
>>> os.rename("copy.txt", "spare.txt")
>>> os.remove("spare.txt")
>>> os.mkdir("today")
>>> os.listdir()
['today', 'myfile.txt']
>>> shutil.copy("myfile.txt", "today")
'today/myfile.txt'
>>>
```
16 **15** **17**

18 Type the following statement, which uses `os.listdir()` to list the contents of the `today` directory. Press **Enter**.

```
os.listdir("today")
```

Python returns `['myfile.txt']`.

19 Type the following statement, which uses the `copytree()` method of the `shutil` module to copy the `today` directory and its contents to a directory named `backup`. Press **Enter**.

```
shutil.copytree("today", "backup")
```

Python returns `'backup'`, indicating that `shutil` has created the directory.

```
● ● ●                    guy — Python — 60×28
...        os.mkdir(tdir)
...
>>> os.chdir(tdir)
>>> os.getcwd()
'/Users/guy/temp1'
>>> f1 = open("myfile.txt", "w")
>>> f1.close()
>>> os.listdir()
['myfile.txt']
>>> import shutil
>>> shutil.copy("myfile.txt", "copy.txt")
'copy.txt'
>>> os.listdir()
['copy.txt', 'myfile.txt']
>>> os.rename("copy.txt", "spare.txt")
>>> os.remove("spare.txt")
>>> os.mkdir("today")
>>> os.listdir()
['today', 'myfile.txt']
>>> shutil.copy("myfile.txt", "today")
'today/myfile.txt'
>>> os.listdir("today")      18
['myfile.txt']
>>> shutil.copytree("today", "backup")   19
'backup'
>>> ▊
```

20 Press **↑** twice to reenter the `os.listdir()` statement, but change the directory to `"backup"` before you press **Enter**:

```
os.listdir("backup")
```

Python returns `['myfile.txt']`, enabling you to see that the copied directory's contents are present.

```
● ● ●                    guy — Python — 60×28
...        os.mkdir(tdir)
...
>>> os.chdir(tdir)
>>> os.getcwd()
'/Users/guy/temp1'
>>> f1 = open("myfile.txt", "w")
>>> f1.close()
>>> os.listdir()
['myfile.txt']
>>> import shutil
>>> shutil.copy("myfile.txt", "copy.txt")
'copy.txt'
>>> os.listdir()
['copy.txt', 'myfile.txt']
>>> os.rename("copy.txt", "spare.txt")
>>> os.remove("spare.txt")
>>> os.mkdir("today")
>>> os.listdir()
['today', 'myfile.txt']
>>> shutil.copy("myfile.txt", "today")
'today/myfile.txt'
>>> os.listdir("today")
['myfile.txt']
>>> shutil.copytree("today", "backup")
'backup'
>>> os.listdir("backup")    20
['myfile.txt']
>>> ▊
```

TIP

How do I move a directory and all its contents?

To move a directory tree, import the `shutil` module and use its `move()` method. For example, to move the directory tree `files` to the directory `archive/files`, first type **import shutil** and press **Enter**, and then type **shutil.move("files", "archive/files")** and press **Enter**. If the directory does not exist, the `move()` method creates it automatically.

Get Information About the User and System

Your code may need to return information about the user running or system running a script. For example, you might want to determine where a user's home directory is so that your code can use it, return the working directory, or learn the computer's operating system.

You use different tools to access different types of information. For example, the os module gives access to the user's home directory, while the sys module lets you determine the operating system. Environment variables offer detailed information about the user and the computing environment on Linux and macOS but provide little information on Windows.

The following subsections explain how to return the user's name from the getpass module, return the user's home directory from the os module, return the computer's operating system via the sys module, and use environment variables to access a wider range of information on Linux and macOS.

Return the User's Username

To return the user's username, first import the getpass module, and then use the getuser() method:

```
import getpass
username = getpass.getuser()
print(username)
```

Return the User's Home Directory

To return the user's home directory, first import the os module, and then use the expanduser() method of the path object in the os module, with the argument ~, as in the second of the following statements. The third statement uses the chdir() method to change directory to the homedir directory.

```
import os
homedir = os.path.expanduser("~")
os.chdir(homedir)
```

Determine the Computer's Operating System

To determine the computer's operating system, first import the sys module:

```
import sys
```

You can then return the platform attribute to get the operating system — for example:

```
print(sys.platform)
```

The value win32 indicates Windows, darwin indicates macOS, and either linux or linux2 indicates Linux.

Return Information Using Environment Variables

Python's environment variables enable you to return a wide range of information about the user and the environment on Linux and macOS, but not on Windows.

Table 4-1 explains the most widely useful environment variables.

Table 4-1: Python's Environment Variables		
Variable Name	**Returns the**	**Example**
USER	User's username	jo
LOGNAME	User's login name	jo
HOME	User's home directory on macOS or Linux	/Users/jo
LANG	Current language encoding	en_US.UTF-8
OLDPWD	Old working directory	/Users/jo
PWD	Current working directory	/Users/jo/samples
SHELL	The shell, the command language interpreter	/bin/zsh on macOS /bin/bash on Linux,

To access the environment variables, you import the os module and then use the environ object. Here are quick examples of returning information from environment variables:

- Import the os module:
  ```
  import os
  ```

- Return the username:
  ```
  os.environ.get("USER")
  ```

- Return the user's home directory and change directory to it on macOS or Linux:
  ```
  homedir = os.environ.get("HOME")
  os.chdir(homedir)
  ```

- Return the language encoding:
  ```
  os.environ.get("LANG")
  ```

- Return the present working directory:
  ```
  os.environ.get("PWD")
  ```

- Return the current shell:
  ```
  os.environ.get("SHELL")
  ```

Split a File Path into Its Components

Python's `os` module enables you to split a file path into its components. By using the `split()` method of the `path` object in the `os` module, you can split the path and the filename. And by using the `splitext()` method of the `path` object, you can split the base filename from the extension. For example, starting from the file path `Users/Ted/Python/Division1.txt`, you can return the path, `/Users/Ted/Python`; the base filename, `Division1`; and the file extension, `.txt`. Using the components, you can then build a different file path — for example, creating the name for an output file for a script.

Split a File Path into Its Components

① Open a terminal window and launch Python.

Ⓐ The Python prompt appears.

② Type the following statement, which imports the `os` module, and then press Enter:

`import os`

③ Type the following statement, which creates a variable named `fp` and assigns to it a file path in macOS format. Press Enter.

`fp = "/Users/Ted/Python/Division1.txt"`

④ Type the following statement, which creates the variables `d` and `f` and uses the `split()` method of the `path` object in the `os` module to assign to them the directory path and the full filename, respectively, from `fp`. Press Enter.

`d, f = os.path.split(fp)`

⑤ Type the following statement, which uses the `print()` function to display the contents of `d`, and then press Enter:

`print(d)`

Python displays `/Users/Ted/Python`.

⑥ Type the following statement to display the contents of `f`, and then press Enter:

`print(f)`

Python displays `Division1.txt`.

```
guy — Python — 63×28                      1
guy@Mac-Pro-2 ~ % python3
Python 3.10.0 (v3.10.0:b494f5935c, Oct  4 2021, 14:59:20) [Clan
g 12.0.5 (clang-1205.0.22.11)] on darwin
Type "help", "copyright", "credits" or "license" for more infor
mation.
>>> import os              2
>>> fp = "/Users/Ted/Python/Division1.txt"       3
>>>
```

```
guy — Python — 63×28
guy@Mac-Pro-2 ~ % python3
Python 3.10.0 (v3.10.0:b494f5935c, Oct  4 2021, 14:59:20) [Clan
g 12.0.5 (clang-1205.0.22.11)] on darwin
Type "help", "copyright", "credits" or "license" for more infor
mation.
>>> import os
>>> fp = "/Users/Ted/Python/Division1.txt"
>>> d, f = os.path.split(fp)         4
>>> print(d)
/Users/Ted/Pytho
>>> print(f)        6
Division1.txt
>>>
```

7 Type the following statement, which creates the variables `fn` and `x` and assigns to them the results of using the `splitext()` method of the `path` object in the `os` module to split the filename and extension in `f`. Press `Enter`.

```
fn, x = os.path.splitext(f)
```

8 Type the following statement to display the contents of `fn`, and then press `Enter`:

```
print(fn)
```

Python displays `Division1`.

9 Type the following statement to display the contents of `x`, and then press `Enter`:

```
print(x)
```

Python displays `.txt`.

10 Type the following statement, which creates a variable named `output` and assigns to it a string formed from `d`, `f`, `/`, and the extension `.rtf`. Press `Enter`.

```
output = d + "/" + fn + ".rtf"
```

11 Type the following statement to display the contents of `output`, and then press `Enter`:

```
print(output)
```

Python displays `/Users/Ted/Python/Division1.rtf`.

```
guy@Mac-Pro-2 ~ % python3
Python 3.10.0 (v3.10.0:b494f5935c, Oct  4 2021, 14:59:20) [Clan
g 12.0.5 (clang-1205.0.22.11)] on darwin
Type "help", "copyright", "credits" or "license" for more infor
mation.
>>> import os
>>> fp = "/Users/Ted/Python/Division1.txt"
>>> d, f = os.path.split(fp)
>>> print(d)
/Users/Ted/Python
>>> print(f)
Division1.txt
>>> fn, x = os.path.splitext(f)    ← 7
   8 → print(fn)
Division1
>>> print(x)    ← 9
.txt
>>>
```

```
guy@Mac-Pro-2 ~ % python3
Python 3.10.0 (v3.10.0:b494f5935c, Oct  4 2021, 14:59:20) [Clan
g 12.0.5 (clang-1205.0.22.11)] on darwin
Type "help", "copyright", "credits" or "license" for more infor
mation.
>>> import os
>>> fp = "/Users/Ted/Python/Division1.txt"
>>> d, f = os.path.split(fp)
>>> print(d)
/Users/Ted/Python
>>> print(f)
Division1.txt
>>> fn, x = os.path.splitext(f)
>>> print(fn)
Division1
>>> print(x)
.txt
>>> output = d + "/" + fn + ".rtf"    ← 10
  11 → print(output)
/Users/Ted/Python/Division1.rtf
>>>
```

TIP

What other methods does the `os.path` object provide?

Here are four highly useful methods. The `basename()` method returns the filename and extension from a file path — for example, typing `os.path.basename("/Users/jill/a.png")` and pressing `Enter` returns `'a.png'`. The `dirname()` method returns the directory path — for example, `os.path.dirname("/Users/jill/a.png")` returns `'/Users/jill'`. The `isabs()` method returns `True` if the specified path is absolute, beginning with / on UNIX-based file systems and \ on Windows after a drive letter and colon, such as `C:\`. The `normcase()` method returns paths unchanged on macOS and Linux but on Windows converts paths to lowercase and changes forward slashes to escaped backslashes; for example, `os.path.normcase("/Users/Jo/Pictures")` returns `'\\users\\jo\\pictures'` on Windows.

Understanding Python's `open()` Function

Python's `open()` function enables you to open a file if it exists and to create the file if it does not exist. The `open()` function has various modes that you specify by including the appropriate argument when you call the function. For example, you can use `open()` with the `w` parameter to open a file in Write Mode, which enables you to make changes to the file. Or you can use `open()` with the `a` parameter to open the file in Append Mode, which lets you append data at the end of the file's existing contents.

The `open()` function enables you to open a file in one of six main modes:

- **Write Mode.** You use Write Mode to write text to the file. Write Mode deletes the current contents of the file and inserts the text at the beginning of the file. Subsequent writes occur at the end of the file unless you specify a different position using the `seek()` method.
- **Read Mode.** You use Read Mode to read the contents of a file. In Read Mode, you cannot make changes to the file's contents.
- **Append Mode.** You use Append Mode to append text to a file without deleting its existing contents. By default, Python inserts the new text at the end of the file unless you specify a different position.
- **Write and Read Mode.** You use Write and Read Mode to open a file, deleting any existing contents, so you can write to the file and then read its contents.
- **Read and Write Mode.** You use Read and Write Mode when you need to open a file both for reading text from it and for writing text to it.
- **Append and Read Mode.** You use Append and Read Mode when you want to append data to a file and be able to read the file's contents.

Table 4-2 explains the modes of the `open()` function.

Table 4-2: Modes of Python's `open()` Function	
Mode	**Explanation**
w	Create the file if it does not exist; delete its contents if it does exist. Open the file in Write Mode with the pointer at the beginning.
r	Open the file in Read Mode with the pointer at the beginning. If the file does not exist, an error occurs.
a	Create the file if it does not exist. Open the file in Append Mode with the pointer at the end.
x	Create the specified file and then open it with the pointer at the beginning. If the file already exists, an error occurs.
w+	Create the file if it does not exist; delete its contents if it does exist. Open the file in Write and Read Mode with the pointer at the beginning.
r+	Open the file in Read and Write Mode with the pointer at the beginning. If the file does not exist, an error occurs.
a+	Create the file if it does not exist. Open the file in Append and Read Mode with the pointer at the end.

Understanding Python's Ways of Closing Files

After opening or creating a file using the open() function and either reading the file's contents or changing them, your scripts will likely need to close that file. You can either close the file explicitly by using the close() method of the file object or have Python close the file automatically for you. Python can close a file automatically either at the end of a script or when it runs a command that implicitly requires the file to be closed. Generally, it is better to close files explicitly, but you should understand how both approaches work.

The first subsection tells you how to close a file manually using the close() method of the file object that references the file. The second subsection explains how you can let Python close files implicitly in your code.

Close a File Manually Using the close() Method

To close a file explicitly, use the close() method at the appropriate point in your code. For example, the first of the following statements creates the variable f6 and uses the open() function to assign to it the file new.txt, creating the file if it does not exist. The second statement closes the f6 file object.

```
f6 = open("new.txt", "w+")
f6.close()
```

Python does not raise an error if you call the close() method on a file object that you or Python have already closed. The file object must exist, but it does not have to be open. This flexibility means that you can safely use the close() method to ensure that a file has been closed, even if it turns out to have been closed earlier.

Let Python Close a File Implicitly

Instead of closing a file explicitly using the close() method, you can let Python close the file for you. Python closes a file automatically if you assign the file object currently assigned to the open file to a different file, as in the following example for macOS or Linux:

```
# open h.txt and assign it to the variable f
f = open("/Users/fi/h.txt", "w")
# write text to f
f.write("Unblock the writer!")
# open j.txt and assign it to the variable f
f = open("/Users/fi/j.txt", "r")
# Python closes h.txt to free up f
```

Python also closes a file automatically if you use the open() function to reopen the file using a different mode. You do not need to close the file explicitly.

Open a File If It Exists; If Not, Create It

Python's `open()` function enables you to open a file in Write Mode, Write and Read Mode, Append Mode, or Append and Read Mode if the file exists, and create the file if it does not exist. Automatically creating a file is especially useful because you need neither write code to check that the file exists before you try to open it nor handle an error if the file does not exist.

Open a File If It Exists; If Not, Create It

1 Open a terminal window and launch Python.

Ⓐ The Python prompt appears.

2 Type the following statement, which imports the `os` module, and then press Enter.

```
import os
```

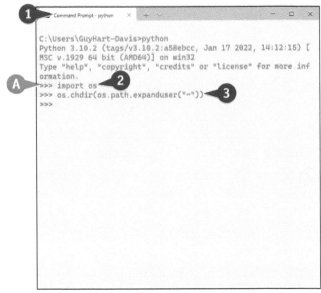

3 Use the `os.chdir()` method to change to a directory in which you can create a sample file. For example, type the following statement, and then press Enter, to change to your home directory:

```
os.chdir(os.path.expanduser("~"))
```

4 Type the following statement, which uses the `getcwd()` method of the `os` module, to display the current directory, confirming you have navigated to where you intended. Press Enter.

```
os.getcwd()
```

Python returns the directory, such as `'C:\\Users\\AJ'` on Windows.

Note: In Windows paths, Python's escaped backslash, `\\`, represents a single "real" backslash, `\`.

5 Type the following statement, which uses the `open()` function with no mode specified to try to open the file `offices.txt` in the current directory and assign it to the variable `olist`, and then press Enter.

```
olist = open("offices.txt")
```

B Python returns a `FileNotFoundError`, because the file does not exist.

6 Press ⬆ once to repeat the command, but edit the end to add the appropriate argument before you press **Enter**. In this case, use the `w` argument.

```
olist = open("offices.txt", "w")
```

Note: Use the `w` argument for Write Mode, the `w+` argument for Write and Read Mode, the `a` argument for Append Mode, and the `a+` argument for Append and Read Mode.

Python creates the file but gives no indication it has done so.

The file is now open in Write Mode.

7 Type the following statement, which uses the `write()` method to write text to the file, and then press **Enter**:

```
olist.write("Anchorage, Boston")
```

8 Type the following statement, which uses the `close()` method to close the file, and then press **Enter**:

```
olist.close()
```

Why does the `open()` function sometimes fail even though I specify the w argument?
The `open()` function with the `w` argument, the `w+` argument, the `a` argument, or the `a+` argument fails if you do not have Write permission for the directory in which Python is trying to create the file.

Check an Open File's Status and Close It

After opening a file using the `open()` function, you can use the resulting file object to manipulate the file. The following sections show you how to read a file's data, replace a file's existing data, and append new data to the existing data.

In this section, you check the properties of a file object to determine information about it. You use the `name` property to return the filename and then use the `closed` property to determine whether the file object is open or has been closed. You then use the `close()` method to close the file.

Check an Open File's Status and Close It

① Open a terminal window and launch Python.

Ⓐ The Python prompt appears.

② Type the following statement, which imports the os module, and then press **Enter**:

`import os`

③ Use the `os.chdir()` method to change to a directory in which you can create a sample file. For example, type the following statement, and then press **Enter**, to change to your home directory:

`os.chdir(os.path.expanduser("~"))`

④ Type the following statement, which uses the `open()` function with the w+ mode specified to open the existing file new.txt, or create it if it does not exist, in the current directory and assign it to the variable f1. Press **Enter**.

`f1 = open("new.txt", "w+")`

⑤ Type the following statement, which returns the name property of f1. Press **Enter**.

`f1.name`

Ⓑ Python displays 'new.txt'.

6 Type the following statement, which returns the `closed` property of f1. Press Enter.

```
f1.closed
```

C Python returns `False`.

7 Type the following statement, which uses the `close()` method to close f1, and then press Enter:

```
f1.close()
```

Python closes the file without confirmation or comment.

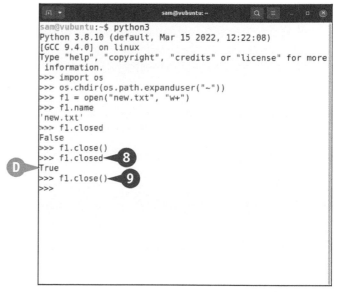

8 Press ⬆ twice to repeat the second-to-last statement, and then press Enter:

```
f1.closed
```

D Python returns `True`.

9 Press ⬆ twice to repeat the now second-to-last statement, and then press Enter:

```
f1.close()
```

Even though the file was already closed, no error occurs.

How can I check which mode an open file is using?

Return the `mode` property of the file object that represents the file. For example, use `f1.mode` to return the `mode` property of the file object represented by f1. The property returns the same string as you use to specify the mode with the `open()` function — for example, `w+`, `r`, or `a+`.

Write Data to a File

To write data to a text file, you open that file in Write Mode by using the `open()` function with the `w` argument. To write data and subsequently read it, you use the `open()` function with the `w+` argument to open the file in Write and Read Mode.

Both modes create the specified file if it does not exist; if it does exist, both modes "truncate" the file, deleting all its contents. Both modes position the pointer at the start of the file, so text you add using the `write()` method lands there.

Write Data to a File

1 Open a terminal window and launch Python.

A The Python prompt appears.

2 Type the following statement, which imports the `os` module, and then press **Enter**.

```
import os
```

3 Use the `os.chdir()` method to change to a directory in which you can create a file. For example, type the following statement, and then press **Enter**, to change to your home directory:

```
os.chdir(os.path.expanduser("~"))
```

4 Type the following statement, which creates a variable named `w1` and assigns to it the file `waters.txt`, which it opens in Write Mode. Press **Enter**.

```
w1 = open("waters.txt", "w")
```

Note: If the file exists, Python "truncates" it, deleting its contents; if not, Python creates it. Either way, the file is empty once opened.

5 Type the following statement, which uses the `write()` method to write text to the `w1` file object. Press **Enter**.

```
w1.write("beck, billabong, bight")
```

6 Type the following statement, which uses the `open()` function with the `r` argument to reopen the text file in Read Mode, reassigning it to `w1`. Press **Enter**.

```
w1 = open("waters.txt", "r")
```

Note: Python automatically closes the file before reopening it.

```
guy@Mac-Pro-2 ~ % python3
Python 3.10.0 (v3.10.0:b494f5935c, Oct  4 2021, 14:59:20) [C
lang 12.0.5 (clang-1205.0.22.11)] on darwin
Type "help", "copyright", "credits" or "license" for more in
formation.
>>> import os
>>> os.chdir(os.path.expanduser("~"))
>>> w1 = open("waters.txt", "w")
>>>
```

```
guy@Mac-Pro-2 ~ % python3
Python 3.10.0 (v3.10.0:b494f5935c, Oct  4 2021, 14:59:20) [C
lang 12.0.5 (clang-1205.0.22.11)] on darwin
Type "help", "copyright", "credits" or "license" for more in
formation.
>>> import os
>>> os.chdir(os.path.expanduser("~"))
>>> w1 = open("waters.txt", "w")
>>> w1.write("beck, billabong, bight")
22
>>> w1 = open("waters.txt", "r")
>>>
```

7 Type the following statement, which uses the print() function to display the output from using the read() method on w1. Press Enter.

```
print(w1.read())
```

Python displays beck, billabong, bight.

8 Type the following statement, which uses the open() function with the w+ argument to reopen the text file in Write and Read Mode, again assigning it to w1. Press Enter.

```
w1 = open("waters.txt", "w+")
```

Note: Again, Python automatically closes the file before reopening it. Python truncates the file, deleting its contents.

9 Type the following statement, which writes two fresh waters to the file, and then press Enter.

```
w1.write("kill, tarn")
```

10 Type the following statement, which reads the file from the pointer position. Press Enter.

```
w1.read()
```

Python displays ' ', an empty string, because the pointer is at the end of the file.

11 Type the following statement, which uses the seek() method to move the pointer to the file's beginning, and then press Enter:

```
w1.seek(0, os.SEEK_SET)
```

12 Press ⬆ twice to repeat the w1.read() statement, and then press Enter:

```
w1.read()
```

Python displays 'kill, tarn', the contents you wrote.

```
guy — Python — 60×28
guy@Mac-Pro-2 ~ % python3
Python 3.10.0 (v3.10.0:b494f5935c, Oct  4 2021, 14:59:20) [C
lang 12.0.5 (clang-1205.0.22.11)] on darwin
Type "help", "copyright", "credits" or "license" for more in
formation.
>>> import os
>>> os.chdir(os.path.expanduser("~"))
>>> w1 = open("waters.txt", "w")
>>> w1.write("beck, billabong, bight")
22
>>> w1 = open("waters.txt", "r")
>>> print(w1.read())
beck, billabong, bight
>>> w1 = open("waters.txt", "w+")
>>>
```

```
guy — Python — 60×28
guy@Mac-Pro-2 ~ % python3
Python 3.10.0 (v3.10.0:b494f5935c, Oct  4 2021, 14:59:20) [C
lang 12.0.5 (clang-1205.0.22.11)] on darwin
Type "help", "copyright", "credits" or "license" for more in
formation.
>>> import os
>>> os.chdir(os.path.expanduser("~"))
>>> w1 = open("waters.txt", "w")
>>> w1.write("beck, billabong, bight")
22
>>> w1 = open("waters.txt", "r")
>>> print(w1.read())
beck, billabong, bight
>>> w1 = open("waters.txt", "w+")
>>> w1.write("kill, tarn")
10
>>> w1.read()
''
>>> w1.seek(0, os.SEEK_SET)
0
>>> w1.read()
'kill, tarn'
>>>
```

TIP

How can I see whether a file is open?
Check the closed property of the appropriate file object. For example, if your code has created a file object named w1, as in the main example, w1.closed returns False if the file object is open and True if it has been closed.

Open a File for Both Reading and Writing

To open a file for both reading and writing, use the `open()` function with the `r+` argument. Because the file is open for writing as well as reading, you will need to be careful to avoid overwriting the existing contents of the file. For example, you can use the `seek()` method to move the pointer to the end of the file before writing new data to the file using the `write()` method. After writing, you can move the pointer back to the beginning of the file to read all its contents using the `read()` method.

Open a File for Both Reading and Writing

1 Open a terminal window and launch Python.

A The Python prompt appears.

2 Type the following statement, which imports the `os` module, and then press **Enter**.

```
import os
```

3 Use the `os.chdir()` method to change to a directory in which you can create a file. For example, type the following statement, and then press **Enter**, to change to your home directory:

```
os.chdir(os.path.expanduser("~"))
```

4 Type the following statement, which creates a variable named `rwf` and assigns to it the file `metals.txt`, which it opens or creates in Write Mode. Press **Enter**.

```
rwf = open("metals.txt", "w")
```

5 Type the following statement, which uses the `write()` method to write text to the `rwf` file object, and then press **Enter**.

```
rwf.write("Calcium\nGallium\n")
```

Python returns `16`, the character position at the end of the file.

6 Type the following statement, which opens the same file in Read/Write Mode and assigns it to `rwf` again. Press **Enter**.

```
rwf = open("metals.txt", "r+")
```

Note: Opening the file with the `r+` argument causes Python to close the file and then reopen it.

```
guy@Mac-Pro-2 ~ % python3
Python 3.10.0 (v3.10.0:b494f5935c, Oct  4 2021, 14:59:20) [C
lang 12.0.5 (clang-1205.0.22.11)] on darwin
Type "help", "copyright", "credits" or "license" for more in
formation.
>>> import os
>>> os.chdir(os.path.expanduser("~"))
>>> rwf = open("metals.txt", "w")
>>>
```

```
guy@Mac-Pro-2 ~ % python3
Python 3.10.0 (v3.10.0:b494f5935c, Oct  4 2021, 14:59:20) [C
lang 12.0.5 (clang-1205.0.22.11)] on darwin
Type "help", "copyright", "credits" or "license" for more in
formation.
>>> import os
>>> os.chdir(os.path.expanduser("~"))
>>> rwf = open("metals.txt", "w")
>>> rwf.write("Calcium\nGallium\n")
16
>>> rwf = open("metals.txt", "r+")
>>>
```

7 Type the following statement, which uses the `seek()` method to move the pointer to the end of the file, and then press `Enter`:

```
rwf.seek(0, os.SEEK_END)
```

Python returns `16`, the character position at the end of the file.

8 Type the following statement, which uses the `write()` method to add text to the file, and then press `Enter`:

```
rwf.write("Cesium")
```

Python returns `6`, the number of characters added.

9 Type the following statement, which uses the `seek()` method to move the pointer to the start of the file, and then press `Enter`:

```
rwf.seek(0, os.SEEK_SET)
```

Python returns `0`, the character position at the start of the file.

10 Type the following statement, which uses the `print()` function to display the result of reading the file's contents. Press `Enter`.

```
print(rwf.read())
```

Python displays this:

```
Calcium
Gallium
Cesium
```

11 Type the following statement, which uses the `close()` method to close `rwf`, and then press `Enter`:

```
rwf.close()
```

TIP

How can I tell whether a file is readable or writable?
Use the `readable()` method of the file object to determine whether a file is readable — for example, `myfile.readable()` returns `True` if the file is readable and `False` if it is not readable. Similarly, you can use the `writable()` method to determine whether a file is writable via the `write()` method and the `seekable()` method to determine whether Python can use the `seek()` method to change the pointer position within the file.

Append Data to a File

Python provides two modes for appending data to the existing contents of a file without affecting the existing contents. Append Mode, which you invoke by using the `a` argument with the `open()` function, lets you add text after the file's existing contents. Append and Read Mode, which you invoke by using the `a+` argument, likewise lets you append text but also lets you read the existing contents.

Both Append Mode and Append and Read Mode automatically create the specified file if it does not exist. Both modes prevent you from modifying the file's existing contents.

Append Data to a File

1 Open a terminal window and launch Python.

A The Python prompt appears.

2 Type the following statement, which imports the `os` module, and then press **Enter**.

```
import os
```

3 Use the `os.chdir()` method to change to a directory in which you can create a file. For example, type the following statement, and then press **Enter**, to change to your home directory:

```
os.chdir(os.path.expanduser("~"))
```

4 Type the following statement, which creates a variable named `s` and assigns to it the file `staples.txt`, which it opens or creates in Append Mode. Press **Enter**.

```
s = open("staples.txt", "a")
```

5 Type the following statement, which uses the `write()` method to append some text to the `s` file object. Press **Enter**.

```
s.write("Staple Foods\n\nCoffee\nEggs")
```

Python returns 25, the number of characters added.

6 Type the following statement, which uses the `close()` method to close the `s` file object explicitly, and then press **Enter**:

```
s.close()
```

```
sam@vubuntu:~$ python3
Python 3.8.10 (default, Nov 26 2021, 20:14:08)
[GCC 9.3.0] on linux
Type "help", "copyright", "credits" or "license" for more
 information.
>>> import os
>>> os.chdir(os.path.expanduser("~"))
>>> s = open("staples.txt", "a")
>>>
```

```
sam@vubuntu:~$ python3
Python 3.8.10 (default, Nov 26 2021, 20:14:08)
[GCC 9.3.0] on linux
Type "help", "copyright", "credits" or "license" for more
 information.
>>> import os
>>> os.chdir(os.path.expanduser("~"))
>>> s = open("staples.txt", "a")
>>> s.write("Staple Foods\n\nCoffee\nEggs")
25
>>> s.close()
>>>
```

7 Type the following statement, which opens the same file in Append and Read Mode, again assigning it to the variable s. Press **Enter**.

```
s = open("staples.txt", "a+")
```

8 Type the following statement, which uses the `write()` method to append text to the end of the file. Press **Enter**.

```
s.write("\nBread\nButter")
```

9 Type the following statement, which uses the `seek()` method to move the pointer to the start of the file. Press **Enter**.

```
s.seek(0, os.SEEK_SET)
```

10 Type the following statement, which uses the `print()` function to display the result of using the `read()` method to read the file's contents. Press **Enter**.

```
print(s.read())
```

Python displays the file's text:

```
Staple Foods

Coffee
Eggs
Bread
Butter
```

11 Type the following statement, which uses the `close()` method to close the file, and then press **Enter**.

```
s.close()
```

TIP

What happens if I move the pointer and then append text?

Python appends the text after the end of the existing text. In Append and Read Mode, moving the pointer to the start of the file enables you to read the file's contents, but Python puts any text you append at the end of the file.

Read a Text File

Python's `open()` function enables you to open a text file in Read Mode by using the `r+` argument or in Read and Write Mode by using the `r+` argument. Usually, the choice between Read Mode and Read and Write Mode is straightforward: Use Read Mode when you need only to read the file's contents, but use Read and Write Mode when you also need to change the contents.

Both modes place the pointer at the start of the file, ready to read from there on. Both modes return a `FileNotFoundError` if the specified file does not exist.

Read a Text File

1 Open a terminal window and launch Python.

Ⓐ The Python prompt appears.

2 Type the following statement, which imports the `os` module, and then press **Enter**.

```
import os
```

3 Use the `os.chdir()` method to change to a directory in which you can create a file. For example, type the following statement, and then press **Enter**, to change to your home directory:

```
os.chdir(os.path.expanduser("~"))
```

4 Type the following statement, which creates a variable named `xr` and assigns to it the file `waters.txt`, which it opens or creates in Write Mode. Press **Enter**.

```
xr = open("waters.txt", "w")
```

5 Type the following statement, which uses the `write()` method to add text to `xr`, and then press **Enter**:

```
xr.write("sound, swamp, wadi")
```

6 Type the following statement, which reopens the same file in Read Mode. Press **Enter**.

```
xr = open("waters.txt", "r")
```

Note: Python automatically closes the text file before reopening it.

7 Type the following statement, which uses the `print()` function to display the result of using the `read()` method to read the contents of `xr`. Press **Enter**.

```
print(xr.read())
```

```
sam@vubuntu:~$ python3
Python 3.8.10 (default, Nov 26 2021, 20:14:08)
[GCC 9.3.0] on linux
Type "help", "copyright", "credits" or "license
 information.
>>> import os
>>> os.chdir(os.path.expanduser("~"))
>>> xr = open("waters.txt", "w")
>>>
```

```
sam@vubuntu:~$ python3
Python 3.8.10 (default, Nov 26 2021, 20:14:08)
[GCC 9.3.0] on linux
Type "help", "copyright", "credits" or "license
 information.
>>> import os
>>> os.chdir(os.path.expanduser("~"))
>>> xr = open("waters.txt", "w")
>>> xr.write("sound, swamp, wadi")
18
>>> xr = open("waters.txt", "r")
>>> print(xr.read())
```

Python displays sound, swamp, wadi.

8 Type the following statement, which uses the close() method to close xr explicitly. Press Enter.

```
xr.close()
```

9 Type the following statement, which opens the file in Read and Write Mode, again assigning it to xr. Press Enter.

```
xr = open("waters.txt", "r+")
```

10 Press ⬆ three times to repeat the print() statement, and then press Enter:

```
print(xr.read())
```

Python displays sound, swamp, wadi again.

11 Type the following statement, which writes another term to the file, and then press Enter:

```
xr.write(", lagoon")
```

12 Press ⬆ twice to repeat the print() statement, and then press Enter:

```
print(xr.read())
```

B Python returns a blank paragraph, because the Write operation has moved the pointer to the end of the file.

13 Type the following statement, which uses the seek() method to move the pointer to the start of the file. Press Enter.

```
xr.seek(0, os.SEEK_SET)
```

14 Press ⬆ twice to repeat the print() command, and then press Enter:

```
print(xr.read())
```

Python displays sound, swamp, wadi, lagoon, the file's entire contents.

```
sam@vubuntu:~$ python3
Python 3.8.10 (default, Nov 26 2021, 20:14:08)
[GCC 9.3.0] on linux
Type "help", "copyright", "credits" or "license" fd
 information.
>>> import os
>>> os.chdir(os.path.expanduser("~"))
>>> xr = open("waters.txt", "w")
>>> xr.write("sound, swamp, wadi")
18
>>> xr = open("waters.txt", "r")
>>> print(xr.read())
sound, swamp, wadi
   xr.close()          ← 8
>>> xr = open("waters.txt", "r+")  ← 9
>>> print(xr.read())   ← 10
sound, swamp, wadi
>>> xr.write(", lagoon")  ← 11
8
>>>
```

```
sam@vubuntu:~$ python3
Python 3.8.10 (default, Nov 26 2021, 20:14:08)
[GCC 9.3.0] on linux
Type "help", "copyright", "credits" or "license" fd
 information.
>>> import os
>>> os.chdir(os.path.expanduser("~"))
>>> xr = open("waters.txt", "w")
>>> xr.write("sound, swamp, wadi")
18
>>> xr = open("waters.txt", "r")
>>> print(xr.read())
sound, swamp, wadi
>>> xr.close()
>>> xr = open("waters.txt", "r+")
>>> print(xr.read())
sound, swamp, wadi
>>> xr.write(", lagoon")
8
>>> print(xr.read())  ← 12
B
>>> xr.seek(0, os.SEEK_SET)  ← 13
0
>>> print(xr.read())  ← 14
sound, swamp, wadi, lagoon
>>>
```

TIP

What happens if I move the pointer to the start of the file and then write text?
If you explicitly move the pointer to the start of the file, the text you write overwrites any text that is in the way. If the text you write is shorter than the existing text, some of the existing text remains.

## CHAPTER 5

Working with Python's Operators

Python provides a wide range of operators for performing operations on values and variables. You use arithmetic operators to perform mathematics, assignment operators to assign data to variables, comparison operators to make comparisons, and logical operators to link conditional statements. You use identity operators to test whether objects are identical, membership operators to determine whether an object includes a particular value, and bitwise operators to compare and manipulate binary numbers.

Meet the Arithmetic Operators

When you need to perform arithmetical operations in Python, such as addition or division, you can use standard arithmetic operators, adapted slightly for the computer keyboard. For example, while the keyboard includes the + key for addition, it has no ÷ key for division, so you use `/` for division instead.

Python performs operations following the standard order used in mathematics. This order is sometimes summarized by the acronym PEMDAS: Parentheses, Exponentiation, Multiplication, Division, Addition, and Subtraction. You can change the order of operations by putting particular operations in parentheses, thus promoting them to earlier positions in the order of operations.

Table 5-1 explains the arithmetic operators you can use in Python. Most of these are instantly recognizable, with the possible exception of these two:

- **Integer division.** Also called *floor division*, this operation returns only the integer component of the result. For example, with regular division, 10 divided by 4 returns 2.5. With integer division, 10 divided by 4 returns 2, discarding the decimal component and returning the integer.
- **Modulus.** This operation returns the remainder — the number left over — from a division operation. For example, 5 modulus 4 returns 1, because 1 is the remainder after dividing 5 by 4. Similarly, 9 modulus 4 also returns 1, and 399 modulus 200 returns 199.

Table 5-1:	Python's Arithmetic Operators		
Operation	**Operator**	**Example**	**Returns**
Addition	+	1 + 1	2
Subtraction	–	2 - 1	1
Multiplication	*	3 * 3	9
Exponentiation	**	2**8	256
Division	/	3 / 3	1.0
Integer Division	//	9 // 4	2
Modulus	%	10 % 3	1

Understanding the Order of Operations

Python implements mathematical operations in the standard order given by the acronym PEMDAS:

1. **P**arentheses
2. **E**xponentiation
3. **M**ultiplication and **D**ivision
4. **A**ddition and **S**ubtraction

When two operations at the same level occur, Python evaluates them reading from left to right.

So take for example the following calculation:

```
4 ** 3 - 5 * 8 + 4 / (1 + 1)
```

This calculation returns 26. Python evaluates it as follows:

- Parentheses: `(1 + 1)` gives 2, so the calculation becomes
  `4 ** 3 - 5 * 8 + 4 / 2`

- Exponentiation: `4 ** 3` gives 64. The calculation becomes
  `64 - 5 * 8 + 4 / 2`

- Multiplication: `5 * 8` gives 40. The calculation becomes
  `64 - 40 + 4 / 2`

- Division: `4 / 2` gives 2. The calculation becomes
  `64 - 40 + 2`

- Addition and subtraction: `64 - 40` occurs first, giving 24. Then `24 + 2` gives 26.

Changing the Order of Operations

You can change the order of operations in a calculation by placing one or more parts of the calculation in parentheses. For example, say you want to add 5 and 5, giving 10, and then multiply that by 10. This gives 100, but if you use the following calculation, you get 55 instead because of the standard order of operations:

```
5 + 5 * 10
```

To change the order of operations, you put the addition component inside parentheses, making Python evaluate it first:

```
(5 + 5) * 10
```

You can nest parentheses within parentheses, as needed. Python performs the most deeply nested calculation first — for example:

```
(5 + ((2 * 3) - 1)) * 10
```

Here, Python multiplies 2 by 3, subtracts 1 from the resulting 6, adds the resulting 5 to the first 5, and multiplies the resulting 10 by 10, giving 100 again.

Work with the Arithmetic Operators

In the previous section, "Meet the Arithmetic Operators," you learned what arithmetic operators Python provides and what they do. In this section, you put the arithmetic operators to work performing calculations.

To work through these examples and those later in this chapter, open a terminal window on your computer. For example, on Windows, click **Search** (🔍), type cmd, and then click **Command Prompt** (⬛) or press Enter. On macOS, click **Launchpad** (⠿), and then click **Terminal** (⬛). On Ubuntu, click **Show Applications** (⊞), and then click **Terminal** (⬛).

Work with the Arithmetic Operators

Launch Python and Perform Arithmetic Calculations

1 Open a terminal window and launch Python.

Ⓐ The Python prompt appears.

2 Type the following addition calculation using the + operator, and then press Enter.

`5 + 4`

Python displays the result, 9.

3 Type the following subtraction calculation, and then press Enter.

`4 - 7`

Python displays the result, -3.

4 Type the following multiplication calculation, and then press Enter.

`6.33 * 9.2`

Python displays the result, 58.236.

5 Type the following exponentiation calculation, and then press Enter.

`2 ** 8`

Python displays the result, 256.

6 Type the following division calculation, and then press Enter.

`77 / 11`

Python displays the result, 7.0.

7 Type the following integer division calculation, and then press Enter.

`90 // 11`

Python displays the result, 8.

114

Note: Integer division returns only the integer component of the result of the division calculation, discarding the remainder.

⑧ Type the following modulus calculation, and then press **Enter**.

`90 % 11`

Python displays the result, `2`.

Note: The modulus gives the amount left over following a division operation. In this case, 11 times 8 produces 88, so the modulus gives 2.

Using Parentheses to Change the Order of Precedence

① In the terminal window, type the following calculation, and then press **Enter**.

`5 + 4 * 8 / 2 + 1`

Python displays the result, `22.0`.

② Type the calculation again, this time adding parentheses around `5 + 4`, and then press **Enter**.

`(5 + 4) * 8 / 2 + 1`

Python display the result of the adjusted calculation, `37.0`.

③ Type the calculation a third time, this time adding parentheses around `2 + 1`, and then press **Enter**.

`(5 + 4) * 8 / (2 + 1)`

Python displays the new result, `24.0`.

TIP

Why does division return a floating-point number with `.0` rather than an integer?
Using the division operator, `/`, always produces a floating-point number, even if the calculation results in an integer with a .0 decimal component.

If necessary, you can use the `int()` function to convert a floating-point number to an integer.

Meet the Assignment Operators

As you have seen earlier in this book, Python uses the equal sign, =, to assign a value to a variable. For example, you can use the statement `userLevel = "Professional"` to create a variable called `userLevel` and assign the string value `Professional` to it.

Python includes a dozen other assignment operators. These operators are for assigning a value to a variable by manipulating its existing value. For example, the `+=` assignment operator adds to a variable's existing value: `myInt += 7` has the same effect as `myInt = myInt + 7` but is quicker and easier to enter.

Table 5-2 explains the assignment operators, showing a brief example of each and giving the equivalent full command.

Table 5-2: Python's Assignment Operators			
Operation	**Operator**	**Example**	**Equivalent**
Assignment Operator			
Assignment only	=	`str1 = "Manager"`	Not applicable
Arithmetic and Assignment Operators			
Addition and assignment	+=	`x += 1`	`x = x + 1`
Subtraction and assignment	-=	`x -= 2`	`x = x - 2`
Multiplication and assignment	*=	`x *= 3`	`x = x * 3`
Division and assignment	/=	`x /= 4`	`x = x / 4`
Percentage and assignment	%=	`x %= 6`	`x = x % 6`
Floor division and assignment	//=	`x //= 7`	`x = x // 7`
Exponentiation and assignment	**=	`x **= 8`	`x = x ** 8`
Bitwise and Assignment Operators			
In-place AND and assignment	&=	`a &= b`	`a = a & b`
In-place OR and assignment	|=	`a |= b`	`a = a | b`
In-place XOR and assignment	^=	`a ^= b`	`a = a ^ b`
Bitwise right shift and assignment	>>=	`x >>= 2`	`x = x >> 2`
Bitwise left shift and assignment	<<=	`x <<= 3`	`x = x << 3`

The first of the assignment operators, =, needs no introduction, as you have already used it extensively to assign values to variables. Beyond this, you will recognize the arithmetic-plus-assignment operators from the earlier section, "Meet the Arithmetic Operators." For example, the + operator performs addition, and the += operator performs addition and assignment.

The five assignment operators that include bitwise operations — &=, |=, ^=, >>=, and <<= — evaluate and manipulate the bit values in binary numbers and then perform assignment. See the section "Meet the Bitwise Operators," later in this chapter, to learn the details of bitwise operations.

Work with the Assignment Operators

In the previous section, "Meet the Assignment Operators," you learned about the assignment operators Python provides and what they do. In this section, you use two of the arithmetic-and-assignment operators to manipulate the existing values of variables and then reassign the result back to the same variables. See the section "Meet the Bitwise Operators," later in this chapter, for examples of working with Python's bitwise operators.

Work with the Assignment Operators

① Open a terminal window and launch Python.

Ⓐ The Python prompt appears.

② Type the following statement, which creates the variable `myNum` and assigns the value 2 to it, and then press **Enter**.

`myNum = 2`

③ Type the following statement, which gets the value in `myNum`, adds 1, and then reassigns the resulting value to `myNum`.

`myNum += 1`

④ Type the following statement, and then press **Enter**, to display the value of `myNum`.

`print(myNum)`

Python displays the value of `myNum`, 3.

⑤ Type the following statement, which uses the exponentiation and assignment operator, and then press **Enter**.

`myNum **= 3`

⑥ Type the following statement, and then press **Enter**, to display the value of `myNum` again.

`print(myNum)`

Python displays the value of `myNum`, 27.

```
guy@Mac-Pro-7 ~ % python3
Python 3.10.0 (v3.10.0:b494f5935c, Oct  4 2021, 14:59:20) [
Clang 12.0.5 (clang-1205.0.22.11)] on darwin
Type "help", "copyright", "credits" or "license" for more i
nformation.
>>> myNum = 2
>>> myNum += 1
>>> print(myNum)
3
>>>
```

```
guy@Mac-Pro-7 ~ % python3
Python 3.10.0 (v3.10.0:b494f5935c, Oct  4 2021, 14:59:20) [
Clang 12.0.5 (clang-1205.0.22.11)] on darwin
Type "help", "copyright", "credits" or "license" for more i
nformation.
>>> myNum = 2
>>> myNum += 1
>>> print(myNum)
3
>>> myNum **= 3
>>> print(myNum)
27
>>>
```

117

Meet the Comparison Operators

When you need to compare values in your code, you use Python's comparison operators. The comparison operators enable you to determine whether two values are equal or not equal; whether one value is greater than or less than another value; and whether one value is greater than or equal to, or less than or equal to, another value.

Table 5-3 explains the comparison operators. Chances are that you will be familiar with most of these from math class.

Table 5-3:	Python's Comparison Operators		
Comparison	**Operator**	**Example**	**Returns**
Equal to	==	1 == 1	True
Not equal to	!=	7 != 7	False
Greater than	>	5 > 3	True
Less than	<	5 < 3	False
Greater than or equal to	>=	7 >= 7	True
Less than or equal to	<=	7 <= 6	False

The exception is the equal-to operator, ==, which uses two equal signs because Python uses a single equal sign, =, as the assignment operator for assigning value to variables. This operator checks whether the two values are mathematically equal but not whether they are the same item. If you need to check whether two items are the same, use the is operator for the comparison; see the section "Meet the Identity Operators," later in this chapter.

Each comparison operator returns the Boolean value True if the comparison is true and the Boolean value False if the comparison is not true.

Examples of Using Comparison Operators

Here are examples of using comparison operators with two variables: a = 1 and b = 2:

a == b returns False.

a != b returns True.

a > b returns False.

a < b returns True.

a >= b returns False.

a <= b returns True.

Work with the Comparison Operators

In the previous section, "Meet the Comparison Operators," you learned about the comparison operators Python provides and how they work. In this section, you try the comparison operators. You start with integer values that make it easy to verify that you are getting the results you expect, move on to comparing strings, and then compare a binary value with a decimal value.

Work with the Comparison Operators

1 Open a terminal window and launch Python.

A The Python prompt appears.

2 Type the following statement, which uses the == operator, and then press Enter.

```
4 == 2 * 2
```

Python returns True, because the result of multiplying 2 by 2 is 4.

3 Type the following statement, which uses the != operator, and then press Enter.

```
2/3 != 4/6
```

Python returns False, because the two operands have the same value.

4 Type the following statement, which uses the > operator, and then press Enter.

```
"expenses" > "expense"
```

Python returns True, because the string expenses evaluates to greater than the string expense.

5 Type the following statement, which uses the >= operator, and then press Enter.

```
0b100000 >= 32
```

Python returns True, because the binary value 100000 is equal to the decimal value 32.

Command Prompt - python — □ ×

```
C:\Users\guy>python
Python 3.10.0 (tags/v3.10.0:b494f59, Oct  4 2021, 19:00:18
) [MSC v.1929 64 bit (AMD64)] on win32
Type "help", "copyright", "credits" or "license" for more
information.
>>> 4 == 2 * 2
True
>>> 2/3 != 4/6
False
>>>
```

Command Prompt — □ ×

```
C:\Users\guy>python
Python 3.10.0 (tags/v3.10.0:b494f59, Oct  4 2021, 19:00:18
) [MSC v.1929 64 bit (AMD64)] on win32
Type "help", "copyright", "credits" or "license" for more
information.
>>> 4 == 2 * 2
True
>>> 2/3 != 4/6
False
>>> "expenses" > "expense"
True
>>> 0b100000 >= 32
True
>>>
```

Meet the Logical Operators

Python provides three logical operators that enable you to make logical comparisons in your code. The and operator returns True if both the operands evaluate as True. The or operator returns True if one or both operands evaluate as True. The not operator reverses the Boolean value of the operand, changing the value True to False and the value False to True.

Table 5-4 lists Python's logical operators.

Table 5-4: Python's Logical Operators		
Comparison	**Operator**	**Explanation**
AND	and	Returns True if each statement tested is True; otherwise returns False.
OR	or	Returns True if one or more of the statements tested is True; returns False if none of the statements is True.
NOT	not	Returns False if the statement tested is True; returns True if the statement tested is False.

Understanding How the Logical Operators Work

The first figure shows how the and operator works. If the first statement is False, the and operator returns False without evaluating the second statement; but if the first statement is True, the and operator evaluates the second statement, returning True if it is True and False if it is False.

The second figure shows how the or operator works. If the first statement is True, the or operator returns True without evaluating the second statement; but if the first statement is False, the or operator evaluates the second statement, returning True if it is True and False if it is False.

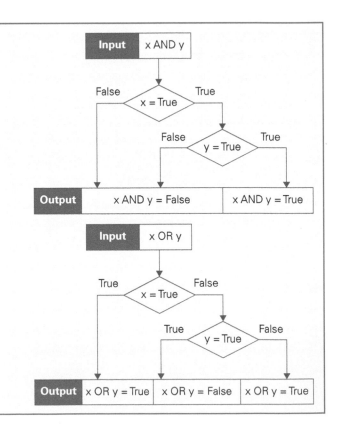

Work with the Logical Operators

In the previous section, "Meet the Logical Operators," you learned about the logical operators Python provides — and, or, and not — and the operations they perform. In this section, you practice using these operators with straightforward examples.

To work through these examples, open a terminal window on your computer. As you work, remember that Python requires initial capitalization on the terms True and False. Any other capitalization, from TRUE to true, produces a NameError error saying that the name is not defined. Similarly, you must use lowercase for and, or, and not.

Work with the Logical Operators

1 Open a terminal window and launch Python.

Ⓐ The Python prompt appears.

2 Type the following statement, which uses the and operator, and then press Enter.

True and True

Python returns True, because both statements are True.

3 Type the following and statement, and then press Enter.

True and False

Python returns False, because only one statement is True.

4 Type the following or statement, and then press Enter.

True or True

Python returns True, because at least one statement is True.

5 Type the following or statement, and then press Enter.

True or False

Again, Python returns True, because one statement is True.

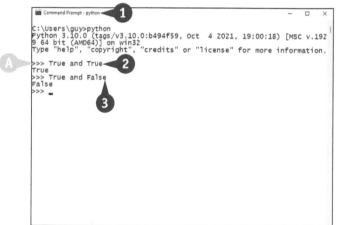

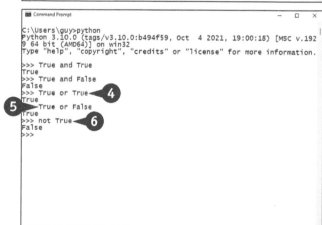

6 Type the following not statement, and then press Enter.

not True

Python returns False.

Meet the Identity Operators

ython provides two identity operators that you can use to compare the identity of objects. Comparing identity means checking that the two objects are actually the same object, in the same memory location. This is different from checking that the objects are equal, which means they have the same value. Two objects can be equal without being the same object.

You use the `is` operator to check that objects have the same identity, and you use the `is not` operator to check that objects have different identities.

Table 5-5 explains the identity operators.

Table 5-5: Python's Identity Operators			
Identity	**Operator**	**Example**	**Returns**
The first operand is the same object as the second operand.	`is`	`item1 is item2`	`True` if the objects are the same object, `False` if they are different objects
The first operand is not the same object as the second operand.	`is not`	`item1 is not item2`	`True` if the objects are not the same object, `False` if they are the same object

Understanding the Identity Operators

Python stores each distinct object at a separate memory location. The `is` operator and the `is not` operator use the memory locations to determine whether two objects are the same object or different objects.

For example, the first of the following statements creates the variable `item1` and assigns the value `7` to it. The second statement creates the variable `item2` and assigns to it the value contained in `item1`. This assignment makes the two objects the same. The third statement uses the `is` operator to compare `item1` and `item2`. Because the objects are the same, this statement returns `True`.

```
item1 = 7
item2 = item1
item1 is item2
```

Another way to determine whether two objects are the same is to see whether they have the same memory location. You can use the `id()` function to display the memory location at which an object is stored.

Work with the Identity Operators

I n the previous section, "Meet the Identity Operators," you learned about Python's two identity operators, `is` and `is not`, and what checking identity entails. In this section, you try using these operators. You also use the `id()` function to return the memory location of two objects, another way of determining whether the objects are the same.

Work with the Identity Operators

1 Open a terminal window and launch Python.

Ⓐ The Python prompt appears.

2 Type the following statement, which creates the variable `item1` and assigns it the value 7, and then press Enter.

```
item1 = 7
```

3 Type the following statement, which creates the variable `item2` and assigns it the value of `item1`, and then press Enter.

```
item2 = item1
```

4 Type the following statement, which uses the `is` operator to compare the objects, and then press Enter.

```
item1 is item2
```

Python returns `True`, because the objects are the same.

5 Type the following statement, which uses the `id()` function to return the memory location of `item1`, and then press Enter.

```
id(item1)
```

Python displays the memory location, such as `1743901755952`.

6 Type the following statement, which returns the memory location of `item2`, and then press Enter.

```
id(item2)
```

Python displays the memory location.

You can see it matches the location for `item1`.

```
C:\Users\guy>python
Python 3.10.0 (tags/v3.10.0:b494f59, Oct  4 2021, 19:00:18)
[MSC v.1929 64 bit (AMD64)] on win32
Type "help", "copyright", "credits" or "license" for more in
formation.
>>> item1 = 7
>>> item2 = item1
>>> item1 is item2
True
>>>
```

```
C:\Users\guy>python
Python 3.10.0 (tags/v3.10.0:b494f59, Oct  4 2021, 19:00:18)
[MSC v.1929 64 bit (AMD64)] on win32
Type "help", "copyright", "credits" or "license" for more in
formation.
>>> item1 = 7
>>> item2 = item1
>>> item1 is item2
True
>>> id(item1)
2458223903152
>>> id(item2)
2458223903152
>>>
```

Meet the Membership Operators

Python's membership operators give you a way to test whether a value appears in a particular sequence or iterable object. For example, if you have a list of machine parts, you can use the membership operators to determine whether the list includes a particular part number.

The `in` operator returns `True` if the sequence is included in the object and returns `False` if it is not. The `not in` operator works the other way around, returning `True` if the sequence is not included in the object and returning `False` if it is.

Table 5-6 explains Python's two membership operators.

Table 5-6:	Python's Membership Operators			
Membership	**Operator**	**Example**		**Returns**
The item is included in the selection.	`in`	`"dog" in ["cat", "dog"]`		`True`
The item is not included in the selection.	`not in`	`"cat" not in ["cat", "dog"]`		`False`

Understanding the Membership Operators

You can use the membership operators with any of Python's sequence objects or iterable objects: dictionary, list, set, string, and tuple.

For example, the first statement in the following code creates a list named `partNumbers` and assigns three alphanumeric strings to it. The second statement tests whether the string `A104` appears in the list.

```
partNumbers = ["A104", "A105", "A106"]
"A104" in partNumbers
```

This example returns `True`.

Similarly, the following statement tests whether the string `Boxing` appears in a classic pangram string:

```
"Boxing" in "The five boxing wizards jump quickly."
```

This example returns `False`, because `Boxing` has an initial capital, whereas `boxing` does not.

Work with the Membership Operators

In the previous section, "Meet the Membership Operators," you learned about Python's two membership operators, in and not in. In this section, you explore some quick examples using these operators to check whether a specific value is present in a list and whether a substring is included in a string.

Work with the Membership Operators

1 Open a terminal window and launch Python.

Ⓐ The Python prompt appears.

2 Type the following statement, which creates the variable myList and assigns to it a short list of integers, and then press Enter.

```
myList = [1, 3, 5, 7, 11]
```

3 Type the following statement, which creates the variable myPrime and assigns the value 7 to it, and then press Enter.

```
myPrime = 7
```

4 Type the following statement, which tests whether myPrime is in myList, and then press Enter.

```
myPrime in myList
```

Python returns True.

5 Type the following statement, which tests whether 8 is in myList, and then press Enter.

```
8 in myList
```

Python returns False.

6 Type the following statement, which creates the variable myString and assigns a string, and then press Enter.

```
myString = "North, South, West"
```

7 Type the following statement, which tests whether East appears in myString, and then press Enter.

```
"East" in myString
```

Python returns False.

125

Meet the Bitwise Operators

Python includes six bitwise operators for performing Boolean logic on individual bits. The first three bitwise operators — AND, OR, and XOR — are for making comparisons between bits. The fourth bitwise operator, NOT, inverts the value of each bit. The last two bitwise operators enable you to shift the bits in the binary number either to the left, by adding zeros to the end of the number and discarding the equivalent number of bits from the start; or to the right, by adding copies of the leftmost bit to the start and discarding the equivalent number of bits from the end.

Table 5-7 explains Python's bitwise operators.

Operation	Operator	Explanation	Example	Returns
Bitwise AND	&	Returns 1 if each bit has the value 1; otherwise, returns 0.	1 & 1 0 & 1	1 0
Bitwise OR	|	Returns 1 if either or both bits have the value 1; otherwise, returns 0.	1 | 1 1 | 0 0 | 0	1 1 0
Bitwise XOR	^	Returns 1 if only one bit has the value 1; otherwise, returns 0.	0 ^ 1 1 ^ 1	1 0
Bitwise NOT	~	Inverts the value of each bit.	~ 1 & 1 ~ 0 & 0 ~ 1 & 0 ^ 1	0 1 1
Zero-fill left shift	<<	Shifts the binary digits left, adding zeros to the right end and discarding the equivalent number of bits from the left end.	1 << 16	65536
Signed right shift	>>	Shifts the binary digits right, adding copies of the leftmost bit at the left end and discarding the equivalent number of bits from the right end.	65536 >> 8	256

Table 5-7: Python's Bitwise Operators

Understanding the Bitwise Operators

Python's bitwise operators enable you to use Boolean logic on individual bits and to perform bit-shifting, moving the digits in a binary number to the left or right.

Table 5-8 shows the output of the bitwise AND, OR, and XOR operators. The difference between the bitwise OR operator and the bitwise XOR operator is that XOR performs an exclusive OR operation, so it returns 1 only if its two inputs differ from each other. By contrast, the bitwise OR returns 1 if each input evaluates to 1 as well as if only one input evaluates to 1.

Earlier in this chapter, you met three assignment operators that include bitwise operations: ^=, >>=, and <<=. These operators work in the same way as the bitwise-only &, >>, and << operators, except that they also reassign the resulting value to the operand.

Table 5-8: Python's Bitwise Operators

Input 1	Input 2	Bitwise AND	Bitwise OR	Bitwise XOR
0	0	0	0	0
0	1	0	1	1
1	0	0	1	1
1	1	1	1	0

Work with the Bitwise Operators

In the previous section, "Meet the Bitwise Operators," you learned about Python's six bitwise operators. In this section, you use these operators to manipulate individual bits. You start by performing bitwise AND, OR, and XOR operations; you then use the bitwise NOT operator to invert bit values; and you finally use the zero-fill left shift operator and the signed right shift operator to shift binary digits to the left and to the right.

Work with the Bitwise Operators

① Open a terminal window and launch Python.

Ⓐ The Python prompt appears.

② Type the following statement, which uses the bitwise AND operator, and then press Enter.

```
1 & 1
```

Python returns 1, because each bit has the value 1.

③ Type the following statement, which uses the bitwise OR operator, and then press Enter.

```
1 | 1
```

Python returns 1, the result of the nonexclusive OR comparison.

④ Type the following statement, which uses the bitwise XOR operator, and then press Enter.

```
1 ^ 1
```

Python returns 0, the result of the exclusive OR comparison.

⑤ Type the following statement, which uses the bitwise NOT operator, and then press Enter.

```
~1
```

Python returns -2, the result of inverting the bit.

⑥ Type the following statement, which uses the zero-fill left shift operator, and then press Enter:

```
1 << 8
```

Python returns 256, which is binary 100000000 — 1 shifted left by 8 places, which are then filled with zeros.

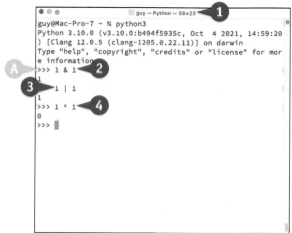

⑦ Type the following statement, which uses the signed right shift operator, and then press Enter:

```
256 >> 8
```

Python returns 1, the result of shifting binary 100000000 right by eight places, placing a copy of the leftmost bit at the left end.

CHAPTER 6

Making Decisions with `if` Statements

Python includes all the tools you need to make decisions easily and effectively in your code. In this chapter, you meet Python's `if` statements, `if... else` statements, and `if... elif` statements and put them to work in your code. You also learn how to nest `if` statements to make complex decisions in your scripts.

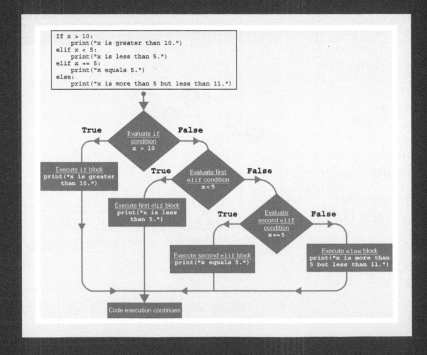

Learn the Essentials of `if` Statements

To make decisions in your code, you use Python's various types of `if` statements. When an `if` statement's condition evaluates to `True`, Python runs the code that follows the statement. An `if... else` statement runs the `if` code when the condition is `True` and the `else` code when it is `False`. An `if... elif` statement can evaluate not only the `if` condition but also one or more `elif` conditions, as needed; you can add an `else` statement that runs code when both `if` and all `elif` conditions evaluate to `False`. You can nest `if` statements to make complex decisions.

Essential Features of `if` Statements

The three main forms of `if` statement are plain `if`, `if... else`, and `if... elif`. The `if` statement looks like this, with italics indicating placeholders:

```
if expression1:
    code block 1
```

The `if... else` statement looks like this and is illustrated nearby:

```
if expression1:
    code block 1
else:
    code block 2
```

The `if... elif` statement looks like this:

```
if expression1:
    code block 1
elif expression2:
    code block 3
```

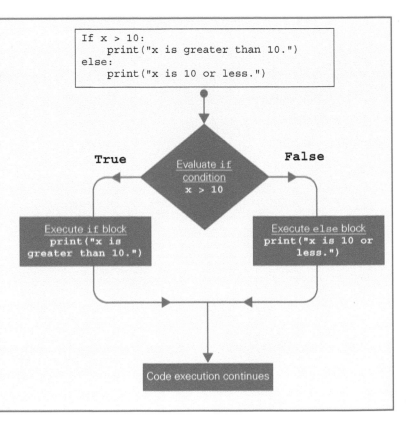

```
If x > 10:
    print("x is greater than 10.")
else:
    print("x is 10 or less.")
```

True

False

Evaluate if condition
x > 10

Execute if block
print("x is greater than 10.")

Execute else block
print("x is 10 or less.")

Code execution continues

The following list explains the components of these if statements:

- The if keyword introduces the if statement.

- *expression1* and *expression2* are expressions that evaluate to a Boolean True value or a Boolean False value. For example, if x = 10: evaluates to True if x equals 10 but evaluates to False if x evaluates to anything other than 10.

- A colon (:) follows *expression1* or *expression2*. This colon is required; Python throws a SyntaxError: expected ':' error if you omit the colon.

- Similarly, a colon (:) follows the else statement. This colon is required.

- *code block 1* is an indented block containing one or more statements that Python executes after the if condition evaluates to True.

- *code block 2* is an indented block containing one or more statements that Python executes after the if condition evaluates to False.

- *code block 3* is an indented block containing one or more statements that Python executes after the elif statement evaluates to True.

  Each code block must be indented; if not, Python returns an IndentationError error, such as expected an indented block after 'if' statement. Visual Studio Code and other editors can automatically apply the required indentation for you.

  The end of the indentation marks the end of the code block attached to the if statement. Execution resumes at the next line that does not have the indentation.

  You may want to leave a blank line after the end of an if block to make your code easier to read, but there is no need to do so.

Understanding the `if` Statement

When your code needs to make a straightforward decision between taking an action and not taking an action, you can use an `if` statement. For example, your code might check the value of a variable to see whether it is 100 or more. If the value is indeed 100 or more, the code would take action by running the `if` code block; if the value is less than 100, the code would take no action.

How the `if` Statement Works

An `if` statement begins with the `if` keyword followed by the expression to be evaluated for the condition. The statement ends with a colon. If the expression evaluates to `True`, the statements in the code block run.

```
if expression:
    code block
```

For example, the following `if` statement checks whether the value of the variable `x` is greater than 10. If so, the `print()` statement runs. The illustration represents the flow of execution.

```
if x > 10:
    print("x is greater than 10.")
```

When an `if` statement's code block contains only a single statement, you can place that statement on the same line of code as the `if` statement. For example, the following `if` statement's code block has only a single statement:

```
if ampm < 12:
    print("Good morning!")
```

Instead, you can place the code block on the same line:

```
if ampm < 12: print("Good morning!")
```

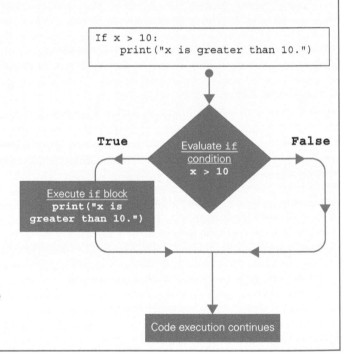

Create an `if` Statement

A straightforward `if` statement enables you to test a condition and take action if that condition evaluates to `True`. For example, your code may need to evaluate input provided by the user and take action if the input is of a certain type. If the condition evaluates to `False`, the code takes no action. Execution continues at the line of code after the end of the `if` statement.

Create an `if` Statement

1 In Visual Studio Code, create a new script, and then save it.

2 Type the following statement, which creates a variable named `x` and assigns to it the string resulting from prompting the user to enter a number between 1 and 20. Press Enter.

```
x = input("Enter a number between
1 and 20 (inclusive): ")
```

3 Type the following statement, which converts the string `x` to an integer and assigns the result back to `x`. Press Enter.

```
x = int(x)
```

4 Type the following `if` statement, which tests whether `x` is greater than `10`. Press Enter.

```
if x > 10:
```

A Visual Studio Code automatically indents the next line for you to enter the code block.

5 Type the following statement, which uses the `print()` function to display a message, and then press Enter.

```
print("x is greater than 10.")
```

6 Click **Run Python File in Terminal** (▷).

The Terminal pane appears.

7 Type a number greater than 10 and press Enter.

B Python displays the message `x is greater than 10.`

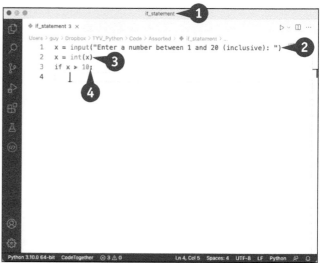

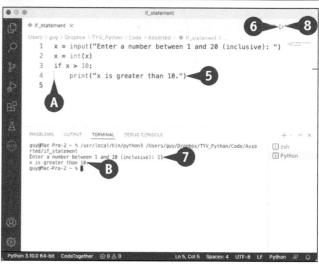

8 Click **Run Python File in Terminal** (▷) again, but this time type a number less than 11, and then press Enter. This time, the condition evaluates to `False`, so the code block does not run, and Python does not display the message.

Understanding the `if... else` Statement

When your code needs to decide between two paths of action, use an `if... else` statement. The `if` line contains an expression that evaluates to a Boolean `True` or a Boolean `False`. If the expression evaluates to `True`, Python runs the statements in the code block that follows the `if` line. After this code block comes the `else` line, followed by the code block containing the statements for Python to run if the expression evaluates to `False`.

How the `if...else` Statement Works

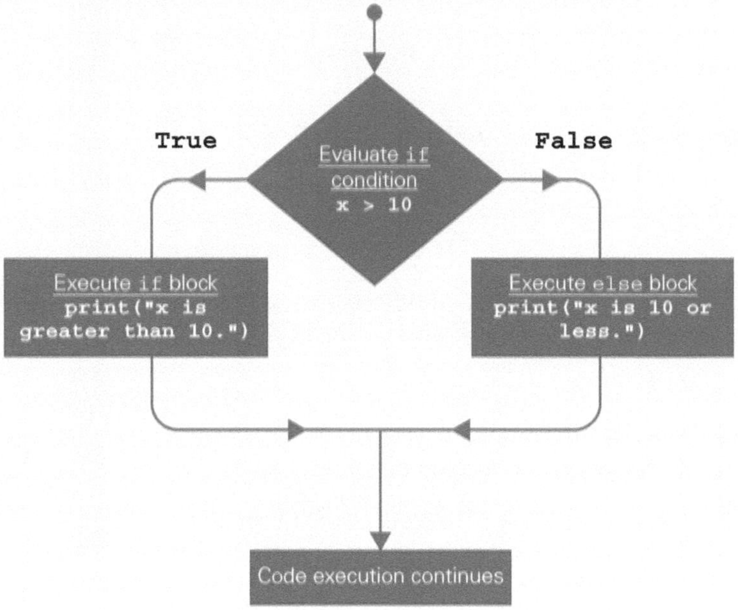

An `if... else` statement begins with the `if` keyword followed by the expression to be evaluated for the condition. The statement ends with a colon. If the expression evaluates to `True`, the statements in the `if` code block run. If the statement evaluates to `False`, execution moves to the `else` line, and the statements in the `else` code block run.

```
if expression:
    code block 1
else:
    code block 2
```

Continuing the previous example, the following `if` statement checks whether the value of the variable `x` is greater than `10`. If so, the `if` code block runs, and the `print()` statement displays a message that x is greater than 10; if not, the `else` statement's code block runs, making its `print()` statement display a message that x is 10 or less. The nearby illustration shows the flow of execution.

```
if x > 10:
    print("x is greater than 10.")
else:
    print("x is 10 or less.")
```

```
If x > 10:
    print("x is greater than 10.")
else:
    print("x is 10 or less.")
```

Evaluate if condition x > 10

True — Execute if block print("x is greater than 10.")

False — Execute else block print("x is 10 or less.")

Code execution continues

Create an `if... else` Statement

An `if... else` statement enables you to test a condition and take one of two courses of action depending on the result. If the condition evaluates to `True`, Python runs the statements in the code block that follows the `if` line; if the condition evaluates to `False`, Python runs the statements in the code block that follows the `else` line.

Create an `if.... else` Statement

1 In Visual Studio Code, create a new script, and then save it.

2 Type the following statement, and then press **Enter**. This statement creates a variable named `x`, prompts the user to enter a number, converts the input string to an integer, and assigns it to `x`.

```
x = int(input("Enter a number between
1 and 20 (inclusive): "))
```

3 Type the `if` condition, the colon, and the `print()` statement, as before. Press **Enter**.

```
if x > 10:
    print("x is greater than 10.")
```

4 Press **Backspace** to remove the indent, type the `else` statement and its colon, and then press **Enter**.

```
else:
```

Ⓐ Visual Studio Code applies an indent after the `else:` line.

5 Type the following `print()` statement, and then press **Enter**.

```
    print("x is 10 or less.")
```

6 Click **Run Python File in Terminal** (▷).

The Terminal pane appears.

7 Type a number less than 11, and then press **Enter**.

Ⓑ Python displays the message from the `else` block.

8 Click **Run Python File in Terminal** (▷) again. This time, type a number 11 or greater, and then press **Enter**.

Python displays the message from the `if` block.

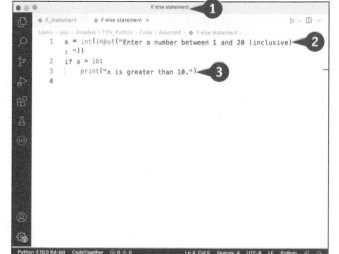

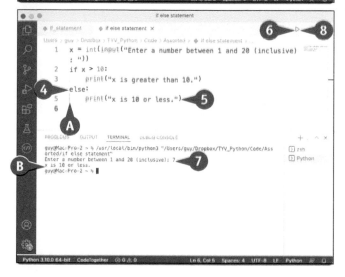

Understanding the `if...` `elif` Statement

When your code needs to evaluate two or more conditions, use an `if...` `elif` statement. After the `if` line (which as usual contains an expression that evaluates to a Boolean `True` or a Boolean `False`) and the `if` code block, the `if...` `elif` statement has one or more `elif` lines, each of which contains another expression to evaluate. After the `if` expression evaluates to `False`, Python evaluates the first `elif` expression, running its code block if it evaluates to `True` or moving along to the next `elif` line if it evaluates to `False`.

How the `if...` `elif` Statement Works

The `if...` `elif` statement consists of an `if` line with an expression to evaluate, ending in a colon; a code block to execute if the expression evaluates to `True`; an `elif` line, likewise with an expression and ending in a colon; and a code block to evaluate if the `elif` expression evaluates to `True`. Here is a pseudocode representation:

```
if expression1:
    code block 1
elif expression2:
    code block 2
```

Here is an example, also illustrated nearby:

```
if x > 10:
    print("x is greater than 10.")
elif x < 5:
    print("x is less than 5.")
```

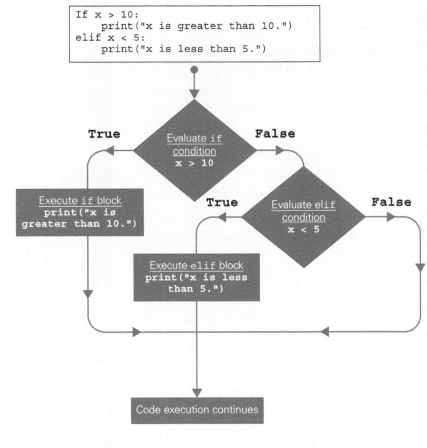

```
If x > 10:
    print("x is greater than 10.")
elif x < 5:
    print("x is less than 5.")
```

You can add as many `elif` statements as you need to test more than two conditions. You can also add an `else` statement after the last `elif` statement, making an `if...` `elif...` `else` statement. See the section "Understanding the if... elif... else Statement," later in this chapter, for an example.

Create an `if... elif` Statement

An `if... elif...` statement enables you to test multiple conditions, taking different actions depending on which condition evaluates to `True` and taking no action if each condition evaluates to `False`. As usual, the `if` line is followed by its code block; similarly, each `elif` line is followed by its code block.

You can use multiple `elif` lines to test more conditions. You must arrange the `elif` lines in the appropriate order for testing, because once a condition evaluates to `True`, Python executes the following code block and does not test any further conditions.

Create an `if... elif` Statement

1 In Visual Studio Code, create a new script, and then save it.

2 Copy and paste — or simply retype — the first three lines from the `if... else` example you created in the previous section:

```
x = int(input("Enter a number between
1 and 20 (inclusive): "))
if x > 10:
    print("x is greater than 10.")
```

3 Press Enter to create a new line, press Backspace to delete the indent, and type the following `elif` line. Press Enter again.

```
elif x < 5:
```

A Visual Studio Code automatically indents the next line following the `elif` line and its colon.

4 Type the following statement, which uses the `print()` function to display a message about the value of `x`, and then press Enter.

```
print("x is less than 5.")
```

5 Click **Run Python File in Terminal** (▷).

The Terminal pane appears.

6 Type a number less than 5 and press Enter.

B Python displays the message `x is less than 5`.

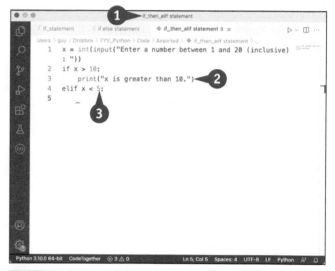

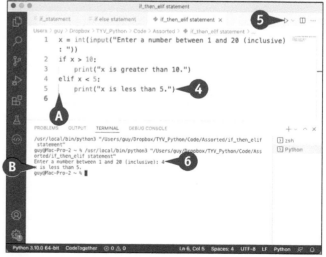

Understanding the `if... elif... else` Statement

An `if... elif... else` statement combines the features of the `if... elif` statement and the `if... else` statement. First, you specify the `if` condition and the code to run if it evaluates to `True`; second, you specify one or more `elif` conditions, each with the code to run if it is `True`; and third, you specify the code to run if both the `if` statement and each `elif` statement evaluates to `False`. You can include as many `elif` lines as required for all the conditions you need to test.

How the `if... elif... else` Statement Works

The `if... elif... else` statement consists of an `if` line with an expression to evaluate, ending in a colon; a code block to execute if the expression evaluates to `True`; one or more `elif` lines, each with an expression, ending in a colon, and followed by a code block to evaluate if that `elif` expression evaluates to `True`; the `else` line, also ending in a colon; and the code block to execute in the `else` case. Here is a pseudocode representation:

```
if expression1:
    code block 1
elif expression2:
    code block 2
[other elif statements]
else:
    code block 3
```

Here is an example, which is illustrated nearby, that uses two `elif` lines:

```
if x > 10:
    print("x is greater than 10.")
elif x < 5:
    print("x is less than 5.")
elif x == 5:
    print("x equals 5.")
else:
    print("x is more than 5 but less than 11.")
```

```
If x > 10:
    print("x is greater than 10.")
elif x < 5:
    print("x is less than 5.")
elif x == 5:
    print("x equals 5.")
else:
    print("x is more than 5 but less than 11.")
```

Create an `if... elif... else` Statement

An `if... elif... else` statement enables you to test multiple conditions, taking appropriate action if any condition evaluates to `True` and taking other action if all the conditions evaluate to `False`. The statement begins with an `if` line and expression, followed by a code block. Similarly, each `elif` line contains an expression and is followed by its code block. Finally, the `else` line appears, without an expression but followed by its code block.

You can include multiple `elif` lines to test multiple conditions.

Create an `if... elif... else` Statement

1 In Visual Studio Code, create a new script, and then save it.

2 Copy and paste — or retype, if you prefer — the first five lines from the `if... else` example you created in the previous section:

```
x = int(input("Enter a number between
1 and 20 (inclusive): "))
if x > 10:
    print("x is greater than 10.")
elif x < 5:
    print("x is less than 5.")
```

3 Press Enter to create a new line, press Backspace to remove the indent, and then type the following `elif` line. Press Enter again.

```
elif x == 5:
```

4 Type the following `print()` statement, and then press Enter.

```
print("x equals 5.")
```

5 Press Backspace to remove the indent, type the following `else` line, and then press Enter.

```
else:
```

6 Type the following statement, which uses the `print()` function to display a message. Press Enter.

```
print("x is more than 5 but less than 11.")
```

7 Click **Run Python File in Terminal** (▷).

The Terminal pane appears.

8 Type a number — this example uses **5** — and press Enter.

Ⓐ Python displays the appropriate message.

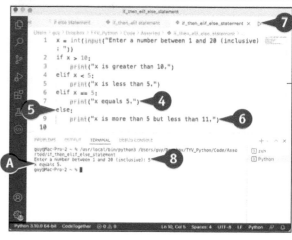

Understanding Nested `if` Statements

When your code needs to make complex decisions, you can nest one or more `if` statements inside another `if` statement. You can use any type of `if` statement — a straightforward `if` statement, an `if... else` statement, an `if... elif` statement, or an `if... elif... else` statement — as either the outer `if` statement or the nested `if` statement, as needed. You may sometimes need to nest further `if` statements within your nested `if` statements.

How Nested `if` Statements Work

To create a nested `if` statement, you create the outer `if` statement of your preferred type and enter the nested `if` statements in the appropriate code block. Here is a pseudocode representation that shows an `if... elif` statement nested in an `if... elif... else` statement:

```
if expression1:
    if expression2:
        code block 1
    if expression3:
        code block 2
elif expression4:
    code block 3
else:
    code block 4
```

Here is a straightforward example of nested `if` statements. The outer statement is `if... elif... elif... else`, and the `if` block contains two nested `if` statements.

```
if n.isalnum():
    if n.isalpha():
        r = "alphabetical"
    if n.isnumeric():
        r = "numeric"
elif n.isspace():
    r = "space-based"
elif n.isascii():
    r = "ASCII text"
else:
    r = "a mystery"
```

This example demonstrates using several string methods on the string stored in the variable n, which we assume has been created already. The `isalnum()` method returns `True` if the string contains alphanumeric characters. The `isalpha()` method returns `True` if the string contains alphabetical characters, while the `isnumeric()` method returns `True` if the string contains numbers. The `isspace()` method returns `True` if the string consists of spaces. The `isascii()` method returns `True` if the string contains ASCII characters.

Create Nested `if` Statements

Nested `if` statements enable you to make complex decisions in your code. You begin the outer `if` statement with an `if` line that contains the `if` keyword, an expression that evaluates to `True` or `False`, and a colon. Within the `if` code block, an `elif` code block, or the `else` code block, you nest `if` statements, as needed. When Python evaluates that `if` condition or `elif` condition as true, or when it reaches the `else` line, Python evaluates the nested `if` statements and continues executing code accordingly.

Create Nested `if` Statements

1 In Visual Studio Code, create a new script, and then save it.

Note: Press **Enter** at the end of each line.

2 Type the following statement, which uses the `input()` method to prompt the user for input:

```python
n = input("Type something: ")
```

3 Type the outer `if` statement, which uses the `isalnum()` function.

```python
if n.isalnum():
```

4 Type the two nested `if` statements, which use the `isalpha()` method and the `isnumeric()` method, respectively, and assign appropriate text to the variable `r`.

```python
if n.isalpha():
    r = "alphabetical"
if n.isnumeric():
    r = "numeric"
```

5 Type the first `elif` statement, which uses the `isspace()` method.

```python
elif n.isspace():
    r = "space-based"
```

6 Type the second `elif` statement, which uses the `isascii()` method.

```python
elif n.isascii():
    r = "ASCII text"
```

7 Type the `else` statement and its text:

```python
else:
    r = "a mystery"
```

8 Type the following `print()` statement to display the information about `n`:

```python
print(n + " is " + r + ".")
```

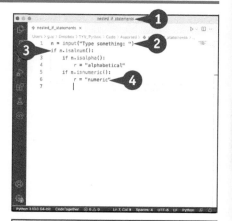

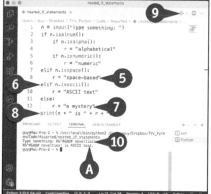

9 Click **Run Python File in Terminal** (▷).

The Terminal pane appears.

10 Type your choice of input, and then press **Enter**.

A Python displays the appropriate message.

CHAPTER 7

Repeating Actions with Loops

In this chapter, you start using Python's loops to repeat actions as needed in your scripts. You learn to create both `for` loops and `while` loops, use loop control statements, and nest loops within each other to implement complex repetition.

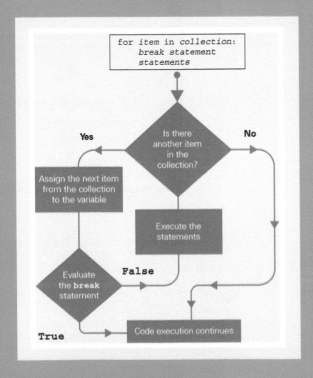

Understanding Python's Loops

When you need to repeat actions in your code, you can use Python's loop structures. A `for` loop lets you *iterate* — repeat — actions either once for each object in a collection, such as once for each letter in a string of text, or a specific number of times, such as 10 times. A `while` loop enables you to repeat actions as long as a condition remains `True` — for example, while a value is above a specified cutoff. When you need more complex repetition, you can nest either type of loop or a mixture of the two types.

Using `for` Loops for Definite Iteration

A `for` loop enables you to repeat actions for a predetermined number of times. This type of repetition is sometimes called *definite iteration*. You can either specify the exact numerical range through which the loop should iterate, such as starting at 1 and ending at 101, or specify that the code should loop once for each element in a collection. For example, your code might create a separate file for each person's name in a list of names.

Looping through a numerical range is preferable when you know in advance exactly how many repetitions you need. Looping through a collection of items is helpful when you need to repeat an action for each item in a specific collection, but you do not know how many items that collection will contain.

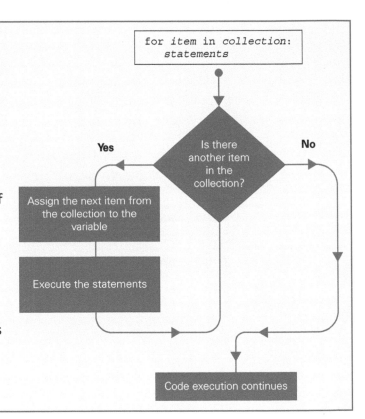

Using `while` Loops for Indefinite Iteration

A `while` loop enables you to repeat actions as long as a condition remains `True`. This type of repetition is sometimes called *indefinite iteration*.

For example, say you want your code to read through a file one line at a time, from start to end. To do this using definite iteration, you could determine how many lines the file contains and then go through line by line, identifying each line by its index number. But indefinite iteration using a `while` loop is typically faster and more efficient. In the `while` loop, the code starts at the beginning of the file, checking that there is at least one line left to read. While there is at least one more line, the loop repeats.

You can also view a `while` loop as continuing until the condition becomes `False`.

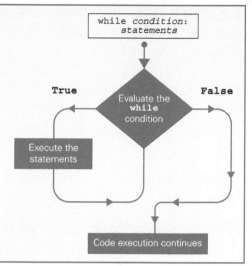

Nesting Loops to Create Complex Repetition

Nesting enables you to run one or more loops inside another loop. For example, while you are reading each line in a file, you may want to perform a task on each word within that line. You can do this by nesting a `for` loop that works with each word on a line within a `while` loop that works on each line in the file.

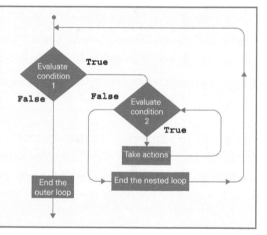

Interrupting and Continuing Loops

When your code is executing within a loop, you may find that you have achieved the result you want and that continuing the loop may waste time or do something counterproductive. In such situations, you can use a `break` statement to interrupt the loop and immediately continue with the code that follows it.

Conversely, conditions may arise in your code that require skipping the rest of the current iteration of the loop but then continue the loop at the next iteration rather than breaking out of the loop. You can achieve this by using the `continue` statement.

Understanding How **for** Loops Work

In Python, a `for` loop enables you to perform definite iteration, repeating an action or a set of actions for a specific number of times. The number of repetitions is controlled by the iterable collection you use for the loop. This collection can be a list, a tuple, a set, a dictionary, or even a string of text; you can also iterate through a collection of open files or a collection of custom objects you have created. For example, a `for` loop that works with a five-item list will iterate five times.

Understanding the Structure of a **for** Loop

The structure of a `for` loop is to use a variable to iterate through an iterable item. The iterable item is usually a collection, such as a list, a tuple, or a set.

A `for` loop starts with the `for` keyword, as in the following pseudocode and diagram, where the italics represent placeholders. The `in` keyword precedes the iterable's name, which a colon follows. After the colon, the loop's statements are indented by four spaces. When the indentation ends, the loop ends.

```
for variable in iterable:
    statements
```

On the first iteration through the loop, Python allocates to `variable` the first item in `iterable` and runs `statements`. On each subsequent iteration, Python allocates the next item in `iterable` to `variable` and runs `statements`. The loop ends after Python has run `statements` for the last item.

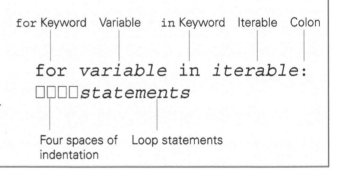

Using a **for** Loop with a List

The following statements show a `for` loop that works through a list:

```
cities = ["Atlanta", "Boston", "Chicago", "Denver"]
for city in cities:
    print(city)
```

The first statement creates the variable `cities` and assigns to it a list of four cities, `Atlanta`, `Boston`, `Chicago`, and `Denver`. The second statement contains the `for` statement, which creates the variable `city` and specifies `cities` as the iterable. The third statement simply uses the `print()` function to display the value of the variable `city`.

When you run this code, Python iterates through the loop four times, once for each city, and displays the following:

```
Atlanta
Boston
Chicago
Denver
```

You can create similar loops for other collections, including sets, tuples, dictionaries, and strings.

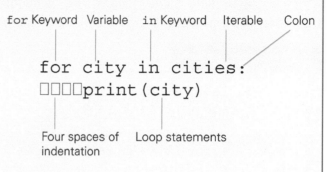

Using the `range()` Function to Create a Numeric `for` Loop

When you need to loop through a sequence of nonsequential numbers, you can put them in a set and loop through the set. For example, the following `for` loop works through the numbers `4`, `7`, and `11` in a set:

```
for num in (4, 7, 11):
    print(num)
```

This approach works fine, and you can use it for sequential numbers as well if you want — for example, `for num in (1, 2, 3)`. But when you have many sequential numbers, using Python's `range()` function is a better solution.

In the following example, the first line creates the variable `r1` and uses the `range()` function to assign to it a range of 20 items. The second line creates the variable `num` and uses it in a `for` loop that iterates through `r1`. The third line, indented four spaces as usual, simply prints the current value of `num`.

```
r1 = range(20)
for num in r1:
    print(num)
```

This example outputs 20 numbers, starting with `0` and ending with `19`.

```
0
1
...
19
```

Create **for** Loops

Python's `for` loops enable you to iterate quickly and easily through various kinds of collection objects. In this section, you create `for` loops that iterate through three widely used types of collections: a list, a string, and a dictionary.

Before we begin, here is one thing to keep in mind: Because Python uses indentation to denote control structures, you must indent each subordinate statement under the `for` statement by four spaces.

Create **for** Loops

Create a **for** Loop That Uses a List

① Open a terminal window and launch Python.

Ⓐ The Python prompt appears.

② Type the following statement, which creates a variable named `cities` and assigns to it a list of four cities. Press **Enter**.

```
cities = ["Atlanta", "Boston", "Chicago",
"Denver"]
```

③ Type the following two-line `for` statement, which uses the variable `city` to iterate through the items in the `cities` list. Press **Enter** at the end of each of these two lines.

```
for city in cities:
    print(city)
```

④ Press **Enter** on the third line to end the `for` loop.

Python runs the loop and displays the following:

```
Atlanta
Boston
Chicago
Denver
```

Create a **for** Loop That Iterates Through a String

① Type the following statement, which creates the variable `st` and assigns a string of text to it. Press **Enter**.

```
st = "duty"
```

② Type the following two-line `for` statement, which uses the variable `s` to iterate through the letters in the `st` string. Press **Enter** at the end of each of these two lines.

```
for s in st:
    print(s)
```

③ Press **Enter** on the third line to end the `for` loop.

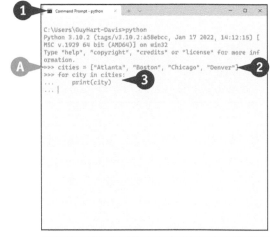

Python runs the loop and displays the following:

```
d
u
t
y
```

Create a `for` Loop That Iterates Through a Dictionary

1 Type the following statement, which creates the variable d1 and assigns a short dictionary to it. Press Enter at the end of each line.

```
d1 = {
    "country": "USA",
    "state": "Alaska",
    "city": "Anchorage"
    }
```

2 Type the following two-line `for` statement, which uses the variable a to iterate through the keys in the d1 dictionary, retrieving the value for each key and displaying it together with the key. Press Enter at the end of each of these two lines.

```
for a in d1:
    print(a + ": " + d1[a])
```

3 Press Enter on the third line to end the `for` loop.

Python runs the loop and displays the following:

```
country: USA
state: Alaska
city: Anchorage
```

TIP

Is there a way to end a `for` loop early?

Yes — you can use a `break` statement to stop executing a loop when a particular condition is met. See the sections "Understanding `break` Statements in Loops" and "Using a `break` Statement to Exit a Loop Early," both later in this chapter, for more information.

Understanding How `while` Loops Work

In Python, a `while` loop enables you to perform indefinite iteration, repeating a block of code as long as a condition remains `True`. Python evaluates the condition before performing the action or actions, so if the condition initially evaluates to `False`, the loop never performs the actions, and execution continues with the next statement after the loop. By contrast, if the condition evaluates to `True`, and continues to do so, the `while` statement can create an infinite loop, a loop that never ends.

Understanding the Structure of a `while` Loop

A `while` loop starts with the `while` keyword, which is followed by the condition to be evaluated. The `while` statement ends with a colon, after which each of the loop's statements is indented by four spaces, as is standard for Python's control structures. When the indentation ends, the loop ends. The following pseudocode and nearby diagram illustrate a `while` loop:

```
while condition:
    statements
```

When execution reaches the `while` statement, Python evaluates the expression. If the result is `True`, Python executes the loop's statements; it then returns to the `while` statement and evaluates it again. If the result is `False`, execution continues with the first statement after the loop.

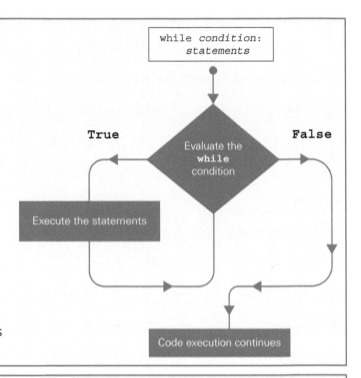

An Example: A `while` Loop Using a Numeric Condition

The following statements show a `while` loop that uses a straightforward numeric condition. The first line declares the variable `a` and assigns it the integer value `100`. The second line starts the `while` loop, which runs while `a` is greater than `50`. The third line uses the `print()` function to display the value of `a`, after which the fourth line decreases the value of `a` by `20`.

```
a = 100
while a > 50:
    print(a)
    a = a - 20
```

When you run this code, Python evaluates the `while` condition four times. The first three times, `a` equals `100`, `80`, and `60`, respectively, so the condition evaluates to `True`, and Python prints those values and performs the subtraction. The fourth time, `a` equals `40`, so the condition evaluates to `False`, and Python does not execute the loop's statements.

Understanding and Avoiding Infinite Loops

If the condition for a `while` loop initially evaluates to `False`, the loop's statements do not run, and execution continues at the first statement after the loop's end. But if the condition initially evaluates to `True`, and continues to do so, the loop will iterate without ending, in what is called an *infinite loop*.

For example, the following `while` loop causes an infinite loop:

```
one = 1
while one == 1:
    print("one: 1")
```

If you run this code in a terminal window, Python displays `one: 1` on each line until you stop it by

pressing `Control`+`C`. This key combination gives a stop command, which Python registers as a `KeyboardInterrupt` event, so you see something like this:

```
one: 1
one: 1
Traceback (most recent call last):
  File "<stdin>", line 2, in <module>
KeyboardInterrupt
>>>
```

To avoid creating infinite loops, you can use one or more `break` statements in your `while` loops. See the sections "Understanding `break` Statements in Loops" and "Using a `break` Statement to Exit a Loop Early," both later in this chapter, for information on adding `break` statements.

```
sam@vubuntu:~$ python3
Python 3.8.10 (default, Mar 15 2022, 12:22:08)
[GCC 9.4.0] on linux
Type "help", "copyright", "credits" or "license" for more
 information.
>>> one = 1
>>> while one == 1:
...     print("one: 1")
...
one: 1
one: 1
one: 1
one: 1
one: 1
one: 1
one: 1
^CTraceback (most recent call last):
  File "<stdin>", line 2, in <module>
KeyboardInterrupt
one: 1
>>>
```

Create `while` Loops

A `while` loop enables you to repeat actions as long as a condition evaluates to `True`. In your scripts, `while` loops can be great for giving your code the flexibility to adapt to the conditions under which it is running.

In this section, you create two straightforward `while` loops that complete without problems. You also create an infinite `while` loop, which you then interrupt by using a key combination.

Create `while` Loops

Create a Straightforward `while` Loop

1 Open Visual Studio Code and create a Python script.

2 Type the following statement, which creates the variable `a` and assigns to it the value `100`. Press **Enter**.

```
a = 100
```

3 Type the following three-line `while` loop, which runs while `a` is greater than `50`, with each iteration using the `print()` function to display the value of `a` and then subtracting `20` from `a`. Press **Enter** at the end of each line.

```
while a > 50:
    print(a)
    a = a - 20
```

4 Click **Run Python File in Terminal** (▷) to run the loop code.

Ⓐ Python displays the following:

```
100
80
60
```

Create an Infinite `while` Loop and Interrupt It

1 In Visual Studio Code, create another Python script.

For example, press `Control`+`N`, click **Select a language**, and then click **Python** in the pop-up menu. Save the script under a name of your choice.

2 Type the following statement, which creates a variable named `myBoolean` and assigns the value `True` to it. Press `Enter`.

```
myBoolean = True
```

3 Type the following two-line `while` loop, which runs while `myBoolean` evaluates to `True` and uses the `print()` command to display `Continuing...`. Press `Enter` at the end of each line.

```
while myBoolean == True:
    print("Continuing...")
```

4 Click **Run Python File in Terminal** (▷) to run the loop code.

Ⓑ The script gets stuck in an infinite loop, outputting `Continuing...` once per iteration.

5 Click in the Terminal pane.

Visual Studio Code moves the focus to the Terminal pane.

6 Press `Control`+`C`.

Ⓒ Visual Studio Code registers a keyboard interrupt, stops the code, and displays the `KeyboardInterrupt` message.

TIP

Can I use the `Control`+`C` keypress in a terminal window?
Yes, you can press `Control`+`C` to interrupt code in a terminal window, such as a Command Prompt window on Windows or a Terminal window on macOS or Linux.

Understanding **break** Statements in Loops

In either a `for` loop or a `while` loop, Python enables you to include a `break` statement to exit the loop before it would otherwise end. You usually use a `break` statement with an `if` condition so as to exit the loop only if the condition is met. In `while` loops, `break` statements can be especially useful for avoiding infinite loops.

To use a `break` statement, you construct your `for` loop or `while` loop as usual but include a `break` statement at the appropriate place, usually with a condition.

The following pseudocode and nearby drawing illustrate the use of a `break` statement in a `for` loop:

```
for item in collection:
    if expression:
        break
    statements
```

The following example creates a variable named `s`, prompts the user to enter some text including a z, and assigns that text to `s`. It creates a variable named `i` to use as a counter. The loop uses the variable `a` to iterate through the user's string input one character at a time. If the character is not z, the `print()` function displays the character, and the code increments the counter variable. If the character is z, the code displays a message giving the character position at which z was found, and the `break` statement ends the loop.

```
s = input("Enter some text including a z: ")
i = 0
for a in s:
    if a == "z":
        print("z found at character " +
str(i))
        break
    print(a)
    i = i + 1
```

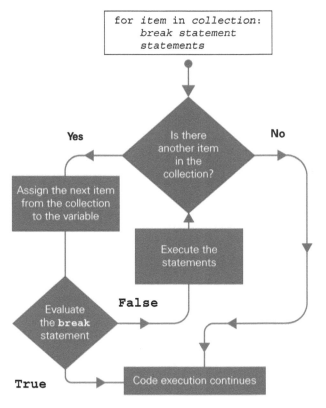

154

Using a **break** Statement to Exit a Loop Early

A break statement enables your code to exit either a for loop or a while loop before the loop's collection or condition causes it to terminate.

In this section, you create a while loop that prompts the user to guess a number between 0 and 10. The while loop simply specifies True as its condition; True cannot become False, so the loop is infinite and keeps running until the break statement is triggered.

Using a **break** Statement to Exit a Loop Early

1 Open Visual Studio Code and create a Python script.

2 Type the following statement, which creates the variable answer and assigns to it the value 7. Press **Enter**.

```
answer = 7
```

3 Type the following statement, which creates the variable prompt and assigns text to it, and then press **Enter**.

```
prompt = "Guess between 0 and 10: "
```

4 Type the following while loop, which creates the variable guess, assigns to it an integer derived from the user's input, and compares guess to answer. If the two match, the loop displays Correct! and then ends.

```
while True:
    guess = int(input(prompt))
    if guess == answer:
        print("Correct!")
        break
```

5 Click **Run Python File in Terminal** (▷) to run the script.

The prompt appears.

6 Type a number other than 7.

The prompt reappears.

7 Type 7.

A The Correct! message appears.

The break statement stops the loop.

Understanding `continue` Statements in Loops

As well as providing the `break` statement that enables your code to exit a loop early, Python provides the `continue` statement, which lets your code skip the remainder of the statements in the current iteration of the loop and proceed to the next iteration. Using a `continue` statement allows you to skip taking actions with particular items in a `for` loop's collection or specific values in a `while` loop without terminating the loop early.

To use a `continue` statement, you construct your `for` loop or `while` loop in the normal way but include a condition followed by the `continue` keyword at the appropriate point in the code.

The following pseudocode and nearby drawing illustrate a `while` loop that includes a `continue` statement. After Python evaluates the `while` condition to `True`, it evaluates the second condition, which precedes the `continue` statement. If this second condition evaluates to `True`, Python skips the rest of the loop, returning to the `while` condition and evaluating it for the next iteration. If the second condition evaluates to `False`, Python executes the loop's statements before returning to the `while` condition.

```
while condition:
    if condition2:
        continue
    statements
```

A `for` loop that includes a `continue` statement works in a similar way, except that the loop's iteration is controlled by its collection rather than by a `while` condition.

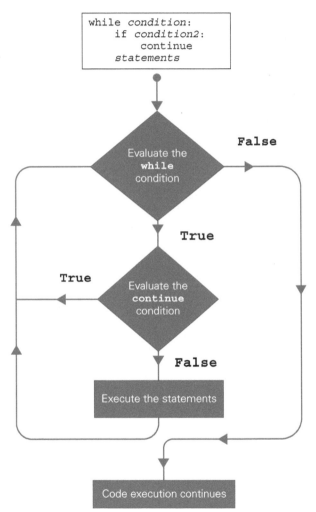

```
while condition:
    if condition2:
        continue
    statements
```

Evaluate the **while** condition — **False** / **True**

Evaluate the **continue** condition — **True** / **False**

Execute the statements

Code execution continues

Using a `continue` Statement in a Loop

A `continue` statement enables you to create a loop that skips a particular value without exiting the loop. You can add multiple `continue` statements to a loop if necessary.

In this section, you create a `for` loop that iterates through a list of names, using a `continue` statement to skip those that consist entirely of uppercase letters, and displaying the remaining names.

Using a `continue` Statement in a Loop

1 Open a terminal window and launch Python.

Ⓐ The Python prompt appears.

2 Type the following statement, which creates the variable `names` and assigns to it a list of first names. Press Enter.

```
names = ["AJ", "Bo", "CC", "CJ",
"Di", "Ed", "El", "Fi"]
```

3 Type the following four-line `for` loop, which uses the variable `n` to iterate through the `names` list. The second line uses the `isupper()` method to check whether the current contents of `n` are all uppercase; if so, the `continue` statement in the third line runs. If not, the `print()` function in the fourth line displays the name. Press Enter at the end of each line.

```
for n in names:
    if n.isupper():
        continue
    print(n)
```

Note: Indent the second line by four spaces, the third line by eight spaces, and the fourth line by four spaces.

4 Press Enter to end the loop.

The loop runs.

Ⓑ Python displays the names that are not all uppercase:

```
Bo
Di
Ed
El
Fi
```

```
sam@vubuntu:~$ python3
Python 3.8.10 (default, Nov 26 2021, 20:14:08)
[GCC 9.3.0] on linux
Type "help", "copyright", "credits" or "license" for more
 information.
>>> names = ["AJ", "Bo", "CC", "CJ", "Di", "Ed", "El", "F
i"]
>>> for n in names:
...     if n.isupper():
...         continue
...     print(n)
...
```

```
sam@vubuntu:~$ python3
Python 3.8.10 (default, Nov 26 2021, 20:14:08)
[GCC 9.3.0] on linux
Type "help", "copyright", "credits" or "license" for more
 information.
>>> names = ["AJ", "Bo", "CC", "CJ", "Di", "Ed", "El", "F
i"]
>>> for n in names:
...     if n.isupper():
...         continue
...     print(n)
...
Bo
Di
Ed
El
Fi
>>>
```

Understanding `else` Statements in Loops

Python enables you to add an `else` statement to either a `for` loop or a `while` loop. Much like the `else` statement in an `if` structure, the `else` statement in a loop runs when the main part of the loop does not. In a `for` loop, the `else` statement runs when there are no more items in the collection through which the loop iterates. In a `while` loop, the `else` statement runs when the `while` condition evaluates to `False` rather than `True`.

To use an `else` statement, you construct your `for` loop or `while` loop in the normal way. Where the loop would normally end, you add the `else` keyword followed by a colon. After that, indented by four spaces, you add the statements you want to run when the `else` condition is triggered.

The following pseudocode and nearby drawing illustrate the use of an `else` statement in a `for` loop:

```
for item in collection:
    statements
else:
    statements2
```

A `while` loop that includes a `continue` statement works in a similar way:

```
while condition:
    statements
else:
    statements2
```

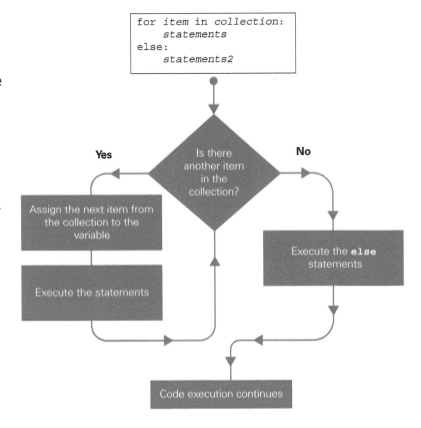

Using an `else` Statement in a Loop

A n `else` statement enables you to add functionality to a loop by running code when the loop has ceased iterating. You can add an `else` statement to either a `for` loop or a `while` loop. This capability is somewhat unusual for programming language, but you may sometimes find it useful.

If the main part of the loop includes a `break` statement and execution hits that `break` statement, the loop's `else` statements do not run.

Using an `else` Statement in a Loop

1 Open Visual Studio Code and create a new script.

2 Type the following statement, which creates the variable `names` and assigns to it a list of first names. Press **Enter**.

```
names = ["AJ", "CC", "CJ", "TJ"]
```

3 Type the following statement, which creates the variable `i` and assigns to it the value `0`. Press **Enter**.

```
i = 0
```

4 Type the following `for` loop, which uses the variable `n` to iterate through the `names` list. If the value of `n` is all uppercase, the `continue` statement skips the rest of the loop; if not, the `print()` function displays the name, and the value of `i` is increased by 1.

```
for n in names:
    if n.isupper():
        continue
    print(n)
    i += 1
```

5 Type the `else` statement, followed by an `if` statement that compares `i` to `0` and displays a message if it matches.

```
else:
    if i == 0:
        print("No mixed-case names")
```

6 Click **Run Python File in Terminal** (▷).

A The `No mixed-case names` message appears, because each name was all uppercase.

Understanding Loop Nesting

When you need to perform more complex repetition than either of Python's types of loops allows, you can nest loops within loops. Nesting works with both types of loops: You can nest one `for` loop inside another `for` loop or nest one `while` loop inside another `while` loop. You can nest a `for` loop inside a `while` loop, or vice versa.

Python enables you to nest loops and other blocks, such as `with` blocks and `try` blocks, up to a maximum of 20 layers deep. Usually, it is most practical to nest only a few levels deep.

To nest loops, you construct the outer look in the usual way, but then you place another loop inside it. The following code snippet and nearby drawing illustrate one `for` loop nested inside another `for` loop, which assumes that the variables `firsts` and `lasts` have already been created:

```
for f in firsts:
    for l in lasts:
        print(f + " " + l)
```

Python begins by executing the outer loop. If that loop is a `for` loop, as in this example, Python determines whether an item in the collection is available. If so, Python assigns the next available item to the loop's variable and moves on to the nested loop; if not, Python ends the outer loop, leaving the nested loop untouched.

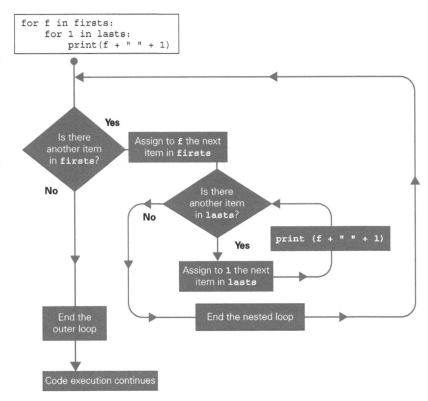

```
for f in firsts:
    for l in lasts:
        print(f + " " + l)
```

Nest Loops to Create Complex Repetition

Nesting loops enables you to create complex repetition in your scripts. You can nest either `for` loops or `while` loops, as needed — or nest both if your code so demands. You can also include `break` statements, `continue` statements, and `else` statements in your nested loops.

In this section, you use two straightforward `for` loops, one nested inside the other. The code is straightforward, but it enables you to see clearly how the nesting works.

Nest Loops to Create Complex Repetition

1 Open a terminal window and launch Python.

A The Python prompt appears.

2 Type the following statement, which creates the variable `firsts` and assigns to it a list of three first names. Press Enter.

```
firsts = ["Ali", "Bee", "Cat"]
```

3 Type the following statement, which creates the variable `lasts` and assigns to it a list of three last names. Press Enter.

```
lasts = ["Clark", "Hill", "Perez"]
```

4 Type the following three-line `for` structure, which implements both `for` loops. The outer loop uses the variable `f` to iterate through `firsts`; the inner loop uses the variable `l` to iterate through `lasts`. The third line uses the `print()` function to display the name produced by the current combination of `f` and `l`. Press Enter at the end of each line.

```
for f in firsts:
    for l in lasts:
        print(f + " " + l)
```

5 Press Enter to run the loop.

Python displays the output, abbreviated here:

```
Ali Clark
Ali Hill
Ali Perez
Bee Clark
...
Cat Perez
```

```
guy@Mac-Pro-3 ~ % python3
Python 3.10.0 (v3.10.0:b494f5935c, Oct  4 2021, 14:59:20) [C
lang 12.0.5 (clang-1205.0.22.11)] on darwin
Type "help", "copyright", "credits" or "license" for more in
formation.
>>> firsts = ["Ali", "Bee", "Cat"]
>>> lasts = ["Clark", "Hill", "Perez"]
>>>
```

```
guy@Mac-Pro-3 ~ % python3
Python 3.10.0 (v3.10.0:b494f5935c, Oct  4 2021, 14:59:20) [C
lang 12.0.5 (clang-1205.0.22.11)] on darwin
Type "help", "copyright", "credits" or "license" for more in
formation.
>>> firsts = ["Ali", "Bee", "Cat"]
>>> lasts = ["Clark", "Hill", "Perez"]
>>> for f in firsts:
...     for l in lasts:
...         print(f + " " + l)
...
Ali Clark
Ali Hill
Ali Perez
Bee Clark
Bee Hill
Bee Perez
Cat Clark
Cat Hill
Cat Perez
>>>
```

Working with Functions

As in other programming languages, a function in Python is a stand-alone section of code that performs a particular task. In this chapter, you learn how functions work, put Python's built-in functions to use, and create custom functions of your own.

Understanding Functions and Their Syntax

A*function* is a stand-alone section of code that performs a particular task. For example, as you have seen earlier in this book, the `input()` function prompts the user to input text, while the `print()` function displays information on-screen. Python includes around 70 built-in functions that you can use immediately, and you can access other prebuilt functions by importing the modules that contain them. You can also create your own custom functions to perform operations that Python's existing functions do not cover.

Understanding the Syntax of a Function

In Python, a function's syntax looks like the following pseudocode and the nearby drawing:

```
def function_name(parameters):
    """function_description"""
    statements
    return [expression]
```

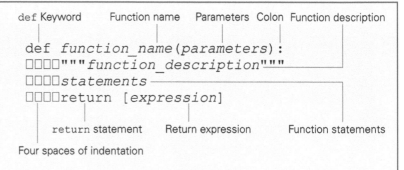

The following list explains the components of a function's syntax:

- `def`. This keyword, short for *definition*, begins the function header.
- `function_name`. Each function must have a name that is unique in its context so that your code can refer to the function unambiguously.
- `parameters`. Parameters are named items used to pass values to a function. The values passed are called *arguments*. Parameters are optional: Some functions have parameters, whereas other functions have none.
- `:` (colon). The colon denotes the end of the function header. After the colon, the function's contents are indented, usually by four spaces, to indicate that they are subordinate to the function header.
- `function_description`. This description is a comment describing what the function does. The description is optional but is usually helpful. It is sometimes called the *documentation string* or *docstring*.
- `statements`. The statements specify the actions that the function performs.
- `return [expression]`. The `return` statement ends the function and returns the function's result to the code that called the function. If the `return` statement specifies an expression, Python returns that expression. If the `return` specifies no expression, Python returns `None`, a special value. The `return` statement is optional, so some functions do not have it. Python returns `None` if there is no `return` statement.

Looking at an Example of a Function's Syntax

The following code shows a custom function. The nearby drawing breaks down the function's components.

```
def odd_even(n):
    """Function to return 'Odd' or 'Even' for a
specified 'n' input."""
    if int(n)%2 == 0:
        odd_or_even = "Even"
    else:
        odd_or_even = "Odd"
    return odd_or_even
```

```
def odd_even(n):
    """Function to return 'Odd' or 'Even'
    for a specified 'n' input."""
    if int(n)%2 == 0:
        odd_or_even = "Even"
    else:
        odd_or_even = "Odd"
    return odd_or_even
```

Function name — Colon

def Keyword — Parameter — Function description

Indentation in four-space increments — Return statement — Function statements

The function begins with the `def` keyword, after which comes the function's name, `odd_even`; its parameter, `n`, in parentheses; and the colon that ends the function header.

The second and third lines contain the function's description in a comment delimited by three double quotes. After those lines is an `if... else` statement that creates the function's output, either `Even` or `Odd`, which is stored in the variable `odd_or_even`. In the final line, the `return` statement returns the value in `odd_or_even`.

Once your code has defined this function, you can call the function by entering its name and the argument for the required parameter, `n`. For example, the following statement creates the variable `x1` and assigns to it the function's output for the number the user types when prompted:

```
x1 = odd_even(input("Enter a number: "))
```

The function returns `Even` for an even number and `Odd` for an odd number.

Understanding Function Parameters and Returns

Most functions use one or more parameters, named items that receive arguments containing the values the user wants the function to manipulate. Parameters can be either required or optional, and a function may use both required parameters and optional parameters. However, some functions use no parameters at all.

Similarly, most functions return one or more values to the code that called them. However, some functions return no values.

Understanding the Four Types of Functions

The combination of parameters-or-no-parameters and values-or-no-values gives four types of functions in Python:

- Functions with both parameters and return values
- Functions with parameters but no return values
- Function with no parameters but with return values
- Functions with no parameters and no return values

The following subsections explore these different types, giving brief examples.

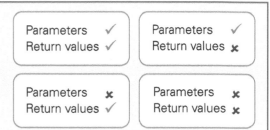

Functions with Both Parameters and Return Values

Many functions both use parameters to accept input and return one or more values after running.

For example, the built-in `abs()` function returns the absolute value of a number, the non-negative value of a number even if it has a minus sign. The `abs()` function has one parameter, to which you provide an argument containing the number for which to return the absolute value. For example, `abs(-2)` returns 2, and `abs(-99*2/50+5)` returns `1.04`.

```
Function name    Argument

>>> abs(-99*2/50+5)
1.04

Return value
```

Functions with Parameters But No Return Values

Some functions use one or more parameters to accept input but return no values. Instead, such functions typically perform an action.

For example, Python's built-in `print()` function displays text on-screen rather than returning a value. This function uses one parameter, the string or other item you want to display. For example, `print("The quick brown fox, etc.")` displays the text `The quick brown fox, etc.` provided as the argument for its parameter.

Functions with No Parameters But with Return Values

Some functions use no parameters but do return one or more values. For example, the built-in `globals()` function returns the dictionary for the current module namespace, the virtual area in which the module is operating. Here is an example of running the `globals()` function:

```
>>> globals()
{'__name__': '__main__', '__doc__': None, '__package__': None, '__loader__':
<class '_frozen_importlib.BuiltinImporter'>, '__spec__': None, '__annotations__':
{}, '__builtins__': <module 'builtins' (built-in)>}
>>>
```

Functions with No Parameters and No Return Values

Some functions — relatively few — use no parameters and return no values. Such a function may either generate or gather its own data automatically or prompt the user to enter data. Rather than returning one or more values to the calling code, the function may display output — for example, by using the `print()` function.

None of Python's built-in functions falls into this category. Here is an example of a custom function that uses no parameters and returns no values:

```
def day_of_week():
    from datetime import datetime
    thisday = datetime.today().strftime("%A")
    print(thisday)
```

This `day_of_week()` function imports the `datetime` object from the `datetime` module. The second line creates a variable called `thisday` and assigns to it a formatted string returned using the `today()` method of the `datetime` object. The third line uses the `print()` function to display the day, such as `Wednesday`.

Using Python's Built-In Functions

Python includes around 70 built-in functions that you can use immediately without needing to load extra modules. These functions perform a variety of widely useful tasks. Some functions help you create and debug your code. For example, the `compile()` function compiles a source file into a code object, the `exec()` function executes a code object, and the `breakpoint()` function switches to the Python debugger at the specified point in a script. Other functions, such as `setattr()` and `delattr()`, enable you to manipulate the attributes of objects.

Table 8-1 explains Python's built-in functions.

Table 8-1: Python's Built-In Functions	
Function Name	**What It Returns or Does**
`abs()`	Returns the absolute value of the specified number.
`aiter()`	Returns an asynchronous iterator for an asynchronous iterable.
`all()`	Returns `True` if all elements of the specified iterable are `True`.
`anext()`	Returns the next item from the specified asynchronous iterator.
`any()`	Returns `True` if any element of the specified iterable is `True`.
`ascii()`	Returns a string containing a printable reproduction of the object with non-ASCII characters escaped using \x, \u, and \U escape codes.
`bin()`	Returns a binary string for the value the specified integer, prefixed with `0b`.
`bool()`	Returns the Boolean value — `True` or `False` — of the specified item.
`breakpoint()`	Switches to the Python debugger.
`bytearray()`	Returns a `bytearray` object containing a new array of bytes.
`bytes()`	Returns a new `bytes` object.
`callable()`	Returns `True` if the object appears callable.
`chr()`	Returns the string for the character representing the specified Unicode code point.
`classmethod()`	Returns a class method from the specified method.
`compile()`	Returns a code object compiled from the specified source file.
`complex()`	Returns a complex number from the specified real value and imaginary value.
`delattr()`	Returns the specified object with the specified attribute deleted.
`dict()`	Returns a new dictionary.
`dir()`	Returns the list of names in the current local scope or in the specified scope.
`divmod()`	Returns the quotient and remainder of the two specified numbers divided using integer division.
`enumerate()`	Returns an `enumerate` object from the specified iterable.
`eval()`	Returns the evaluated expression from the specified expression and arguments.
`exec()`	Executes the specified Python code object.
`filter()`	Returns an iterator constructed from the specified function and iterable.
`float()`	Returns a floating-point number from the specified number or string.
`format()`	Returns a formatted representation of the specified value.

Table 8-1:   Python's Built-In Functions (continued)

Function Name	What It Returns or Does
frozenset()	Returns a new frozenset object.
getattr()	Returns the value of the specified attribute of the given object.
globals()	Returns the dictionary for the current module namespace.
hasattr()	Returns True if the specified object includes the specified attribute.
hash()	Returns the integer hash value of the object, if the object has one.
help()	Calls Python's built-in help system.
hex()	Returns the hexadecimal string, prefixed with 0x, for the specified integer.
id()	Returns the specified object's identity, a unique integer.
input()	Prompts the user for input.
int()	Returns an integer from the specified number or string.
isinstance()	Returns True if the specified object is an instance of the specified class.
issubclass()	Returns True if the specified object is a subclass of the specified class.
iter()	Returns an iterator object for the specified object.
len()	Returns the length of the specified object. The length is the number of items the object contains — for example, the number of characters in a string.
list()	Returns a list, tuple, or range.
locals()	Returns the updated dictionary for the current local symbol table.
map()	Returns an iterator showing the specified function applied to every item in the specified iterable.
max()	Returns the largest item in the specified iterable or group.
memoryview()	Returns a memory view object for the specified object.
min()	Returns the smallest item in the specified iterable or group.
next()	Returns the next item from the specified iterator.
object()	Returns a new object of the object class, the base for all other classes.
oct()	Returns an octal string, prefixed with 0o, for the specified integer.
open()	Opens the specified file and returns a file object representing it.

continued ▶

Python's built-in functions include functions for converting values to particular data types. For example, the int() function returns an integer, the str() function returns a string, the list() function returns a list, and the tuple() function returns a tuple. Similarly, the bin(), oct(), and hex() functions return strings containing binary, octal, and hexadecimal representations of the value supplied.

Other functions that are widely useful include three you have used already in this book. The input() function prompts the user for input, the open() function opens a file and returns a file object representing it, and the print() function displays output.

Table 8-1: Python's Built-In Functions (continued)	
Function Name	**What It Returns or Does**
ord()	Returns an integer representing the Unicode code point for the specified string.
pow()	Returns the specified base number raised to the specified power, optionally using a modulo.
print()	Prints the specified objects to the text stream file.
property()	Returns the specified property.
range()	Returns a range object.
repr()	Returns a string containing a printable representation of the specified object.
reversed()	Returns a reverse iterator for the specified object.
round()	Returns the specified number rounded to the specified precision.
set()	Returns a new set object.
setattr()	Returns the specified object with the specified attribute set.
slice()	Returns a slice object for the given set of indices.
sorted()	Returns a sorted list from the specified iterable.
staticmethod()	Returns a static method from the specified method.
str()	Returns a string from the specified object.
sum()	Returns the total of items in the specified iterable.
super()	Returns a proxy object for delegating method calls to a parent or sibling class.
tuple()	Returns a tuple from the specified iterable.
type()	Returns either the type of the specified object or a new type object.
vars()	Returns the __dict__ attribute for the specified object.
zip()	Returns tuples from the specified iterables.

The following sections provide brief examples of putting some of the most widely used of Python's built-in functions to use.

Using the input() Function

The input() function enables you to prompt the user for input. Python receives the input as a string, but you can cast it to a different data type if needed, as in the following example:

```
>>> n1 = input("Type a number
between 1 and 20: ")
Type a number between 1 and 20: 17
>>> n1
'17'
>>> n1 = int(n1)
>>> n1
17
```

Using the sorted() Function

The `sorted()` function lets you sort an iterable into either ascending order or descending order. The following example creates a variable named `locs`, assigns five place names to it, and then sorts them alphabetically.

```
>>> locs = ["Cobb", "Berg", "Eden", "Alba", "Dyer"]
>>> sorted(locs)
['Alba', 'Berg', 'Cobb', 'Dyer', 'Eden']
```

To sort backward, use `sorted()` with `reverse=True`:

```
>>> sorted(locs, reverse=True)
['Eden', 'Dyer', 'Cobb', 'Berg', 'Alba']
```

Returning Binary, Octal, or Hexadecimal Strings

The `bin()` function returns a string consisting of the prefix `0b` and the binary value of the specified integer. Similarly, the `oct()` function returns a string consisting of the prefix `0o` and the octal value, and the `hex()` function returns a string consisting of the prefix `0x` and the hexadecimal value.

For example, `bin(100)` returns the string `0b1100100`, `oct(100)` returns the string `0o144`, and `hex(100)` returns the string `0x64`.

Converting Binary, Octal, or Hexadecimal Strings to Decimal Values

The `int()` function enables you to convert a binary, octal, or hexadecimal string to a decimal value. For example, `int(0b1100100)` returns `100`.

To convert a binary, octal, or hexadecimal number that is not in string format to a decimal value, use the `int()` function, specifying the value as a string and providing the second argument `2` for binary, `8` for octal, or `16` for hexadecimal. For example, `int("1100100", 2)` returns `100` from the binary number `1100100`.

Using the print() Function to Display Information

The `print()` function enables you to print objects to the text stream file, giving you an easy way to display information to the user. For example, `print("New file created")` displays the text `New file created`.

Create a Function with Parameters and a Return

In this section, you create a function that uses parameters and returns a value. The function, `calculate_tip`, calculates the amount of a service gratuity. The function uses two required parameters: The `bill` parameter accepts the amount of the bill, and the `percent` parameter accepts the tip percentage. The function divides `percent` by `100` so that the user can enter the percentage as a round number, such as `15`, rather than as the number that actually produces that percentage, such as `0.15`. The function returns a single value, `tip`, which contains the amount of the tip.

Create a Function with Parameters and a Return

1 Open a terminal window and launch Python.

A The Python prompt appears.

2 Type the following function header, and then press Enter:

```
def calculate_tip(bill, percent):
```

Note: After the function header, indent each line of the function by four spaces to indicate that the line is part of the function.

3 Type the following statement, which divides the `percent` value by `100`, assigning it back to `percent`. Press Enter.

```
percent = percent / 100
```

4 Type the following statement, which declares the variable `tip` and assigns to it the product of `bill` and `percent`. Press Enter.

```
tip = bill * percent
```

5 Type the following statement, which returns `tip` to the calling code. Press Enter once, and then press Enter again to end the function.

```
return tip
```

6 Type the following statement, which uses the `print()` function to display the result of calculating a 15% tip on a $50 bill. Press Enter.

```
print(calculate_tip(50,15))
```

Python returns `7.5`, indicating a $7.50 tip.

```
guy@Mac-Pro-3 ~ % python3
Python 3.10.0 (v3.10.0:b494f5935c, Oct  4 2021, 14:59:20) [C
lang 12.0.5 (clang-1205.0.22.11)] on darwin
Type "help", "copyright", "credits" or "license" for more in
formation.
>>> def calculate_tip(bill, percent):
...     percent = percent / 100
...
```

```
guy@Mac-Pro-3 ~ % python3
Python 3.10.0 (v3.10.0:b494f5935c, Oct  4 2021, 14:59:20) [C
lang 12.0.5 (clang-1205.0.22.11)] on darwin
Type "help", "copyright", "credits" or "license" for more in
formation.
>>> def calculate_tip(bill, percent):
...     percent = percent / 100
...     tip = bill * percent
...     return tip
...
>>> print(calculate_tip(50,15))
7.5
>>>
```

Create a Function with a Parameter But No Return

In this section, you create a function that uses a parameter but that returns no values to the code that calls it. Instead of returning values, the function uses the `print()` function to display information to the user. The function is called `convert_liters_to_pints()` and converts liters to U.S. pints.

To create a function that returns no value explicitly, you can include the `return` statement but not specify a return value. Alternatively, you can omit the `return` statement. Both approaches have the same effect: The function returns no value explicitly, but implicitly it returns the value `None`.

Create a Function with a Parameter But No Return

1 Open a terminal window and launch Python.

A The Python prompt appears.

2 Type the following function header, which declares the function name and a parameter called `liters`, and then press Enter.

```
def convert_liters_to_pints(liters):
```

3 Type the following statement, which creates the variable `pints` and assigns to it the result of multiplying the `liters` argument by `2.11338`, the appropriate factor. Press Enter.

```
pints = 2.11338 * liters
```

4 Type the following statement, which uses the `round()` function to round `pints` down to one decimal place, and then press Enter:

```
pints = round(pints, 1)
```

5 Type the following statement, which creates a variable named `msg` and assigns to it a string derived from `liters` plus literal text. Press Enter.

```
msg = str(liters) + " liters is "
```

6 Type the following statement, which completes the `msg` string by adding a string derived from `pints` plus literal text. Press Enter.

```
msg = msg + str(pints) + " pints."
```

7 Type the following statement, which uses the `print()` function to display `msg`. Press Enter twice.

```
print(msg)
```

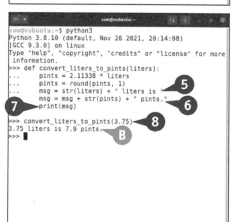

8 Type the following statement, which calls the function and supplies the `liters` value:

```
convert_liters_to_pints(3.75)
```

B Python displays the result:

```
3.75 liters is 7.9 pints.
```

173

Create a Function with No Parameters But a Return

In this section, you create a function that uses no parameters but that does return a value to the code that calls it. The function is called `generate_name()` and returns a name created by combining a random first name, a random middle initial, and a random last name.

For space reasons, the lists of names and the list of initials shown here are unrealistically short. Feel free to extend them with as many names as you wish.

Create a Function with Parameters But No Return

1 Open Visual Studio Code and create a new Python script.

2 Type the following function header, and then press **Enter**.

```
def generate_name():
```

3 Type the following four lines of function description:

```
# This function returns a character
name
# by taking a first name from one
list,
# a middle initial from another list,
# and a last name from a third list.
```

4 Type the following statement, which creates a variable named `first` and assigns to it a list of first names. Press **Enter**.

```
first = ["Al", "Bo", "Cy", "Dot",
"Ed", "Em"]
```

5 Type the following statement, which creates a variable named `middle` and assigns to it a list of initials. Press **Enter**.

```
middle = ["A.", "B.", "C.", "D.",
"E.", "F."]
```

6 Type the following statement, which creates a variable named `last` and assigns to it a list of last names. Press **Enter**.

```
last = ["Adams", "Bain", "Col",
"Dunn", "Ely"]
```

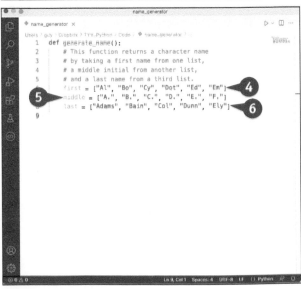

7 Type the following statement, which imports the choice item from the random module, and then press Enter.

```
from random import choice
```

8 Type the following statement, which creates the variable cname and assigns to it a random item chosen from the first list. Press Enter.

```
cname = choice(first)
```

9 Type the following statement, which adds to cname a space and a random item chosen from the middle list. Press Enter.

```
cname = cname + " " + choice(middle)
```

10 Type the following statement, which adds to cname another space and a random item chosen from the last list. Press Enter.

```
cname = cname + " " + choice(last)
```

11 Type the following statement to return cname, and then press Enter twice to end the function.

```
return cname
```

12 Press Backspace to remove the indentation, and then type the following for loop, which uses range(0,9) with the print() function to output ten names.

```
for i in range(0,9):
    print(generate_name())
```

13 Click **Run Python File in Terminal** (▷).

Visual Studio Code displays the Terminal pane.

A The sample names appear.

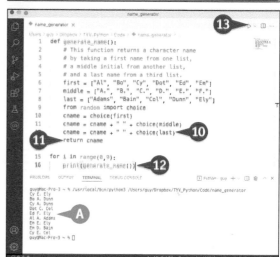

TIP

What other way can I get a random letter?

You can import the string module and then use one of its tools for returning letters. As in the main text, type **from random import choice** and press Enter to import the choice item from the random module. Next, type **import string** and press Enter to import the string module. You can then use choice(string.ascii_lowercase) to return a random lowercase letter, use choice(string.ascii_uppercase) to return a random uppercase letter, or use choice(string.ascii_letters) to return a random letter of one case or the other.

Create a Function with No Parameters and No Return

A function with no parameters and no return is relatively unusual because it lacks flexibility in both input and output. Without parameters to receive values from arguments passed by the calling code, the function either must contain any values it needs or must derive them from other sources. Without a return value, the function needs to rely on other means of communication, such as using the `print()` function to display text.

In this section, you create a parameter-free and return-free function named `show_username()` that uses the `print()` function to display the username under which the user is currently logged in.

Create a Function with No Parameters and No Return

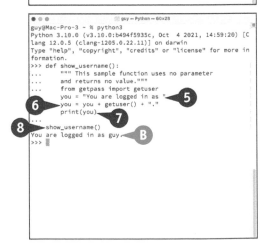

1 Open a terminal window and launch Python.

Ⓐ The Python prompt appears.

2 Type the following function header, which specifies no parameter, and then press Enter.

```
def show_username():
```

3 Type the following two-line function definition, pressing Enter at the end of each line:

```
"""This sample function uses no parameter
and returns no value."""
```

4 Type the following statement, which imports the `getuser()` method from the `getpass` module, and then press Enter:

```
from getpass import getuser
```

5 Type the following statement, which creates the variable `you` and assigns a string of text to it. Press Enter.

```
you = "You are logged in as "
```

6 Type the following statement, which completes the `you` string by adding the username, returned by the `getuser()` method, and a period. Press Enter.

```
you = you + getuser() + "."
```

7 Type the following statement, which uses the `print()` function to display the `you` string. Press Enter twice.

```
print(you)
```

8 Type the function's name, and then press Enter.

Ⓑ The function runs and displays the message including the username.

Create a Function That Returns Multiple Values

Many functions return just a single value, but Python enables you to create functions that return multiple values. In this section, you create a function that uses one required parameter and that returns three values. The function is called `convert_miles_yards_feet_inches()`; it uses a parameter called `miles`, and it returns the equivalent numbers of yards, feet, and inches.

Create a Function That Returns Multiple Values

1 Open a terminal window and launch Python.

Ⓐ The Python prompt appears.

2 Type the following function header, which declares the function with one parameter, `miles`. Press **Enter**.

```
def convert_miles_yards_feet_
inches(miles):
```

3 Type the following statement, which creates the variable `yards` and assigns to it the result of multiplying `miles` by `1760`. Press **Enter**.

```
yards = miles * 1760
```

4 Type the following statement, which creates the variable `feet` and assigns to it the result of multiplying `miles` by `5280`. Press **Enter**.

```
feet = miles * 5280
```

5 Type the following statement, which creates the variable `inches` and assigns to it the result of multiplying `miles` by 63,360. Press **Enter**.

```
inches = miles * 63360
```

6 Type the following `return` statement, which returns `yards`, `feet`, and `inches`. Press **Enter**.

```
return yards, feet, inches
```

7 Type the following statement, which uses the `print()` function to display the result of calling the function with the argument `2`, and then press **Enter**.

```
print(convert_miles_yards_feet_
inches(2))
```

Ⓑ Python displays the resulting tuple:

```
(3520, 10560, 126720)
```

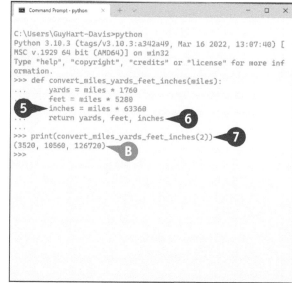

Create a Function with Optional Parameters

Including optional parameters in a custom function enables you to make your code more flexible. In this section, you create a custom function that calculates the odds for a parlay bet, a cumulative bet on multiple outcomes. The function lets the user calculate the odds for a parlay involving two, three, four, or five bets using decimal odds. The function uses required parameters for the first two bets, because a parlay must have at least two bets. The function uses optional parameters for the remaining three bets, thus allowing the user to include these bets or omit them.

Create a Function with Optional Parameters

1 Open a terminal window and launch Python.

Ⓐ The Python prompt appears.

2 Type the following function header, which declares the function `parlay` with five parameters, `odds1` through `odds5`, making the last three parameters optional by assigning the value `None` to them. Press Enter.

```
def parlay(odds1, odds2, odds3 =
None, odds4 = None, odds5 = None):
```

3 Type the function description, and then press Enter.

```
"""Calculate the odds for a parlay
that contains two, three, four, or
five bets"""
```

4 Type the following statement, which declares the variable `p` and assigns to it the result of multiplying `odds1` and `odds2`. Press Enter.

```
p = odds1 * odds2
```

5 Type the following `if` statement, which checks whether `odds3` has the value `None` and, if not, multiplies `p` by `odds3`. Press Enter at the end of each line.

```
if odds3 != None:
    p = p * odds3
```

```
guy@Mac-Pro-3 ~ % python3
Python 3.10.0 (v3.10.0:b494f5935c, Oct  4 2021, 14:59:20) [C
lang 12.0.5 (clang-1205.0.22.11)] on darwin
Type "help", "copyright", "credits" or "license" for more in
formation.
>>> def parlay(odds1, odds2, odds3 = None, odds4 = None, odd
s5 = None):
...     """Calculate the odds for a parlay that contains two
, three, four, or five bets"""
...
```

```
guy@Mac-Pro-3 ~ % python3
Python 3.10.0 (v3.10.0:b494f5935c, Oct  4 2021, 14:59:20) [C
lang 12.0.5 (clang-1205.0.22.11)] on darwin
Type "help", "copyright", "credits" or "license" for more in
formation.
>>> def parlay(odds1, odds2, odds3 = None, odds4 = None, odd
s5 = None):
...     """Calculate the odds for a parlay that contains two
, three, four, or five bets"""
...     p = odds1 * odds2
...     if odds3 != None:
...         p = p * odds3
...
```

6 Type two similar `if` statements for `odds4` and `odds5`, again pressing Enter at the end of each line:

```
if odds4 != None:
    p = p * odds4
if odds5 != None:
    p = p * odds5
```

7 Type the following `return` statement, which causes the function to return the value of `p` to the calling code, and then press Enter.

```
return p
```

8 Press Enter again to end the function.

The Python prompt appears again.

9 Type the following statement, which uses the `print()` function to display the result of calling the `parlay()` function and supplying four bets at low odds. Press Enter.

```
print(parlay(1.72, 2, 3.6, 1.72))
```

Python displays the accumulated odds for the fourfold bet.

10 Press ⬆ to reenter the previous statement, but this time edit the end to include a fifth argument. Press Enter.

```
print(parlay(1.72, 2, 3.6, 1.72, 4))
```

Python displays the accumulated odds for the fivefold bet — `85.20192` for the example.

```
guy — Python — 60×28
guy@Mac-Pro-3 ~ % python3
Python 3.10.0 (v3.10.0:b494f5935c, Oct  4 2021, 14:59:20) [C
lang 12.0.5 (clang-1205.0.22.11)] on darwin
Type "help", "copyright", "credits" or "license" for more in
formation.
>>> def parlay(odds1, odds2, odds3 = None, odds4 = None, odd
s5 = None):
...     """Calculate the odds for a parlay that contains two
, three, four, or five bets"""
...     p = odds1 * odds2
...     if odds3 != None:
...         p = p * odds3
...     if odds4 != None:    ◀─ 6
...         p = p * odds4
...     if odds5 != None:
...         p = p * odds5
...     return p    ◀─ 7
...
>>>
```

```
guy — Python — 60×28
guy@Mac-Pro-3 ~ % python3
Python 3.10.0 (v3.10.0:b494f5935c, Oct  4 2021, 14:59:20) [C
lang 12.0.5 (clang-1205.0.22.11)] on darwin
Type "help", "copyright", "credits" or "license" for more in
formation.
>>> def parlay(odds1, odds2, odds3 = None, odds4 = None, odd
s5 = None):
...     """Calculate the odds for a parlay that contains two
, three, four, or five bets"""
...     p = odds1 * odds2
...     if odds3 != None:
...         p = p * odds3
...     if odds4 != None:
...         p = p * odds4
...     if odds5 != None:
...         p = p * odds5
...     return p
...
>>> print(parlay(1.72, 2, 3.6, 1.72))   ◀─ 9
21.30048
>>> print(parlay(1.72, 2, 3.6, 1.72, 4))   ◀─ 10
85.20192
>>>
```

TIP

What data types can I use for default values?
You can use most data types, including `None`, as in this example; an integer, such as `0` or `1`; a Boolean, such as `True`; or a string. However, in general, it is best to avoid mutable data types because although they work correctly the first time you call the function, subsequent calls to the function will return the value the last call assigned to the data type. For example, if you use an empty list as a default value, the first call returns an empty list, as expected, but the next call returns a list containing the values you assigned to the list.

## CHAPTER 9

Working with Text

In this chapter, you learn how to use Python to work with text, which Python handles as strings of characters. You start by learning the essentials of strings and then perform essential moves with strings, such as returning part of a string; concatenating multiple strings into a single string; searching for specific values; and building strings using the interpolation operator, using the `.format` method, using f-strings, and using template strings.

```python
 2
 3   def make_title(sT):
 4       rlist = []
 5       rs = ""
 6       for word in sT.split():
 7           if not word.isupper() and word not in lwords:
 8               word = word.title()
 9           rlist.append(word)
10
11       if not rlist[0].isupper():
12           rlist[0] = rlist[0].title()
13       if not rlist[-1].isupper():
14           rlist[-1] = rlist[-1].title()
15
16       for word in rlist:
17           rs += " " + word
18
19       rs = rs.strip()
20       return rs
21
22   def main():
23       sT = input("Enter the title: ")
24       print(make_title(sT))
25
26   if __name__ == "__main__":
27       main()
```

Learn the Essentials of Strings

In this section, you learn the essentials of strings: with what strings are in Python, how you create single-line strings and multiline strings, and the tools that Python provides for working with strings. You also learn a little about character codes and character sets, the symbols that computers use to represent text — and emoji — on the screen.

Understanding What a String Is

A *string* is an ordered sequence of characters, such as `abcd` or `The quick brown fox`. You can create a string by assigning text within quotes to a variable. For example, the following statement creates a variable named `animal1` and assigns `The quick brown fox` to it:

```
animal1 = "The quick brown fox"
```

Because the characters have a specific order, each string is immutable, which means you cannot change it. However, you can take the string, manipulate it, and then assign the manipulated string either to the same variable again or to another variable.

A string can contain anywhere from zero characters up to as many characters as your computer's memory can handle. Most strings fall between these two extremes.

Understanding How You Create Strings

When creating a string, you delimit its contents with quotes. To delimit any particular string, you can use either a single quote at the beginning and the end or double quotes at the beginning and the end. You cannot mix single and double quotes to delimit a single string — for example, you cannot start a string with a single quote and then end it with double quotes.

The following example creates a variable named `str1` and assigns a string to it using single quotes:

```
str1 = 'New York'
```

Similarly, the following example creates a variable named `str2` and assigns a string to it using double quotes:

```
str2 = "Grand Canyon Junction"
```

Using single quotes enables you to include double quotes as part of the string. Here is an example:

```
str3 = 'Ann said, "I want to go to New York."'
```

Likewise, using double quotes enables you to include single quotes inside the string. Here is an example:

```
str4 = "Bill replied, 'We should stay here.'"
```

To create a multiline string, you can use either triple single quotes or triple double quotes to mark the start and end of the string. Creating a multiline string enables you to control where the line breaks occur in the output. Here is an example:

```
str5 = """Conference Room C

This meeting room is for senior management only."""
```

In a multiline string, you can also control the layout of text by including tab characters and new-line characters.

Understanding Python's Tools for Manipulating Strings

Python provides a wide variety of methods for manipulating strings. Each string method returns a new value, so it does not change the original string. However, you can assign a changed string back to the variable that contained it, which gives a similar effect to having changed the original string.

The section "Meet Python's String Methods," later in this chapter, gives you an overview of the string methods that Python offers. Subsequent sections of the chapter show you how to put many of the string methods to work.

Understanding Character Codes and Character Sets

A *character set* is a list of symbols used to display text and emoji on a computer. Different character sets may have different characters for the same character codes, the numbers that identify particular characters within a character set.

For example, the widely used American Standard Code for Information Interchange — ASCII for short — contains 255 characters, including uppercase and lowercase Roman letters, such as ABC and abc; Arabic numerals, such as 123; punctuation marks, such as ? and !; and control characters such as Delete, Escape, and space. The Unicode character set, which greatly extends ASCII, has many more than 100,000 characters that include the characters used in more than 100 languages, not to mention thousands of emoji.

When using Python 3, you will normally use the Unicode character set, which Python 3 is designed to support fully. However, earlier versions of Python 2 may use ASCII rather than Unicode.

Unicode supports different formats for encoding its characters. These formats are called Unicode Transformation Formats, abbreviated to UTF. The most widely used Unicode Transformation Format is UTF-8, which uses 8-bit character units to encode the characters. UTF-8 uses up to four character units to encode a character. Eight bits is one byte, so UTF-8 uses up to four bytes of space to encode a given character.

This book assumes you are working with UTF-8.

Create Single-Line Strings

To store text, Python enables you to create either single-line strings or multiline strings. Single-line strings are good for general use in code, whereas multiline strings can be useful for presenting text laid out with line breaks and indentation. This section shows you how to create single-line strings; the next section, "Create Multiline Strings," covers multiline strings.

To delimit a single-line string, you use either paired single quotes or paired double quotes. If needed, the string text can include quotes of the opposite kind — for instance, a string delimited with double quotes can include single quotes for quotation or apostrophes.

Create Single-Line Strings

1 In Visual Studio Code, create a new script, and then save it.

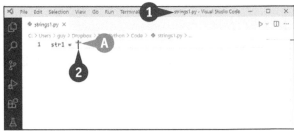

2 Type the following partial statement, which creates a variable named `str1`, and then press Enter:

```
str1 = "
```

A Visual Studio Code's Auto Closing Quotes feature automatically inserts the closing double quotes for you. Normally, this is helpful.

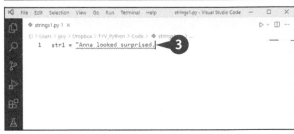

3 For this example, press Del to delete the second pair of double quotes, and then type **Anna looked surprised.**, including the period.

Visual Studio Code places a wavy red underline beneath the string text to indicate there is a problem.

4 Move the pointer over the underlined string.

B The pop-up balloon shows the error that the Pylance extension has identified: *String literal is unterminated*.

5 Type the missing double quotes to close the string, and then press Enter.

Visual Studio Code removes the wavy red underline.

6 Type the following statement, which creates a variable named `str2` and assigns to it a string that contains quotes, and then press Enter:

```
str2 = 'Anna said "Who?" to Bill.'
```

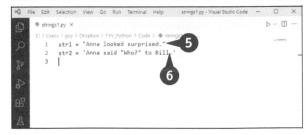

Visual Studio Code starts a new line.

7 Type **print(str**.

C Visual Studio Code displays the Auto Complete list, showing the available items starting with the letters *str*, *st*, and *s*, in that order.

8 Click the item you want to enter — in this case, str1.

Note: You can also select an item from the Auto Complete list by "typing down" to it — typing further characters until you identify it unambiguously — or by pressing ⬇ or ⬆. Once you have selected the item, press Tab to enter it.

Visual Studio Code enters that item in the code, including the closing parenthesis required to complete the function statement.

9 Press Enter to create a new line, type the following statement to display str2, and then press Enter again:

```
print(str2)
```

10 Click **Run Python File in Terminal** (▷).

Visual Studio Code displays the Terminal pane.

Visual Studio Code runs your code.

D The two strings appear in the Terminal pane.

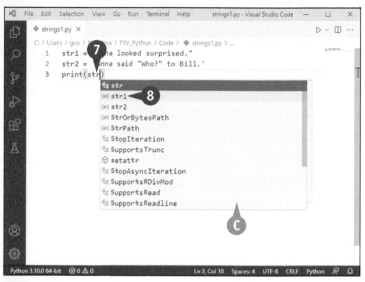

TIPS

Is there another way of including quotes inside a string?

Yes. You can "escape" the quotes, telling Python to treat them specially. To escape a quote character, you put a backslash before it. For example, in str1 = 'Ann is Bill\'s cousin', the \' escapes the apostrophe.

How do I include a backslash in a string?

You can either escape the backslash by preceding it with another backslash — for example, path = "C:\\Windows\\Temp" stores the string C:\Windows\Temp — or create a raw string by preceding the string with R or r, such as path = R"C:\Windows\Temp". Escaping works for other special characters — such as \b for Backspace and \f for form feed — as well, but it causes an error with any nonspecial character.

Create Multiline Strings

When you need to include line breaks and spacing in a string, you can create a multiline string in either of two ways. The first way is to place either triple single quotes or triple double quotes at the beginning and end of the string; between the delimiting quotes, you lay out the string on as many lines as you want using carriage returns, spaces, and tabs, as needed. The second way to create a multiline string is to enter it on a single line of code but include new-line characters or carriage-return characters within the string.

Create Multiline Strings

Create a Multiline String Using Triple Quotes

1 In Visual Studio Code, create a new script, and then save it.

2 In the Editor pane, type the following partial statement, which creates a variable named `strMulti` and starts assigning a string to it:

```
strMulti = """To:
```

Note: You can use either triple single quotes or triple double quotes for any multiline string, but you cannot mix and match single quotes and double quotes for the same string.

A As you enter each double-quote character, Visual Studio Code automatically enters a matching one to the right of the insertion point, closing the string for you.

3 Press Enter.

The insertion point and the three closing double-quote characters move to a new line.

4 Type the contents of the string, using spaces for indentation and pressing Enter to create new lines, as needed. Here is an example:

```
strMulti = """To:
    Indefinite Distributors
    555 Industry Blvd.
    Anytown, IN 46555"""
```

5 Press ↓.

The insertion point moves to after the three closing double-quote characters.

Note: You can also press End to move the insertion point to the end of the line.

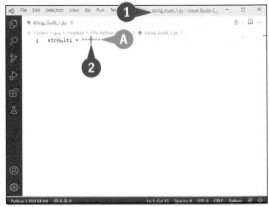

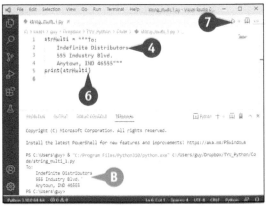

6 Type the following `print()` statement to display `strMulti`, and then press Enter:

```
print(strMulti)
```

7 Click **Run Python File in Terminal** (▷).

B The multiline string appears in the Terminal pane.

Create a Multiline String Using Carriage-Return and New-Line Characters

1 In Visual Studio Code, create a new script, and then save it.

2 In the Editor pane, type the following statement, which creates a variable named `Multi2` and assigns to it a string that includes tab characters and new-line characters. Press **Enter**.

```
Multi2 = "\t\tIntroduction\n\
nMaking a strong first impression
has never been more important."
```

3 Type the following statement, which adds further text to `Multi2`, and then press **Enter**:

```
Multi2 = Multi2 + "\n\n\tHere is a
handy technique you can use to add
impact to your first impression."
```

Note: If Visual Studio Code does not wrap long lines of code, click **View** on the menu bar, and then click **Word Wrap**, placing a check mark next to it.

4 Type the following `print()` statement to display `Multi2`, and then press **Enter**:

```
print(Multi2)
```

5 Click **Run Python File in Terminal** (▷).

C The multiline string appears in the Terminal pane with the tab characters replaced by tabs and the new-line characters replaced by new lines.

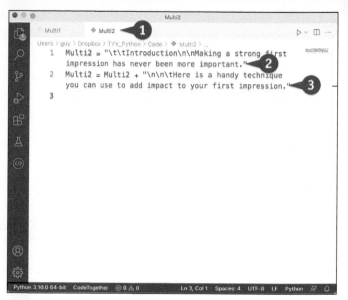

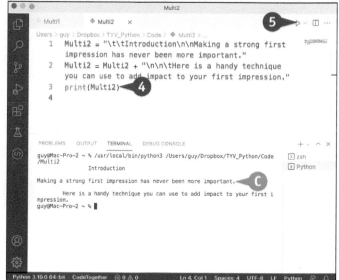

TIP

What is the difference between a carriage-return character and a new-line character?

In a string, the carriage-return character, `\r`, makes the following text start at the beginning of the line, but it does not move down to the next line. By contrast, the new-line character, `\n`, moves down to the next line and makes the text start at the beginning of the line.

Usually, you will want to use `\n` to start the text on a new line. Using `\r` on its own causes any subsequent text to overwrite part of the existing text, which is not what you normally want.

Meet Python's String Methods

Python includes nearly four dozen methods for working with strings. This section gives you an overview of these methods, dividing them into five categories: methods for checking and changing the case of text, such as `islower()` and `lower()`; methods for returning information about strings, such as `isalpha()` and `startswith()`; methods for finding and replacing in strings, including `find()` and `replace()`; methods for laying out string data, such as `center()` and `format()`; and methods for transforming string data, from `encode()` to `zfill()`.

Later in this chapter, you put the most useful of these methods into action.

Methods for Checking and Changing Case

Table 9-1 lists Python's methods for checking and changing the case of strings.

Table 9-1: Methods for Checking and Changing Case	
Method	**What It Returns**
`capitalize()`	The string with an initial capital applied
`casefold()`	The string in lowercase letters
`islower()`	True if all characters in the string are lowercase
`istitle()`	True if the string is lowercase with initial caps
`isupper()`	True if all characters in the string are uppercase
`lower()`	The string in lowercase letters
`swapcase()`	The string with its original casing reversed
`title()`	The string in title case — with the first letter of each word capitalized
`upper()`	The string in uppercase letters

Methods for Returning Information About Strings

Table 9-2 lists Python's methods for returning information about strings.

Table 9-2: Methods for Returning Information About Strings	
Method	**What It Returns**
`count()`	The count of occurrences of the string in another string
`endswith()`	True if the string ends with the specified string
`isalnum()`	True if all characters in the string are alphanumeric
`isalpha()`	True if all characters in the string are alphabetical
`isascii()`	True if all characters in the string are ASCII characters
`isdecimal()`	True if all characters in the string are decimals
`isdigit()`	True if all characters in the string are digits
`isidentifier()`	True if the string is a valid identifier
`isnumeric()`	True if all characters in the string are numeric
`isprintable()`	True if all characters in the string are printable
`isspace()`	True if all characters in the string are whitespaces
`startswith()`	True if the string starts with the specified string

Methods for Finding Within Strings

Table 9-3 lists Python's methods for performing find operations in strings.

Table 9-3: Methods for Finding and Replacing in Strings	
Method	**What It Returns**
find()	The position of the specified value in the string
index()	The position of the specified value in the string
rfind()	The position of the specified value in the string, searching from the end
rindex()	The position of the specified value in the string, starting from the end

Methods for Laying Out String Data

Table 9-4 lists Python's methods for laying out string data.

Table 9-4: Methods for Laying Out String Data	
Method	**What It Returns**
center()	A centered string
format_map()	The string formatted as specified
format()	The string formatted as specified
ljust()	The left-justified version of the string
rjust()	The right-justified version of the string

Methods for Transforming String Data

Table 9-5 lists Python's methods for transforming string data.

Table 9-5: Methods for Transforming String Data	
Method	**What It Returns**
encode()	The string encoded in the specified way
expandtabs()	Sets the tab size to the specified number of white spaces (default 8)
join()	A string containing an iterable's elements joined together
lstrip()	The string with leading spaces removed
maketrans()	A translation table
partition()	A three-element tuple containing the text before the specified string (searching from the beginning), the specified string, and the text after the specified string
replace()	A string with the specified search value replaced with the specified replacement value
rpartition()	A three-element tuple containing the text before the specified string (searching from the end), the specified string, and the text after the specified string
rsplit()	Splits the string at the specified separator, and returns a list
rstrip()	The string with trailing spaces removed
split()	A list consisting of strings split at the specified value
splitlines()	A list containing strings created by splitting the specified string at the line breaks
strip()	The string with leading and trailing spaces removed
translate()	A translated string
zfill()	The string filled with zeros at the beginning to bring it to the specified length

Return Information About a String

Python includes a wide variety of string methods that enable you to return information about strings. For example, you can use the `isupper()` method or the `islower()` method to determine whether the string is uppercase or lowercase, respectively; or use the `isalpha()` method, the `isnumeric()` method, or the `isalnum()` method to check whether the string is numeric, alphabetic, or alphanumeric — again, respectively. You can use the `startswith()` method to check a string's start, use the `endswith()` method to check its end, or use the `count()` method to return the number of occurrences of another string inside that string.

Return Information About a String

1 Open a terminal window and launch Python.

Ⓐ The Python prompt appears.

2 Type the following statement, which creates a variable named `str1` and assigns a string to it, and then press **Enter**:

```
str1 = "Sometimes a string is just a string."
```

3 Type the following statement, which uses the `isalnum()` method, to check whether the string's characters are all alphanumeric, and then press **Enter**:

```
str1.isalnum()
```

Python returns `False`, because the spaces and the period are not alphanumeric characters.

Note: You could also try other tests, such as `str1.isalpha()`, `str1.isdecimal()`, or `str1.isnumeric()`.

4 Type the following statement, which uses the `endswith()` method to check the string's end, and then press **Enter**:

```
str1.endswith(".")
```

Python returns `True` because the string ends with a period.

5 Type the following statement, which uses the `startswith()` method to see if `str1` starts with "The", and then press **Enter**:

```
str1.startswith("The")
```

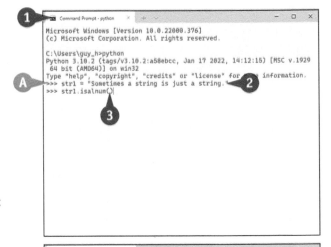

190

Python returns `False`.

⑥ Type the following statement, which uses the `count()` method to return the number of instances of "string" in `str1`, and then press Enter:

```
str1.count("string")
```

Python returns 2, because `str1` contains two instances of "string".

⑦ Type the following statement, which uses the `isprintable()` method to determine whether all the string's characters are printable, and then press Enter:

```
str1.isprintable()
```

Python returns `True`, because all the string's characters are printable.

Note: Characters such as a line feed or a carriage return are nonprintable and cause the `isprintable()` method to return `False`.

⑧ Type the following statement, which checks whether the string is a valid identifier in Python, and then press Enter:

```
str1.isidentifier()
```

Note: A valid identifier must contain only alphanumerics — the letters *a* to *z* and the numbers 0 to 9 — and underscores. It cannot contain spaces. It can start with a letter or an underscore, but not with a number.

Python returns `False`, because the string contains spaces and punctuation.

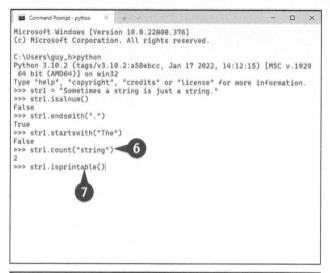

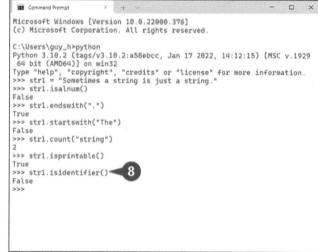

TIP

How can I return the number of characters in a string?

Use the `len()` function, which returns the length of the string as a number of characters. For example, `print(len(str1))` makes Python display the number of characters in `str1`, including spaces.

The `len()` function works on sequences and collections but returns a `TypeError` error if you use it on an object that has no length. For example, if you run `len()` on an `int` object, Python returns `TypeError: object of type 'int' has no len()`.

Transform and Clean Up a String

As you saw in the section "Meet Python's String Methods," earlier in this chapter, Python provides a comprehensive suite of methods for manipulating strings. In this section, you use some of those methods to clean up a string by trimming off *leading spaces* — extra spaces at the beginning of the string — and *trailing spaces* —extra spaces at the end — and replacing double internal spaces with a single space. You then use the `split()` method to split the string into a list and the `partition()` method to split the string into a three-element tuple.

Transform a String

1 Open a terminal window and launch Python.

A The Python prompt appears.

2 Type the following statement, which creates a variable named `lm` and assigns a string to it, and then press Enter:

```
lm = "   West   Oregon   19411   "
```

Note: The `lm` string has three leading spaces, double spaces between the words, and three trailing spaces.

3 Type the following statement, which assigns to `lm` the string with its leading spaces and trailing spaces removed, and then press Enter:

```
lm = lm.strip()
```

Note: To remove only leading spaces, use the `lstrip()` method — for example, `lm.lstrip()`. To remove only trailing spaces, use the `rstrip()` method.

4 Type the following statement, which displays the contents of `lm`, and then press Enter:

```
print(lm)
```

Python displays the trimmed string:

```
West   Oregon   19411
```

5 Type the following statement, which uses the `replace()` method to replace each instance of two spaces with a single space and assigns the results to `lm`. Press Enter.

```
lm = lm.replace("  ", " ")
```

```
guy@Mac-Pro-2 Code % python3
Python 3.10.0 (v3.10.0:b494f5935c, Oct  4 2021, 14:59:20) [Clang 1
2.0.5 (clang-1205.0.22.11)] on darwin
Type "help", "copyright", "credits" or "license" for more informat
ion.
>>> lm = "   West   Oregon   19411   "
>>>
```

```
guy@Mac-Pro-2 Code % python3
Python 3.10.0 (v3.10.0:b494f5935c, Oct  4 2021, 14:59:20) [Clang 1
2.0.5 (clang-1205.0.22.11)] on darwin
Type "help", "copyright", "credits" or "license" for more informat
ion.
>>> lm = "   West   Oregon   19411   "
>>> lm = lm.strip()
>>> print(lm)
West   Oregon   19411
>>> lm = lm.replace("  ", " ")
>>>
```

6 Again, use the `print()` function to display the contents of `lm`. Press Enter.

```
print(lm)
```

Python displays the string, now with a single space between words.

```
West Oregon 19411
```

7 Type the following statement, which creates a variable named `list1` and assigns to it the list of strings created by splitting the string in `lm` at its spaces using the `split()` method. Press Enter.

```
list1 = lm.split(" ")
```

8 Type the following statement, which uses the `print()` method to display `list1`, and then press Enter:

```
print(list1)
```

Python displays the list of three strings:

```
['West', 'Oregon', '19411']
```

9 Type the following statement, which creates a variable named `tuple1` and assigns to it the three-element tuple resulting from dividing `lm` using the `partition()` method. Press Enter.

```
tuple1 = lm.partition('Oregon')
```

10 Type the following print statement to display the contents of `tuple1`, and then press Enter:

```
print(tuple1)
```

Python displays the three-element tuple:

```
('West ', 'Oregon', ' 19411')
```

Note: The tuple appears in parentheses rather than brackets. Note also that the tuple's first string includes a trailing space and the third string includes a leading space.

TIP

How do I pad a string with zeros to make it a specific length?

Use the `zfill()` method, which fills the beginning of the string with zeros so that it contains the specified number of characters altogether. For example, if the variable named `a5` contains the string `628` but you need an 8-digit number, you could use `a5.zfill(8)` to produce the string `00000628`. Note that the `zfill()` method is working with strings that appear to contain integer data, not with integers themselves.

Return Part of a String via Slicing

Often, you will want to return part of a string rather than a whole string. For example, you may want to get the first three characters, the last ten characters, or a specific part in the middle.

Python uses the term *slice* to mean chopping up a string like this; you can also slice other objects, such as lists, tuples, and sets. When slicing, you specify the start point and the end point for the substring you are returning. You can also specify a step argument — for example, to return every other character or every third character.

Return Part of a String via Slicing

1 Open a terminal window and launch Python.

A The Python prompt appears.

2 Type the following statement, which creates a variable named `txt1` and assigns a string to it, and then press Enter:

```
txt1 = "Cantilever production
statistics Q3"
```

3 Type the following statement, which creates a variable named `first3` and assigns to it the first three characters of `txt1`. Press Enter.

```
first3 = txt1[0:3]
```

4 Type the following statement, which uses the `print()` function to display `first3`, and then press Enter:

```
print(first3)
```

Python displays `Can`, the first three characters in `txt1`.

5 Type the following statement, which creates a variable named `last2` and assigns to it the last two characters of `txt1`. Press Enter.

```
last2 = txt1[-2:]
```

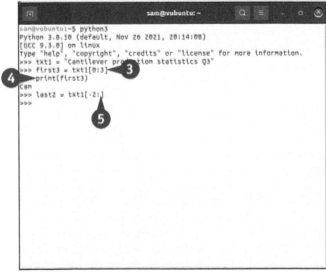

6 Type the following statement, which uses the print() function to display last2, and then press Enter:

```
print(last2)
```

Python displays Q3, the last two characters in txt1.

7 Type the following statement, which creates a variable named middle10 and assigns to it 10 characters from the mid part of txt1. Press Enter.

```
middle10 = txt1[22:32]
```

8 Type the following statement, which uses the print() function to display middle10, and then press Enter:

```
print(middle10)
```

Python displays statistics, the characters in positions 22 to 32 in txt1.

9 Type the following statement, which creates a variable named m10odd and assigns to it every other character from middle10. Press Enter.

```
m10odd = middle10[::2]
```

10 Type the following statement, which uses the print() function to display m10odd, and then press Enter:

```
print(m10odd)
```

Python displays saitc, every other character from statistics.

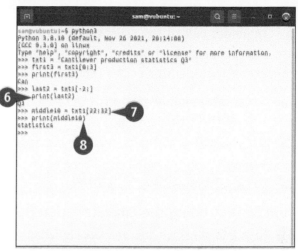

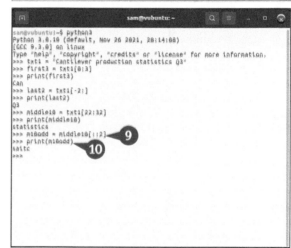

TIPS

How do you use colons when slicing a string?
Slicing as shown here takes three arguments — start, end, and step — separated by colons. For example, txt1[1:5] returns the second through the fifth characters of txt1; txt1[1:5:2] uses a step value of 2 and so returns the second and fourth characters of txt1. You can omit start to use the object's start, omit end to use the object's end, and omit step to use the default step, 1.

What does a negative number mean in slicing?
A negative number indicates starting from the end of the string rather than the beginning. For example, txt1[-13:] returns the portion of txt1 from the 13th character, counting back from the end of the string.

Concatenate and Repeat Strings

Python enables you to join two or more strings together to make a single longer string. Computer languages call this *concatenating* strings — literally, "chaining them together." In Python, you use the concatenation operator, +, to concatenate strings. You can repeat strings using either the concatenation operator or the repetition operator, *.

The + operator simply appends the second string to first string, so if you concatenate the string Anita and the string Hernandez, you get the string AnitaHernandez. When concatenating strings, you will sometimes need to add spaces or punctuation to produce the string you need.

Concatenate and Repeat Strings

Join Strings Using the Concatenation Operator

1 Open a terminal window and launch Python.

A The Python prompt appears.

2 Type the following statement, which creates a variable named fname and assigns a string to it, and then press **Enter**:

```
fname = "Anita"
```

3 Type the following statement, which creates a variable named mi and assigns a string to it, and then press **Enter**:

```
mi = "C"
```

4 Type the following statement, which creates a variable named lname and assigns a string to it, and then press **Enter**:

```
lname = "Hernandez"
```

5 Type the following statement, which creates a variable named fullname and assigns to it a concatenated string, and then press **Enter**:

```
fullname = fname + " " + mi + ". " + lname
```

6 Type the following statement, which displays fullname, and then press **Enter**:

```
print(fullname)
```

Python returns Anita C. Hernandez, the full name made up of fname, mi, and lname, with spaces and a period.

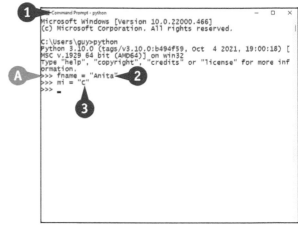

Repeat a String Using the Concatenation Operator

1 Type the following statement, which creates a variable named `myText` and assigns a string to it, and then press `Enter`:

`myText = "* Draft *"`

Note: The `myText` string uses spaces to increase readability.

2 Type the following statement, which uses the concatenation operator to repeat `myText` three times, and then press `Enter`:

`myText + myText + myText`

Python returns `* Draft ** Draft ** Draft *`.

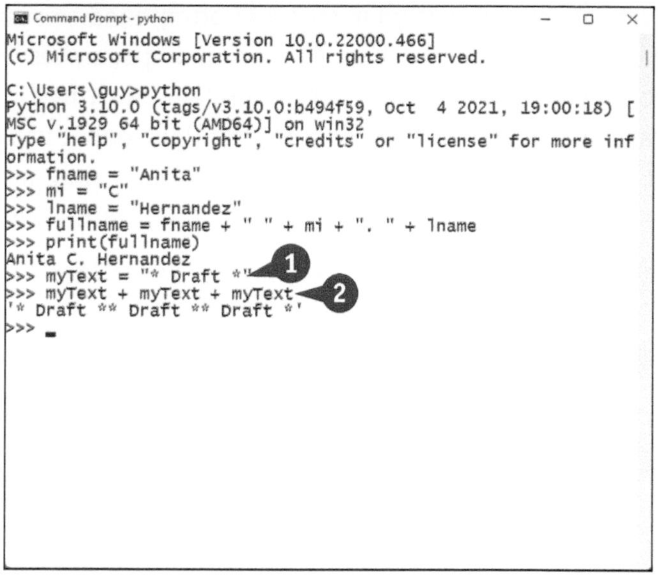

Repeat a String Using the Repetition Operator

1 Type the following statement, which creates a variable named `sChar` and assigns a string to it, and then press `Enter`:

`sChar = "#"`

2 Type the following statement, which uses the repetition operator to repeat `sChar` 12 times:

`sChar * 12`

Python returns `'############'`, which you might use as a display element, such as a separator.

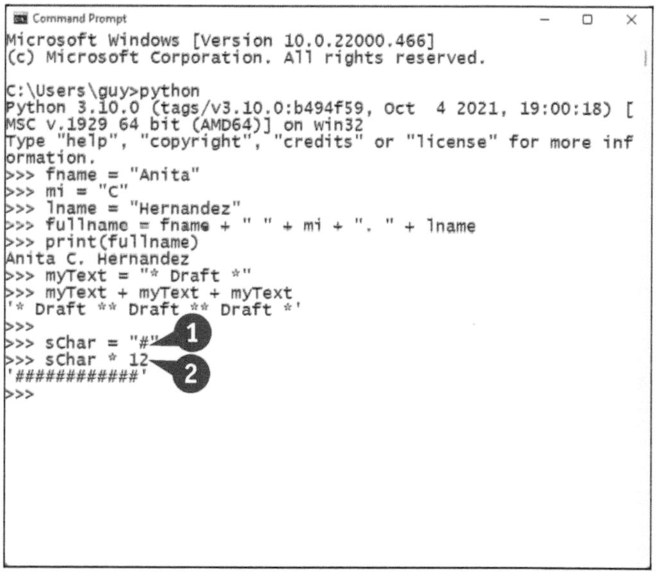

TIP

How do I concatenate a string and an integer?

You need to cast the integer to a string; the same goes for any other nonstring data type you want to concatenate with a string. For example, say you have a variable named `int1` that contains an integer and a variable named `str1` that contains a string. You could use `str(int1) + str1` to concatenate an integer version of `int1` with `str1`; trying to concatenate the two without casting the integer to a string, such as `int1 + str1`, returns a `TypeError`.

Search for One String Inside Another String

Chances are that your code will often need to search for one string inside another string. Python provides four methods for performing searches within strings. You can use the `find()` method to search for one string within another, starting from the left end of the string; and the `rfind()` method to search starting from the right end. Similarly, you can use the `index()` method to return the position of one string within another string, again starting from the left end; or the `rindex()` method to return the position starting from the right end.

Search for One String Inside Another String

1 Open a terminal window and launch Python.

Ⓐ The Python prompt appears.

2 Type the following statement, which creates a string called `text1`, and then press **Enter**:

```
text1 = "It's raining cats, dogs,
and more cats."
```

3 Type the following statement, which uses the `find()` method to find the word "cats", and then press **Enter**:

```
text1.find("cats")
```

Python returns 13, the character position at which the first instance of "cats" starts in the string, counting from the beginning and including spaces.

4 Type the following statement, which uses the `index()` method to locate the word "cats", and then press **Enter**:

```
text1.index("cats")
```

Python again returns 13, the character position at which the first instance of "cats" starts.

Note: See the tip for information on the difference between the `find()` method and the `index()` method.

5 Type the following statement, which uses the `find()` method again but adds two optional arguments, and then press **Enter**:

```
text1.find("cats", 20, len(text1))
```

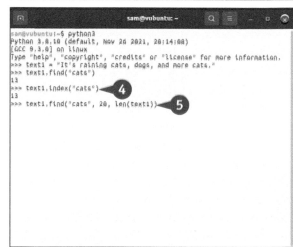

Python returns 34, the character position at which the second instance of "cats" starts.

Note: The `find()`, `index()`, `rfind()`, and `rindex()` methods all take three arguments. The first argument, `value`, is required and gives the search value. The second, `start`, is optional and gives the start position; the default is 0. The third, `end`, is optional and gives the end position; the default is the string's end.

⑥ Type the following statement, which uses the `rfind()` method to find the word "cats", but this time finding the instance nearest the right end of the string. Press Enter.

```
text1.rfind("cats")
```

Python again returns 34, the character position of the instance of "cats" nearest the end of the string.

⑦ Type the following statement, which uses the `rindex()` method to find the instance of "cat" nearest the end of the string, and then press Enter:

```
text1.rindex("cats")
```

Python once more returns 34.

```
sam@vubuntu:~$ python3
Python 3.8.10 (default, Nov 26 2021, 20:14:08)
[GCC 9.3.0] on linux
Type "help", "copyright", "credits" or "license" for more information.
>>> text1 = "It's raining cats, dogs, and more cats."
>>> text1.find("cats")
13
>>> text1.index("cats")
13
>>> text1.find("cats", 20, len(text1))
34
>>> text1.rfind("cats")  ⑥
```

```
sam@vubuntu:~$ python3
Python 3.8.10 (default, Nov 26 2021, 20:14:08)
[GCC 9.3.0] on linux
Type "help", "copyright", "credits" or "license" for more information.
>>> text1 = "It's raining cats, dogs, and more cats."
>>> text1.find("cats")
13
>>> text1.index("cats")
13
>>> text1.find("cats", 20, len(text1))
34
>>> text1.rfind("cats")
34
>>> text1.rindex("cats")  ⑦
34
>>>
```

TIP

What is the difference between `find()` and `index()`?
The `find()` method and the `index()` method work almost alike, and you can use whichever you prefer; similarly, `rfind()` is almost identical to `rindex()`. But there is one key difference: Whereas `find()` and `rfind()` return -1 if they cannot locate the search string, `index()` and `rindex()` return an error — specifically, `ValueError: substring not found`. When searching, your code should either handle this error or use `find()` instead of `index()` and `rfind()` instead of `rindex()`.

Check and Change String Capitalization

Python includes various string methods for determining the capitalization of a string of text and applying your preferred capitalization. For example, you can use the `isupper()` method to check whether the string is all capitals and then use the `title()` method to apply "title case" — the first letter of each word capitalized, the remaining letters lowercase.

In formal English grammar, however, title case uses all lowercase for articles, some prepositions, and some conjunctions that are not the title's first word or last word. In this section, you create a function that applies such "real" title case to a string.

Check and Change String Capitalization

1 In Visual Studio Code, create a new script, and then save it.

2 In the Editor pane, type the following statement, which creates the variable `lwords` and assigns to it the list of words that should appear in lowercase. Press **Enter**.

```
lwords = {"a", "an", "and", "as",
"at", "but", "by", "for", "how",
"if", "in", "of", "on", "off", "nor",
"or", "so", "the", "to", "up", "via",
"with", "yet"}
```

Note: The example list of words is not complete.

3 Press **Enter** again to leave a line blank, and then type the following statement, which declares the `make_title()` function and specifies that it uses the `sT` argument. Press **Enter** again.

```
def make_title(sT):
```

4 Type the following statement, which declares the variable `rlist`. This variable will hold the list of results. Press **Enter**.

```
rlist = []
```

5 Type the following statement, which declares the variable `rs`. This variable will hold the string that the `make_title` function returns to the code that calls it. Press **Enter**.

```
rs = ""
```

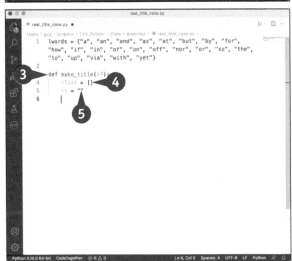

6 Type the following statement, which begins a `for` loop. The loop uses the `split` method to divide the value in the `sT` variable into words and uses the `word` variable to iterate through those words. Press **Enter**.

```
for word in sT.split()
```

7 Type the following statement, which uses an `if` statement to check whether the value in `word` is both not uppercase and not one of the words in `lwords`. Press **Enter**.

```
if not word.isupper() and word not in
lwords:
```

8 Type the following statement, which uses the `title()` function to apply title case to the string in the `word` variable, assigning the result to the `word` variable. Press **Enter**.

```
word = word.title()
```

9 Type the following statement, which uses the `append()` method to append the string in the `word` variable to the list in `rlist`. Press **Enter**.

```
rlist.append(word)
```

10 Press **Enter** again, creating a blank line, and then type the following statement, which checks whether the first item in `rlist` is uppercase and, if not, uses the `title()` method to apply title case to it. Press **Enter** once more.

```
if not rlist[0].isupper():
rlist[0] = rlist[0].title()
```

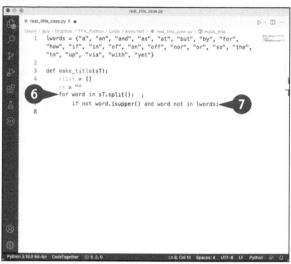

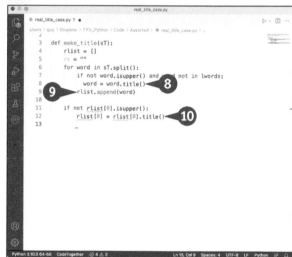

TIP

Why does the `make_title()` function check whether the word is all uppercase?

As written, this function assumes that any word in all uppercase is an abbreviation or acronym that should remain in uppercase. So `if not word.isupper()` verifies that the word is not uppercase before the function changes the word's case.

In a fuller implementation, the function might first check whether the entire string was uppercase and, if so, prompt the user to choose suitable casing.

continued ▶

The code you write in this section contains a function called `make_title()` that iterates through the words in a string you enter — for example, a paragraph that will be a heading. The function ignores words in uppercase, assuming them to have been entered that way deliberately. Uppercase aside, the function ensures that the first word and the last word in the string each have an initial capital; it compares each other word to a list of words that need to be lowercase and applies an initial capital or all lowercase, as appropriate.

Check and Change String Capitalization (continued)

⑪ Press `Backspace` to reduce the indent, and then type the following statement, which checks whether the last item in `rlist` is uppercase and, if not, uses the `title()` method to apply title case to it. Press `Enter`.

```
if not rlist[-1].isupper():
rlist[-1] = rlist[-1].title()
```

⑫ Press `Enter` again, creating a blank line, and then press `Backspace` to reduce the indent.

⑬ Type the following `for` loop, which creates the variable `rs`, iterates through each item in `rlist`, and adds to it each item, preceded by a space. Press `Enter`.

```
for word in rlist:
rs += "" + word
```

⑭ Press `Enter` again, creating a blank line, and then type the following statement, which uses the `strip()` method to remove any leading and trailing spaces from the string in `rs`, assigning the result back to `rs`. Press `Enter`.

```
rs = rs.strip()
```

⑮ Type the following statement, which returns the `rs` string as the output of the `make_title` function. Press `Enter`.

```
return rs
```

⑯ Press `Enter` again to create another blank line, and then type the following statement to declare the `main()` function. Press `Enter`.

```
def main():
```

17 Type the following statement, which creates the variable sT and assigns to it the string that the user types. Press **Enter**.

```
sT = input("Enter the title: ")
```

18 Type the following statement, which displays the result of running the make_title function on the sT string. Press **Enter**.

```
print(make_title(sT))
```

19 Press **Enter** again, creating a blank line, and then type the following if statement to verify that the main() function is being called from within the script:

```
if __name__ == "__main__":
    main()
```

Run the Script

1 Click **Run Python File in Terminal** (▷).

The script starts running.

Ⓐ The prompt appears.

2 Type the text to which you want to apply title case, and then press **Enter**.

Ⓑ Include an uppercase word if you want to verify the casing of abbreviations and acronyms.

Ⓒ Put one of the lowercase words last to verify the casing.

Ⓓ The title-case string appears.

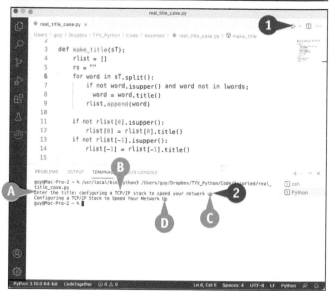

Meet Python's Tools for Building Strings

To build the text strings you need, you can use Python's string-formatting tools. In this case, "formatting" means getting the text in the string into the appropriate order and presenting its characters in the way you want — for example, as a number with a certain number of decimal places.

Python provides four different ways to format strings: string interpolation, the `.format` method, f-strings, and template strings. Each has its own strengths and weaknesses, and you may well find some more useful than others. You should be familiar with all four ways for when you encounter them in others' code.

Learn Python's Four Ways of Formatting Strings

Python offers four means of formatting strings. Each uses a different method of indicating where you want to substitute your variables.

Formatting Method	Example
Interpolation operator	`sayHi = "Hello, %s!" %"Vanessa"`
`.format` method	`str1 = "{} uses {}.".format("New York", "EST")`
f-strings	`str4 = f"1 {unit1}"`
Template strings	`from string import Template` `t1 = Template("Destination: $place.")`

The following subsections discuss these four methods in more detail. The following four main sections provide examples of working with each method.

Format Strings with the Interpolation Operator

Interpolation means putting one thing into another thing — in this case, inserting one string or other value into another string.

Python uses the interpolation operator, `%`, to indicate a placeholder at which you want to place an interpolated value. You can insert values of different types by using the codes in the following list.

Value Type	Interpolation Code
String	`%s`
Single character	`%c`
Integer	`%i` or `%d`
Float	`%f`
Exponential	`%e`
Hexadecimal	`%x`
Octal	`%o`

To insert a single value, you mark the spot in the string with the appropriate interpolation code. The following example specifies interpolating a string where `%s` appears:

```
sayHi = "Hello, %s!"
```

After the string, you enter the interpolation operator, %, followed by the value. The following example specifies a name as the string value:

```
sayHi = "Hello, %s!" %"Vanessa"
```

This statement produces the string `"Hello, Vanessa!"`.

If you have two or more items to interpolate, you put the values in a tuple after the interpolation operator. The following example interpolates a string and two integers:

```
myMsg = "%s, you have %i fingers and %d thumbs." %("Sam", 8, 2)
```

This statement produces the string `"Sam, you have 8 fingers and 2 thumbs."` Both `%i` and `%d` specify interpolating an integer, so use whichever you prefer.

String interpolation using the interpolation operator is straightforward for a small number of interpolations but becomes awkward for larger numbers of interpolations.

Using the Interpolation Operator, %

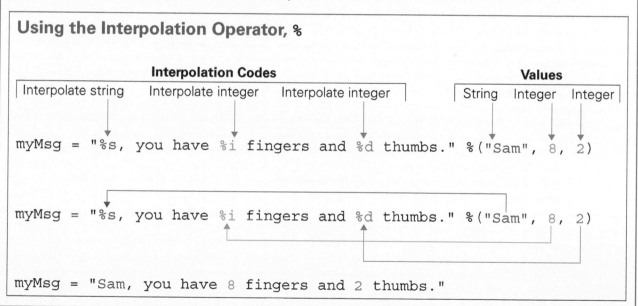

continued ▶

Python's f-strings provide a streamlined method of inserting strings from variables, from a dictionary, or from a class object. Introduced in Python 3.6, f-strings make your code easier to read and run faster than code using the interpolation operator or the `.format` method, so they are generally your best option for interpolating strings.

Format Strings with the `.format` Method

The second method of formatting strings uses the `.format` method of the `string` object. The `.format` method uses a pair of braces, `{}`, as a placeholder for each item you want to insert in the string. The following example uses two placeholders:

```
str1 = "{} uses {}."
```

After the string, you enter the `.format` method, followed by a tuple containing the items you want to insert. Here is an example:

```
str1 = "{} uses {}.".format("New York", "EST")
```

This statement creates the variable `str1` and assigns to it the string `"New York uses EST."`.

In this example, Python inserts the items in the order in which they appear in the `.format` tuple. This is easy enough, but you can also use zero-based index numbers or keywords to insert the items in a different order. The following example uses index numbers:

```
str2 = "{2} is GMT {0}{1} hours.".format("+", 5, "EST")
```

Using the `.format` Method by Position

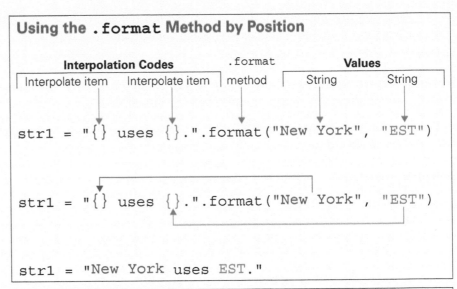

Using the `.format` Method with Index Numbers

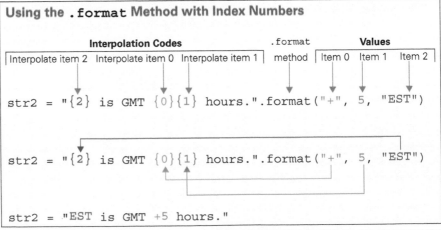

Format Strings with the `.format` Method (continued)

This statement creates the variable `str2` and assigns to it the string `"EST is GMT +5 hours."`. Python inserts the third item, `"EST"`, at the {2} placeholder; the first item, `"+"`, at the {0} placeholder; and the second item, `5`, at the {1} placeholder.

Similarly, you can use keywords to insert terms in your preferred order. The following example uses keywords:

```
s1 = "{w1} {u1} is {w2} {u2}.".format(w1=1, w2=2.2, u1="kg", u2="lb")
```

This statement creates the variable `s1` and assigns to it the string `"1 kg is 2.2 lb."`. Python inserts each value at the place specified by its keyword: the value `1` at the `w1` keyword, the string `"kg"` at the `u1` keyword, and so on.

Using the `.format` Method with Keywords

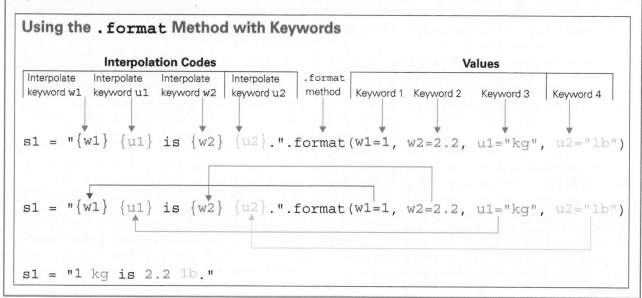

Format Strings with f-Strings

The third method of formatting strings is to use *formatted string literals*, known as *f-strings* for short.

To build an f-string, you use the `f` prefix and then create the string, including the placeholders needed for the items you want to insert. The f prefix can be either lowercase or uppercase, but lowercase is more common.

continued ▶

As you saw earlier in this section, f-strings are the string-building tool recommended for general purposes because of their ease of use and their speed of execution. However, if your Python code gets the user to input strings, use template strings rather than f-strings for the input. Template strings provide greater security, preventing a user from entering a carefully crafted formatted string that accesses variables within your code and exports data from them.

Format Strings with f-Strings (continued)

Unlike with the `.format` method, the placeholders in an f-string cannot be blank. You can populate the placeholders with variables, with items from a dictionary, or with items from a class.

The following example creates two variables and then includes them in an f-string:

```
unit1 = "qt"
unit2 = "oz"
str4 = f"1 {unit1} equals 32 {unit2}."
```

This statement creates the variable `str4` and assigns to it the f-string `1 qt equals 32 oz.`, inserting the contents of the `unit1` and `unit2` variables at their placeholders.

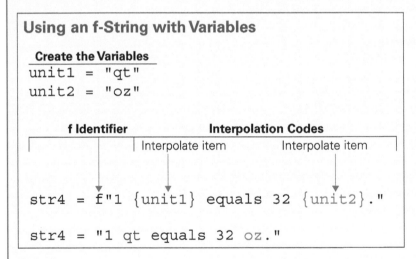

Using an f-String with Variables

Create the Variables
```
unit1 = "qt"
unit2 = "oz"
```

f Identifier   **Interpolation Codes**

Interpolate item   Interpolate item

```
str4 = f"1 {unit1} equals 32 {unit2}."

str4 = "1 qt equals 32 oz."
```

In the following example, the first statement creates a dictionary called `d1` that contains values named `u1`, `u2`, `a1`, and `a2`. The second statement then inserts these values in an f-string.

```
d1 = {
    "u1": "gal",
    "u2": "oz",
    "a1": 2,
    "a2": 256
    }
str5 = f'{d1["a1"]} {d1["u1"]} equals {d1["a2"]} {d1["u2"]}.'
```

This statement contains the variable str5 and assigns to it the f-string 2 gal equals 256 oz., inserting the contents of the a1, u1, a2, and u2 items from the d1 dictionary at their placeholders.

Using an f-String with a Dictionary

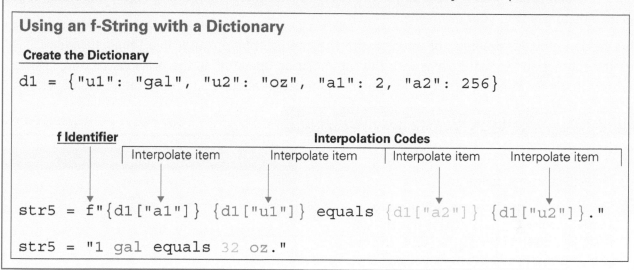

Create the Dictionary

```
d1 = {"u1": "gal", "u2": "oz", "a1": 2, "a2": 256}
```

f Identifier　　　　　　　　　　　**Interpolation Codes**

Interpolate item　　　Interpolate item　　　Interpolate item　　　Interpolate item

```
str5 = f"{d1["a1"]} {d1["u1"]} equals {d1["a2"]} {d1["u2"]}."

str5 = "1 gal equals 32 oz."
```

Format Strings with Template Strings

The fourth method of formatting strings is to use template strings. Template strings enable you to define placeholders and then insert strings in them by using a mapping object.

You would normally use template strings when your code gets the user to enter input. Template strings provide security features that f-strings, string interpolation, and the .format method do not, preventing the possibility that the user might enter a formatted string that accesses variables and exports data.

To use a template string, you first import the Template class from the string library. The following statement shows an example:

```
from string import Template
```

You then create an instance of the Template object containing a string that has the format you want the input to have. You include one or more $ placeholders in the string to indicate where you want to insert data. For example, the following statement creates a template called t1:

```
t1 = Template("Destination: $place.")
```

You then use the substitute method of the Template object to tell Python which variable you want to substitute for which placeholder.

```
t1.substitute(place=input("Enter the destination: "))
```

This statement makes Python prompt the user for the location, which it then substitutes for the placeholder, giving a string such as "Destination: Alaska".

Build Strings with the Interpolation Operator

Using the interpolation operator, %, is Python's oldest method of building strings. Although Python now offers more efficient methods of building strings, the interpolation operator still works fine and is still widely used, so you are likely to encounter it in other people's code even if you decide not to use it in your own code.

This section provides examples of working with the interpolation operator in a terminal window. See the subsection "Format Strings with the Interpolation Operator" in the previous section, "Meet Python's Tools for Building Strings," for general information about using the interpolation operator.

Build Strings with the Interpolation Operator

1 Open a terminal window and launch Python.

Ⓐ The Python prompt appears.

2 Type the following statement, which creates a variable named `myDay`, assigns text and the string interpolation operator `%s` to it, and then provides the string to insert. Press Enter.

```
myDay = "Today is %s." %"Friday"
```

3 Type the following statement to display the contents of `myDay`, and then press Enter:

```
myDay
```

Python displays the string `'Today is Friday.'`

4 Type the following statement, which creates a variable named `dte`; assigns a string including three interpolation codes; and provides a tuple containing the data to interpolate. Press Enter.

```
dte = "%i %s %d" %(21, "June", 2022)
```

5 Type the following statement to display the contents of `dte`, and then press Enter:

```
dte
```

Python displays the string `'21 June 2022'`.

6 Type the following statement, which creates a variable named `calc1`, assigns a string including three interpolation codes; and provides a tuple containing two integers and a float. Press `Enter`.

```
calc1= = "%i/%i = %f" %(10,4,2.5)
```

7 Type the following statement to display the contents of `calc1`, and then press `Enter`:

```
calc1
```

Python displays the string `'10/4 = 2.500000.'`

8 Type the following statement, which prompts the user to enter their name, and then press `Enter`:

```
print("Your initial is " +
input("Enter your name: ")
[0] + ".")
```

Python displays the `Enter your name:` prompt.

9 Type a name, and then press `Enter`.

Python displays a message including the first letter of the name, such as `Your initial is W`.

TIPS

What is the difference between the %d operator and the %i operator?
There is no real difference. Both codes are for signed integer decimals.

To make my code run faster, should I rewrite my code that uses the interpolation operator?
This is up to you — but it may not be worth the effort. Although f-strings provide better performance than the interpolation operator, the improvement is unlikely to be significant unless your code builds many strings. That said, you may want to update the code to use f-strings in the long run because they make your code easier to write, read, and maintain.

Build Strings with the `.format` Method

Introduced in Python 2.6, the `.format` method for building strings is still widely used, so you are likely to encounter it in other people's code even if you do not use it yourself. The `.format` method uses a pair of braces, {}, as a placeholder for each item to insert in the string; after the string, the `.format` keyword is followed by a tuple containing the items to insert.

See the subsection "Format Strings with the .format Method" in the section "Meet Python's Tools for Building Strings," earlier in this chapter, for general information about the `.format` method.

Build Strings with the `.format` Method

1 Open a terminal window and launch Python.

A The Python prompt appears.

2 Type the following statement, which creates the variable `loc1` and assigns to it a string containing two placeholders. Press **Enter**.

`loc1 = "{} is in {}."`

3 Type the following statement, which creates the variable `loc2` and assigns to it the result of using the `.format` method to insert two strings in `loc1`. Press **Enter**.

```
loc2 = loc1.format("Utica", "New York
State")
```

Note: Inserting items by order is straightforward for small numbers of items but can become awkward with many items. To reuse an item, you must enter it again in the appropriate position in the tuple.

4 Type the following statement, and then press **Enter**, to display the contents of `loc2`.

`loc2`

Python displays the string `'Utica is in New York State.'`.

```
● ● ●          Code — Python — 57×27      1
guy@Mac-Pro-3 Code % python3
Python 3.10.0 (v3.10.0:b494f5935c, Oct  4 2021, 14:59:20)
 [Clang 12.0.5 (clang-1205.0.22.11)] on darwin
Type "help", "copyright", "credits" or "license" for more
 information.
>>> loc1 = "{} is in {}."      2
>>> loc2 = loc1.format("Utica", "New York State")     3
>>>
```

```
● ● ●          Code — Python — 57×27
guy@Mac-Pro-3 Code % python3
Python 3.10.0 (v3.10.0:b494f5935c, Oct  4 2021, 14:59:20)
 [Clang 12.0.5 (clang-1205.0.22.11)] on darwin
Type "help", "copyright", "credits" or "license" for more
 information.
>>> loc1 = "{} is in {}."
>>> loc2 = loc1.format("Utica", "New York State")
>>> loc2
'Utica is in New York State.'
>>>
```

5 Type the following statement, which creates the variable m1 and assigns to it a string containing four placeholders that use zero-based index numbers. Press `Enter`.

```
m1 = "{2} {1} equals {0} {3}."
```

6 Type the following statement, which creates the variable m2 and assigns to it the result of using the `.format` method to insert four items in m1. Press `Enter`.

```
m2 = m1.format("1/16", "hammer", 1,
"foot")
```

7 Type the following statement, and then press `Enter`, to display the contents of m2.

```
m2
```

Python displays the resulting string, `'1 hammer equals 1/16 foot.'`.

8 Type the following statement, which creates a variable named wt, assigns a string that includes two placeholders using keywords, and then uses the `.format` method to provide the keywords. Press `Enter`.

```
wt = "{w1} {u1} equals {w2} {u2}.".
format(w1=1, w2=112, u1="cwt", u2="lb")
```

9 Type the following statement, and then press `Enter`, to display the contents of wt.

```
wt
```

Python displays the string `'1 cwt equals 112 lb.'`.

```
guy@Mac-Pro-3 Code % python3
Python 3.10.0 (v3.10.0:b494f5935c, Oct  4 2021, 14:59:20)
 [Clang 12.0.5 (clang-1205.0.22.11)] on darwin
Type "help", "copyright", "credits" or "license" for more
 information.
>>> loc1 = "{} is in {}."
>>> loc2 = loc1.format("Utica", "New York State")
>>> loc2
'Utica is in New York State.'
>>> m1 = "{2} {1} equals {0} {3}."
>>> m2 = m1.format("1/16", "hammer", 1, "foot")
>>> m2
'1 hammer equals 1/16 foot.'
>>>
```

```
guy@Mac-Pro-3 Code % python3
Python 3.10.0 (v3.10.0:b494f5935c, Oct  4 2021, 14:59:20)
 [Clang 12.0.5 (clang-1205.0.22.11)] on darwin
Type "help", "copyright", "credits" or "license" for more
 information.
>>> loc1 = "{} is in {}."
>>> loc2 = loc1.format("Utica", "New York State")
>>> loc2
'Utica is in New York State.'
>>> m1 = "{2} {1} equals {0} {3}."
>>> m2 = m1.format("1/16", "hammer", 1, "foot")
>>> m2
'1 hammer equals 1/16 foot.'
>>> wt = "{w1} {u1} equals {w2} {u2}.".format(w1=1, w2=11
2, u1="cwt", u2="lb")
>>> wt
'1 cwt equals 112 lb.'
>>>
```

TIP

Is it better to use keywords than index numbers with the `.format` method?
Both index numbers and keywords work fine, so use whichever you prefer. You can also mix and match index numbers and keywords in the same tuple if you so wish — for example, `print("Hello, {0} and {n2}!".format("John", n2="Jane"))` displays the string `Hello, John and Jane!`.

Build Strings with f-Strings

Python 3.6 introduced formatted string literals, known as *f-strings* for short. An f-string starts with the letter *f*, either uppercase or lowercase, followed by the string's contents inside either single quotes or double quotes. Inside the string, you include placeholders to indicate where to insert items; each placeholder contains the name of the appropriate item. You can provide the items via variables, from a dictionary, or from a class.

See the subsection "Format Strings with f-Strings" in the section "Meet Python's Tools for Building Strings," earlier in this chapter, for general information about working with f-strings.

Build Strings with f-Strings

① Open a terminal window and launch Python.

Ⓐ The Python prompt appears.

② Type the following statement, which creates the variables o1, o2, and o3 and assigns a city name to each. Press **Enter**.

```
o1, o2, o3 = "Albuquerque",
"Bakersfield", "Cleveland"
```

③ Type the following statement, which uses the print() function to display a string containing the three variables inserted by name. Press **Enter**.

```
print(f"We have offices in {o1}, {o2},
and {o3}.")
```

Python displays the string `We have offices in Albuquerque, Bakersfield, and Cleveland..`

④ Type the following statement, which creates a dictionary named a_dict and assigns values named France, Germany, Spain, and Finland to it. Press **Enter**.

```
a_dict = {
    "France": "Toulouse",
    "Germany": "Siegen",
    "Spain": "Valladolid",
    "Finland": "Rovaniemi"
    }
```

⑤ Type the following statement, which uses the print() function to display an f-string that includes two items from the dictionary, and then press **Enter**:

```
print(f'We have associates in {a_dict["Germany"]} and {a_dict["Finland"]}.')
```

Python displays the resulting f-string, We have associates in Siegen and Rovaniemi..

Note: Chapter 12, "Working with Classes," shows you how to create classes and work with them.

6 Type the following statement, which creates a class named c1 and gives it properties named quantity, type, returnable, and status. Press Enter twice to end the class definition.

```
class c1:
...     quantity = 500
...     type = "nonsequential"
...     returnable = "approval"
...     status = "new"
```

Note: Be sure to indent the quantity, type, returnable, and status lines by two spaces beyond the class line.

7 Type the following statement, which creates a variable named order1 and assigns to it an f-string that incorporates two properties from the c1 class. Press Enter.

```
order1 = f'The order is for
{c1.quantity} units in {c1.type}
combinations.'
```

8 Type the following statement, which uses the print() function to display the contents of order1, and then press Enter:

```
print(order1)
```

TIP

Can I create an f-string on multiple lines of code?
Yes, you can create an f-string on multiple lines. You must start each line with an f, as in the following example:

```
dy, dt, mth = "Wednesday", 24, "June"
>>> d = (
...     f'Today is {dy}. '
...     f'The date is {mth} {dt}.'
```

This produces the f-string Today is Wednesday. The date is June 24..

Build Strings with Template Strings

If you need to build strings that include text that the user inputs, you can use template strings rather than f-strings. A template string is a string that contains one or more placeholders into which you insert strings by using a mapping object. Template strings are more secure than f-strings, because the use of placeholders prevents users from entering a formatted string designed to access variables within your code and export data from them.

See the subsection "Format Strings with Template Strings" in the section "Meet Python's Tools for Building Strings," earlier in this chapter, for general information about template strings.

Build Strings with Template Strings

Launch Python and Import the Template Class

① Open a terminal window and launch Python.

Ⓐ The Python prompt appears.

② Type the following statement, which imports the `Template` class from the `string` library, and then press Enter:

```
from string import Template
```

Note: The word `Template` requires the capital *T*. Using lowercase `template` returns an `ImportError` error.

The Python prompt appears again, but Python gives no other response indicating that it has imported the `Template` class.

③ Type the following statement, which creates a variable named `temp1` and assigns to it an instance of the `Template` class containing the string in the format you want the input to have. Press Enter.

```
temp1 = Template('Location: $where')
```

④ Type the following statement, which uses the `print()` function to display the result of using the `substitute()` method to prompt the user to enter the office location. Press Enter.

```
print(temp1.substitute(where=input
('Type the office location: '))
```

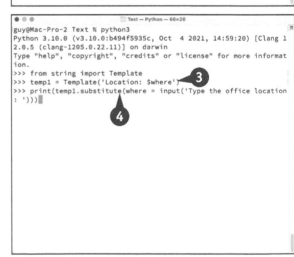

Python displays the prompt:

```
Type the office location:
```

5 Type the location, and then press `Enter`.

Python displays the resulting string, such as `Location: Sacramento`.

6 Type the following statement, which creates a variable named `temp2` and assigns to it an instance of the `Template` class containing the string in the format you want the input to have. Press `Enter`.

```
temp2 = Template('Status: ${dn}denominational')
```

Note: See the tip for details about including `{}` in a template string.

7 Type the following statement, which creates a variable named `s5` and assigns to it the template string resulting from using the `substitute()` method to prompt the user to enter the denomination type. Press `Enter`.

```
s5 = temp2.substitute(dn = input('Type
"non"/"extra"/"intra" to specify the
denomination type: '))
```

Python displays the prompt:

```
Type "non"/"extra"/"intra" to specify the denomination type:
```

8 Type **non**, **extra**, or **intra**, and then press `Enter`.

9 Type the following statement, which uses the `print()` function to display `s5`, and then press `Enter`:

```
print(s5)
```

Python displays the string, such as `Status: extradenominational`.

TIP

Why do template strings sometimes use `{}` as well as `$`?
Template strings use the dollar sign, `$`, to indicate a placeholder in the string. For example, `Template('$item is wet').substitute(item="Water")` uses `$` as a placeholder marking where to insert `item` in the string, returning `Water is wet`. But when the placeholder is not demarcated by a space or punctuation character, a template string needs `{}` to demarcate it. For example, `Template('$xshine is hot').substitute(x="Sun")` returns a `KeyError` error on `xshine`, because Python cannot pick out `x` from `xshine`. In such cases, you use `{}` to demarcate the placeholder — for example, `Template('${x}shine is hot').substitute(x="sun")` returns `Sunshine is hot`.

## CHAPTER 10

Handling Errors

In this chapter, you learn how to handle errors in Python. First, we quickly review the different types of errors that occur in computer code and the ways you can catch the different types. We then focus on using `try...except` blocks to handle errors in your Python code. You learn to cause errors, trap exceptions, and create custom exceptions.

Understanding the Various Types of Errors

In this section, you learn about the different types of errors that can occur in code, what causes them, and what you can do to eliminate them.

We start with compile-time errors, errors that occur when Python is unable to create workable instructions from the commands in a script. Many compile-time errors are syntax errors, mistakes in the structure of the code. We then move on to runtime errors, errors that occur after Python has compiled a script successfully and has moved on to executing it. Runtime errors include semantic errors and logical errors.

Compile-Time Errors

Python is generally considered an interpreted language, which is often understood to mean that it is not a compiled language. But the difference between interpreted computing languages and compiled computing languages is not clear cut, and Python does perform compilation.

Before running a script, Python *compiles* it to a form called *byte code*, interpreting the commands the script contains and creating from them instructions that the computer can execute. The instructions need to be specific to the computer's operating system, such as Windows or macOS, and to the processor type, such as Intel or Apple Silicon.

A *compile-time error* occurs when the script's commands are incomplete, incorrect, or otherwise will not work. A compile-time error occurs before the script runs, so Python does not run the script. You need to fix the problem in order to make the script run.

Runtime Errors

After compiling the code in the script, Python tells the computer to run the script. At this point, you may get a *runtime error* — an error that occurs while the code is running, as opposed to while the code is being compiled.

A runtime error may manifest itself as an exception that stops the script from running and causes Python to display an error message. Alternatively, the script may freeze or crash, it may return an unexpected result, or it may damage data.

Syntax Errors

A *syntax error*, also called a *syntactical error*, is an error where the problem lies in the structure of the code statements. Syntax errors have various causes, including the following:

* Straightforward typos, such as the wrong character, missing punctuation, or an extra space
* Missing required elements of a statement
* Extra, and incorrect, elements of a statement
* Confusion about variables, such as unintentionally creating the new variable `firstname` when you mean to reassign the existing variable `firstName`

Python itself or your code editor may be able to identify a syntax error for you. For example, the illustration shows Python flagging the cause of a syntax error in the following statement, which contains an extra comma after the `"Bill"` item in the list. The caret (A) points to the problem, and the `SyntaxError` statement (B) briefly explains what is wrong.

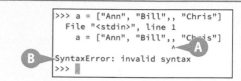

```
a = ["Ann", "Bill",, "Chris"]
```

Semantic Errors

A *semantic error* is an error in which your code is syntactically correct but does not execute the way you intend it to. The word *semantic* means "related to meaning in language or logic" — in other words, the meaning of the code is wrong.

For example, if a script gets stuck in an infinite loop because the `break` statement you included never gets triggered, you have likely committed a semantic error. Similarly, if a `while` loop never runs because its condition cannot be met, that might be a semantic error.

Your code editor or IDE will typically not catch semantic errors. Instead, you will normally discover them while testing and debugging your scripts.

How you discover semantic errors will vary depending on the error's effects. Continuing the previous example, you will notice an infinite loop quickly, because the script will not finish and you will need to break out of the loop. By contrast, a `while` loop that never runs may be less obvious.

Logical Errors

A *logical error* occurs when you, the developer, have told the script to take the wrong action. Even though the script is syntactically correct and semantically correct, what the script does is incorrect. For example, a logical error might occur if you make a mistake with operator precedence when performing calculations or if you use integer division where you should use floating-point division.

Identify Common Python Errors

Python includes a wide variety of built-in exceptions for handling types of errors that occur frequently. For example, a `SyntaxError` error occurs when Python's parser encounters syntax it cannot convert into valid code, such as when you omit a comma or include an extra parenthesis. A `TypeError` error occurs when the code specifies the wrong type of object for an operation, such as trying to add an integer and a string. A `ValueError` error occurs when the code specifies the correct type of object but an incorrect value, such as trying to return the square root of a negative number.

Table 10-1 explains common error types in Python.

Table 10-1: Common Errors in Python	
Exception	**Occurs When**
AssertionError	An `assert` statement fails. An `assert` statement is a tool used for debugging code.
AttributeError	An attribute assignment or attribute reference is incorrect.
EOFError	The `input()` function reaches the end-of-file condition.
FloatingPointError	An error occurs in a floating-point calculation.
GeneratorExit	Code calls the `close()` method of a generator.
ImportError	Importing the specified module fails.
IndexError	The index number of a sequence is out of range.
KeyError	The specified key is not in the dictionary.
KeyboardInterrupt	The user gave a keyboard interrupt by pressing `Ctrl`+`C` or `Del`.
MemoryError	An operation runs out of memory.
ModuleNotFoundError	Python cannot find the specified module.
NameError	The specified variable is not found.
NotImplementedError	An abstract method requires a derived class to override the method; or a developer uses this error as a placeholder to show a real implementation is still needed.
OSError	An operating system–related error occurs.
OverflowError	An arithmetic operation returns an error too large to represent.
ReferenceError	A weak reference proxy accesses an attribute of an item that has been garbage collected.
RuntimeError	A runtime error occurs that does not fall into any other category.

Exception	Occurs When
StopIteration	The next() function finds no further items in the iterator to return.
SyntaxError	The parser encounters a syntax error.
IndentationError	The indentation level of a statement is incorrect — for example, some indentation is missing.
TabError	The indentation consists of a mixture of tabs and spaces instead of only tabs or only spaces.
SystemError	An internal error occurs in the Python interpreter.
SystemExit	The sys.exit() method runs.
TypeError	An object is of the wrong type for the specified operation.
UnboundLocalError	A function or method refers to a local variable that has no value.
UnicodeError	Encoding or decoding Unicode characters causes an error.
UnicodeEncodeError	Encoding Unicode characters causes an error.
UnicodeDecodeError	Decoding Unicode characters causes an error.
UnicodeTranslateError	A Unicode-related error occurs during translation.
ValueError	An argument passed to a function or method has the correct type but an incorrect value.
ZeroDivisionError	Division or modulo by zero is attempted.

Meet the `try... except` Block

Python uses a type of object called an *exception* to handle errors. Python includes many built-in exceptions, which are all derived from the same base class of exception. For example, using the wrong name may cause a `NameException` exception, whereas supplying the wrong kind of value may cause a `ValueException` exception.

When an error occurs, Python *raises* or *throws* an exception. You can catch or *trap* an exception so that you can determine what has gone wrong and do something about it.

Python's tool for handling exceptions is the `try... except` block, which looks like the following pseudocode. Italics indicate placeholders, and the sections in brackets are optional.

```
try:
    statements1
[except error:
    statements2]
except:
    statements3
[else:
    statements4]
[finally:
    statements5]
```

Here is how the `try... except` block works:

- `try:`. This keyword starts the `try` block.
- *statements1*. This block contains one or more statements that may cause an exception. The `try` block is said to *wrap* these statements.
- `except error:`. The except keyword starts an `except` block for the specified error. For example, `except NameError:` starts an `except` block that controls what happens when a `NameError` error occurs.
- *statements2*. This block contains one or more statements to run when the specified error occurs.
- `except:`. The except keyword without a specific error starts an `except` block for any error.
- *statements3*. This block contains one or more statements to run when any error occurs.
- `else:`. The `else` keyword starts a block specifying what to do if no error has occurred.
- *statements4*. This block contains one or more statements to run if no error has occurred.
- `finally:`. This keyword starts a block specifying what to do after the rest of the `try... except` block has completed, whether an error has occurred or not.
- *statements5*. This block contains one or more statements to run after execution reaches the `finally` keyword.

The following subsections contain brief examples of `try... except` blocks.

Trap Any Exception

If you just want to trap any exception that Python raises, you can use a plain `except` statement, as in the following example:

```
try:
    x = 5/0
except:
    print("An error occurred.")
```

Trap One or More Particular Exceptions

A generic error message offers little help, so you will often do better to trap one or more specific exceptions that are likely to occur, as in the following example:

```
try:
    x = 5/0
except(NameError):
    print("A name is missing.")
except(ZeroDivisionError):
    print("A divide-by-zero error
occurred.")
except:
    print("An error occurred.")
```

This example contains three `except` blocks:

- `except(NameError):`. This block catches `NameError`, the type of error that occurs when your code specifies an item that does not exist.

- `except(ZeroDivisionError):`. This block catches `ZeroDivisionError`, the error that occurs when your code tries to divide by zero. As the code stands, the `x = 5/0` statement triggers a `ZeroDivisionError` error.

- `except:`. This block catches any other errors.

The unqualified `except` block must be the last `except` statement in the `try... except` block. You cannot use `except` with a specific error after an unqualified `except` block. Doing so causes the error `SyntaxError: default 'except:' must be last`.

Add an `else` Block

Python supports adding an `else` block to a `try... except` block. Here is an example:

```
try:
    x = 5/0
except:
```

```
    print("An error occurred.")
else:
    print("No error occurred.")
```

An `else` block can be useful, but many `try... except` blocks do not need one.

Add a `finally` Block

You can include a `finally` block in your `try... except` blocks to specify an action that Python should always perform, whether or not an exception has occurred. Here is an example:

```
try:
    x = 5/0
except:
    print("An error occurred.")
finally:
    print("The try block has finished.")
```

Cause Errors and Trap Exceptions

In this section, you cause errors in your code deliberately and observe the exceptions that Python throws as a result. You then handle the exceptions by using `try... except` blocks. The first `try... except` block you create is generic, returning the same error message for every exception it catches. After that, you create a more sophisticated `try... except` block that displays specific error messages for the exceptions you raised earlier, plus a generic error message for any other exception.

Cause Errors and Trap Exceptions

Cause Errors and Create a Generic Exception Trap

1 Open a terminal window and launch Python.

Ⓐ The Python prompt appears.

2 Type the following statement, which creates the variable `x` and assigns to it the result of 5 divided by 0. Press Enter.

```
x = 5/0
```

An error occurs.

Ⓑ Python displays the exception for the error:

```
ZeroDivisionError: division by zero
```

3 Type the following statement, which assigns to `x` the value of variable `y`, and then press Enter.

```
x = y
```

An error occurs, because `y` does not yet exist.

Ⓒ Python displays the exception for the error:

```
NameError: name 'y' is not defined
```

4 Type the following `try... except` block, which uses a single unspecified exception. Press Enter at the end of each line, and press Enter again at the end.

```
try:
    x = 5/0
except:
    "An error occurred."
```

Ⓓ Python returns `'An error occurred.'` because the `try` block catches the error.

```
● ● ●                 guy — Python — 56×27
Last login: Mon Apr  4 18:22:49 on console
guy@Mac-Pro-3 ~ % python3
Python 3.10.0 (v3.10.0:b494f5935c, Oct  4 2021, 14:59:20
) [Clang 12.0.5 (clang-1205.0.22.11)] on darwin
Type "help", "copyright", "credits" or "license" for mor
e information.
>>> x = 5/0
Traceback (most recent call last):
  File "<stdin>", line 1, in <module>
ZeroDivisionError: division by zero
>>> x = y
```

```
● ● ●                 guy — Python — 56×27
Last login: Mon Apr  4 18:22:49 on console
guy@Mac-Pro-3 ~ % python3
Python 3.10.0 (v3.10.0:b494f5935c, Oct  4 2021, 14:59:20
) [Clang 12.0.5 (clang-1205.0.22.11)] on darwin
Type "help", "copyright", "credits" or "license" for mor
e information.
>>> x = 5/0
Traceback (most recent call last):
  File "<stdin>", line 1, in <module>
ZeroDivisionError: division by zero
>>> x = y
Traceback (most recent call last):
  File "<stdin>", line 1, in <module>
NameError: name 'y' is not defined
>>> try:
...     x = 5/0
... except:
...     "An error occurred."
...
'An error occurred.'
>>> 
```

Trap Specific Errors

1 In the same terminal window, type the following `try...`
`except` block, which includes specific messages for the
`ZeroDivisionError` exception and the `NameError` exception
you raised earlier. Press Enter at the end of each line.

```
try:
    x = 5/0
except(ZeroDivisionError):
    "A divide-by-zero error occurred."
except(NameError):
    "A name is missing."
except:
    "An error occurred."
```

2 Press Enter to end the block.

E Python returns the message `'A divide-by-zero error`
`occurred.'`, because `except(Zero`
`DivisionError)` catches the error.

3 Type the same `try... except` block, but this time include
`x = y` to produce the `NameError` exception. Press Enter at
the end of each line.

```
try:
    x = y
except(ZeroDivisionError):
    "A divide-by-zero error occurred."
except(NameError):
    "A name is missing."
except:
    "An error occurred."
```

4 Press Enter to end the block.

F Python returns the message `'A name is missing.'`,
because the `except(NameError)` catches the error.

TIPS

**How many `except` statements can I include in a
`try... except` block?**
You can have pretty much as many `except` statements as
you need, as long as only the last of them is the `except`
statement with no arguments. Each of the earlier `except`
statements must have an argument, such as
`except(NameError)` or `Except(ZeroDivisionError)`.

**Can I use a `try` block without an
`except` block?**
No. Each `try` block must be part of a
`try... except` block that includes at least
one `except` block. However, you can enter
`pass` as the sole statement in the `except`
block to have the block exist but do nothing.

Raise an Exception Manually

In the previous section, "Cause Errors and Trap Exceptions," you caused the `ZeroDivisionError` and `NameError` errors deliberately by entering statements guaranteed not to work. This approach is straightforward for some errors, but you might need to get creative to produce other errors. So Python offers an alternative: You can raise specific exceptions manually to test your code.

To raise an exception, you use the `raise` command and specify the type of exception — for example, `raise Exception` or `raise RuntimeError`. You can also specify the text to display to the user when the exception or error is raised.

Raise an Exception Manually

Raise an Exception Outside of a `try... except` Block

1 Open a terminal window and launch Python.

Ⓐ The Python prompt appears.

2 Type the following statement, which uses the `raise` keyword to raise a `ValueError` error with a custom message. Press Enter.

```
raise ValueError("This value is not valid.")
```

Ⓑ Python returns the following:

```
Traceback (most recent call last):
  File "<stdin>", line 1, in <module>
ValueError: This value is not valid.
```

Raise an Exception Inside of a `try... except` Block

1 Still in the same terminal window and Python session, type the following `try` block, which contains a statement that raises a `TypeError`. Press Enter at the end of each line.

```
try:
    raise TypeError
```

2 Type the following `except` block, which catches the `TypeError` exception. Press Enter at the end of each line, and then press Enter again to end the block.

```
except TypeError:
    print("A TypeError exception has occurred.")
```

Ⓒ Python displays the resulting message:

```
A TypeError exception has occurred.
```

Add an `else` Block or a `finally` Block

You can add an `else` block to a `try...` `except` block to execute statements when no exception has occurred. You can also add a `finally` block containing statements that you want to execute when the `try...` `except` block has finished running, whether or not any exception arises. This section shows a `finally` block that displays information, but the block can be useful for performing cleanup operations, such as closing files.

Add an `else` Block or a `finally` Block

1 Open a terminal window and launch Python.

2 Type the following `try` block, which creates the variable n and assigns 51 to it; creates the variable d and assigns the user's input divisor, cast to an integer; and creates the variable msg and assigns a message to it.

```
try:

    n = 51

    d = int(input("Enter the
integer divisor: "))

    msg = str(n) + " divided
by " + str(d) + " equals " +
str(n/d)
```

3 Type the following `except` block to handle a potential `ZeroDivisionError` exception:

```
except ZeroDivisionError:

    msg = "You cannot divide
by zero."
```

4 Type the following `finally` block, which displays the contents of msg:

```
finally:

    print(msg)
```

5 Press `Enter` again to end the block.

6 Type an integer at the prompt.

B The result appears.

```
● ● ●                     guy — Python — 62×25    ──1
guy@Mac-Pro-3 ~ % python3
Python 3.10.0 (v3.10.0:b494f5935c, Oct  4 2021, 14:59:20) [Cla
ng 12.0.5 (clang-1205.0.22.11)] on darwin
Type "help", "copyright", "credits" or "license" for more info
rmation.
A ─▶>>> try:
...     n = 51
...     d = int(input("Enter the integer divisor: "))
...     msg = str(n) + " divided by " + str(d) + " equals " + ──2
str(n/d)
... except ZeroDivisionError:
...     msg = "You cannot divide by zero."──3
...
```

```
● ● ●                     guy — Python — 62×25
guy@Mac-Pro-3 ~ % python3
Python 3.10.0 (v3.10.0:b494f5935c, Oct  4 2021, 14:59:20) [Cla
ng 12.0.5 (clang-1205.0.22.11)] on darwin
Type "help", "copyright", "credits" or "license" for more info
rmation.
>>> try:
...     n = 51
...     d = int(input("Enter the integer divisor: "))
...     msg = str(n) + " divided by " + str(d) + " equals " +
str(n/d)
... except ZeroDivisionError:
...     msg = "You cannot divide by zero."
... finally:
...     print(msg)──4
...
Enter the integer divisor: 4──6
51 divided by 4 equals 12.75
>>> ▊             B
```

Create Nested `try...` `except` Blocks

Python enables you to nest `try...` `except` blocks inside other `try...` `except` blocks. Nesting blocks enables you to perform more complex error handling.

If an exception is raised in the outer `try...` `except` block, the outer block handles the exception. If the inner `try...` `except` block raises an exception, the inner block handles the exception; if it fails to do so — for example, because it has no unqualified `except` statement — the outer block takes over responsibility for handling the exception.

Create Nested `try...` `except` Blocks

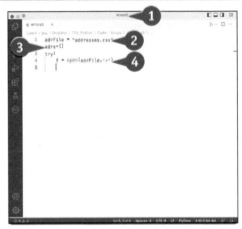

1. Open Visual Studio Code and create a new Python script.

2. Type the following statement, which creates a variable called `adrFile` and assigns to it the file `addresses.csv`. Press Enter.

```
adrFile = "addresses.csv"
```

3. Type the following statement, which creates a variable named `addresses` and assigns to it an empty list. Press Enter.

```
adrs = []
```

4. Type the following `try` block, which uses the `open()` function to open `addressFile` in Read Mode. Press Enter.

```
try:
    f = open("adrFile", "r")
```

5. At the same level of indentation, type the nested `try` block, which uses two `for` loops to iterate through the lines in `f`, split the addresses at the commas, and assign the resulting fields to the `adrs` list. Press Enter at the end of each line.

```
try:
    for line in f.readlines():
        currAdr=[]
        for field in line.strip('\n').
split(','):
            currAdr.append(field)
            adrs.append(currAdr)
```

6. Indented to the level of the inner `try` block, type the inner `except` block, which uses the `print()` function to display an error message. Press Enter at the end of each line.

```
except:
    print("An error occurred in the inner
try... except block.")
```

230

7 Press `Backspace` twice to remove the indent, and then type the following `except` block, which runs if the `FileNotFoundError` occurs. Press `Enter` at the end of each line.

```
except FileNotFoundError:
    print(f"The file '{adrFile}' was
not found.")
```

8 Press `Backspace` to remove the indent again, and then type the following unqualified `except` block, pressing `Enter` at the end of each line.

```
except:
    print("An error occurred in the
outer try... except block.")
```

9 Press `Backspace` to remove the indent once more, and then type the following `else` block, which closes `f` and displays the addresses. Press `Enter` at the end of each line.

```
else:
    f.close()
    print(adrs)
```

10 Click **Run Python File in Terminal** (▷).

The Terminal pane appears.

A `FileNotFoundError` occurs, because `addresses.csv` does not exist.

The `except FileNotFoundError:` block catches the exception.

A The error message appears.

11 Create a file named `addresses.csv` containing address information in the folder Python is using. Put each address on one line, with commas separating the fields.

12 Click **Run Python File in Terminal** (▷).

B The address information appears.

TIP

Can I have multiple levels of nested `try... except` blocks?
Yes, Python enables you to nest `try... except` blocks multiple layers deep. But your code is likely to become confusing, especially to others.

Create Custom Exceptions

As you have seen earlier in this chapter, Python includes a wide range of built-in exceptions. But Python also lets you create your own custom exceptions, which enables you to track exactly what is going wrong in your code.

To create custom exceptions, you create a class based on Python's base class of exceptions. You can then use a `raise` statement to raise instances of the exception, assigning a custom error message to make clear the problem to the user. See Chapter 12, "Working with Classes," for more information on classes.

Create Custom Exceptions

① Open Visual Studio Code and create a new Python script.

② Type the following class header, which creates a class named `InvalidTitle` based on the `Exception` object.

```
class InvalidTitle(Exception):
```

③ Type the `pass` keyword as the only statement for the class, allowing the code to run without taking any action. Press Enter twice, creating a blank line.

```
pass
```

④ Press Backspace to delete the indent, and then type the start of a `try` block. Press Enter.

```
try:
```

⑤ Type the following statement, which creates a variable named `title` and assigns to it the result of the `input()` function prompting the user to enter the title. Press Enter.

```
title = input("Type the title: ")
```

⑥ Type the following `if` block, which uses the `isnumeric()` method to check whether `title` is entirely numeric and, if so, raises an `InvalidTitle` instance with a custom error message. Press Enter at the end of each line.

```
if title.isnumeric():
    raise InvalidTitle("The title is
entirely numeric.")
```

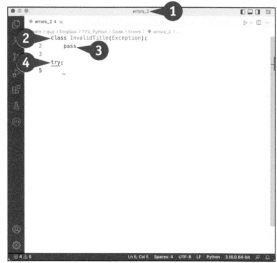

7 Press `Backspace` to remove one step of indentation, and then type the following two `elif` blocks, which use the `len()` function to check the length of `title` and raise `InvalidTitle` instances if it is too short or too long:

```
elif len(title) < 5:
    raise InvalidTitle("The title is too
short.")
elif len(title) > 50:
    raise InvalidTitle("The title is too
long.")
```

8 Press `Backspace` once, and then type the following two `elif` blocks, which raise `InvalidTitle` instances for all uppercase and all lowercase:

```
elif title.isupper():
    raise InvalidTitle("The title is all
uppercase.")
elif title.islower():
    raise InvalidTitle("The title is all
lowercase.")
```

9 Press `Backspace` twice to remove the indentation, and then type the following `except` statement, which casts an `InvalidTitle` exception to `IT` and prints that object:

```
except InvalidTitle as IT:
    print(IT)
```

10 Press `Backspace` once to remove the indent, and then type the following `if` block, which displays `title` if no exception has been raised:

```
else:
    print(title)
```

11 Click **Run Python File in Terminal** (▷).

The Terminal pane appears.

12 When prompted, type a title.

Ⓐ If the title provokes an exception, the relevant message appears.

TIP

How should I test the custom exceptions further?

Click **Run Python File in Terminal** (▷) again, and then type a title designed to raise one of the errors. For example, type a title that is all numbers, all uppercase, or all lowercase. Alternatively, type a title that has fewer than 4 characters or more than 50 characters.

## CHAPTER 11

Working with Lists and Dictionaries

Python provides lists and dictionaries for storing data efficiently in variables. A *list* is a collection that can store multiple items of the same type or of different types and provides access to its items via an index. A *dictionary* is similar to a list but more powerful, allowing you to create collections of information that you access through named elements called *keys*.

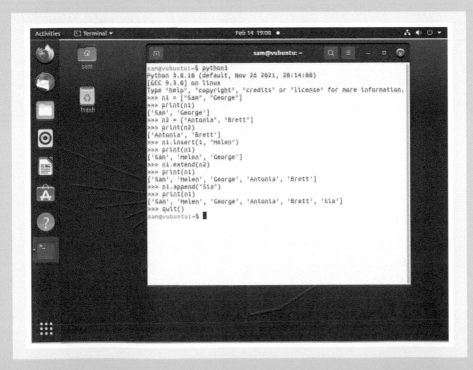

Understanding Lists and Their Use

In Python, a *list* is an object that enables you to store multiple items within a single variable. The items can be of the same type or of different types. The list contains an index that enables you to set or retrieve the individual items. Technically, a list is a mutable sequence, so you can change the order of its items, add and remove items, sort the items, and so on.

A List Is Ordered and Indexed

In Python, a list is an ordered and indexed collection:

- **Ordered.** The items in a list appear in the order you set. You can change the order by adding items, removing items, or reversing the order.
- **Indexed.** The list items are indexed using zero-based numbering, so the first list item is item 0, the second item is item 1, and so on. You use the index numbers to access the list items.

List Items Are Mutable

The items in a list are mutable, so you can change a list after creating it. For example, you can add items to a list, remove items from it, or reverse its order.

Lists Can Contain Duplicate Values

A list can contain duplicate values, as there is no constraint requiring each value to be unique.

You can use the count() method to count the number of items in a list that have a particular value.

Understanding How Lists Compare to Tuples and Sets

Table 11-1 summarizes the three key attributes of lists, tuples, and sets in Python.

Table 11-1: Attributes of Lists, Tuples, and Sets			
Collection	**Mutable**	**Ordered**	**Duplicates Allowed**
List	Yes	Yes	Yes
Set	Yes	No	No
Tuple	No	Yes	Yes

Understanding How Lists Compare to Sets

In Python, both a list and a set can contain various types of data, which gives you great flexibility at the risk of occasionally running into the wrong data type for your needs. Beyond that, however, lists differ significantly from sets.

First, a list is ordered, while a set is unordered. Second, a list can contain duplicates, whereas a set cannot contain duplicates. Third, and more technically, Python sets use hashing to store their values, which makes lookups in sets fast and efficient but means the order of a set's items may vary.

Understanding How Lists Compare to Tuples

The key difference between a list and a tuple is that a list is mutable whereas a tuple is immutable. Both lists and tuples are ordered and can contain duplicate items. Both lists and tuples are sequential, which enables you to iterate through the items they contain.

Tuples' immutability means that they are more memory efficient than lists and require less processing time. When your code contains data that will not need to be changed, you may be able to improve performance by using tuples rather than lists.

Understanding How Python Lists Compare to Arrays in Other Programming Languages

Python lists are similar to arrays in other programming languages, but lists offer greater flexibility. There are two main differences between lists and arrays.

First, when you create an array, you specify its data type, such as float; the array can contain only items that have that data type. By contrast, a list in Python can contain items of different data types, as needed.

Second, when you create an array, you specify the number of items it contains. Python allocates memory to store each potential item, but you do not need to populate each item immediately, or indeed ever. By contrast, a list's size is dynamic, increasing as items are added, but each item must contain data, even if the data type is None.

Create a List

To create a list, you declare a variable; enter the assignment operator, =; and then enter the list items, separated by commas, within square brackets. For example, the statement list1 = [1, 2, 3] declares a variable named list1 and assigns to it three integers — 1, 2, and 3.

In this section, you create three lists in a terminal window. The first list contains integers, the second list contains strings, and the third list contains four different data types.

Create a List

1 Open a terminal window and launch Python.

ⓐ The Python prompt appears.

2 Type the following statement, which creates a variable named list1 and assigns five integers to it, and then press Enter:

`list1 = [1, 2, 3, 4, 5]`

3 Type the following statement, which uses the print() function to display the contents of list1, and then press Enter:

`print(list1)`

Python displays [1, 2, 3, 4, 5]. The brackets indicate that the variable's contents are a list.

4 Type the following statement, which creates a variable named list2 and assigns two strings to it, and then press Enter:

`list2 = ["Evie", "Frank"]`

5 Type the following statement, which creates a variable named list3 and assigns several kinds of data to it. Press Enter.

`list3 = [11.5, "cats", True, 0]`

6 Type the following statement to display the contents of list2. Press Enter.

`print(list2)`

Python displays ['Evie', 'Frank'].

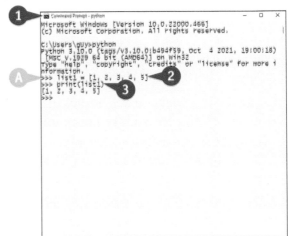

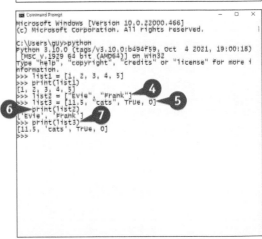

7 Type the following statement to display the contents of list3. Press Enter.

`print(list3)`

Python displays [11.5, 'cats', True, 0].

Meet Python's List Methods

Python provides 11 methods for working with lists. Three of these methods — `append()`, `extend()`, and `insert()` — enable you to add items to the list. Conversely, three other methods — `clear()`, `pop()`, and `remove()` — enable you to remove one or all methods from the list. The other five methods enable you to sort the list, return an element by its position in the list, return the number of items that match specific criteria, and create a copy of the list.

Table 11-2 explains Python's methods for working with lists.

Table 11-2: Methods for Working with Lists	
Method	**Use This Method To**
`append()`	Add an element to the end of the list.
`clear()`	Remove all the elements from the list.
`copy()`	Create a copy of the list.
`count()`	Count the number of list elements that match the specified value.
`extend()`	Extend the list by adding the elements from another list or other iterable.
`index()`	Return the index number of the first list element that matches the specified value.
`insert()`	Insert an element in the list at the specified index position.
`pop()`	Remove the list element at the specified index position.
`remove()`	Remove the first list element that matches the specified value.
`reverse()`	Reverse the order of the whole list.
`sort()`	Sort the list in ascending order, descending order, or ordered by the function specified.

The following list provides examples of using these methods. You will use the methods more extensively during the first half of this chapter.

- Create a list named `list4` and a list named `list5`:
  ```
  list4 = ["Brian", "Charlene", "Dan"]
  list5 = ["Eva", "Finn"]
  ```
- Insert an item at the first index position in the list `list4`:
  ```
  list4.insert(0, "Abigail")
  ```
- Extend the list `list4` by adding the elements from `list5`:
  ```
  list4.extend(list5)
  ```
- Add the item `Gloria` to the end of the list `list4`:
  ```
  list4.append("Gloria")
  ```
- Sort the list `list4` alphabetically:
  ```
  list4.sort()
  ```
- Remove the second item from the list `list4`:
  ```
  list4.pop(1)
  ```
- Remove all the items from the list `list4`:
  ```
  list4.clear()
  ```

Add Items to a List

python's lists are mutable, so you can change a list after creating it. Often, you will want to add items to the list, as explained here, or remove items from it, as explained in the following section, "Remove Items from a List." You can use the `append()` method to add a single element to the end of a list, use the `insert()` method to insert an item at a specific index position in the list, or use the `extend()` method to extend the list by adding items from another list or from another iterable element.

Add Items to a List

1 Open a terminal window and launch Python.

Ⓐ The Python prompt appears.

2 Type the following statement, which creates the variable n1 and assigns a list of two strings to it. Press Enter.

```
n1 = ["Sam", "George"]
```

3 Type the following print() statement, and then press Enter, to display the contents of n1:

```
print(n1)
```

Python displays ['Sam', 'George'].

4 Type the following statement, which creates the variable n2 and assigns a list of two other strings to it. Press Enter.

```
n2 = ["Antonia", "Brett"]
```

5 Type the following print() statement, and then press Enter, to display the contents of n2:

```
print(n2)
```

Python displays ['Antonia', 'Brett'].

6 Type the following statement, which uses the insert() method to insert a string at position 1 — second — in n1. Press Enter.

```
n1.insert(1, "Helen")
```

7 Press ⬆ four times, making Python enter the `print(n1)` statement again, and then press [Enter].

`print(n1)`

Python displays `['Sam', 'Helen', 'George']`.

8 Type the following statement, which uses the `extend()` method to add `n2` to the end of `n1`, and then press [Enter]:

`n1.extend(n2)`

9 Press ⬆ twice to enter the `print(n1)` statement once more, and then press [Enter]:

`print(n1)`

Python displays `['Sam', 'Helen', 'George', 'Antonia', 'Brett']`.

10 Type the following statement, which uses the `append()` method to add a string to the end of `n1`, and then press [Enter]:

`n1.append("Sia")`

11 Press ⬆ twice to enter the `print(n1)` statement yet again, and then press [Enter].

`print(n1)`

Python displays `['Sam', 'Helen', 'George', 'Antonia', 'Brett', 'Sia']`.

```
sam@vubuntu: ~
sam@vubuntu:~$ python3
Python 3.8.10 (default, Nov 26 2021, 20:14:08)
[GCC 9.3.0] on linux
Type "help", "copyright", "credits" or "license" for more information.
>>> n1 = ["Sam", "George"]
>>> print(n1)
['Sam', 'George']
>>> n2 = ["Antonia", "Brett"]
>>> print(n2)
['Antonia', 'Brett']
>>> n1.insert(1, "Helen")
>>> print(n1)
['Sam', 'Helen', 'George']
>>> n1.extend(n2)
>>> print(n1)
['Sam', 'Helen', 'George', 'Antonia', 'Brett']
>>>
```

```
sam@vubuntu: ~
sam@vubuntu:~$ python3
Python 3.8.10 (default, Nov 26 2021, 20:14:08)
[GCC 9.3.0] on linux
Type "help", "copyright", "credits" or "license" for more information.
>>> n1 = ["Sam", "George"]
>>> print(n1)
['Sam', 'George']
>>> n2 = ["Antonia", "Brett"]
>>> print(n2)
['Antonia', 'Brett']
>>> n1.insert(1, "Helen")
>>> print(n1)
['Sam', 'Helen', 'George']
>>> n1.extend(n2)
>>> print(n1)
['Sam', 'Helen', 'George', 'Antonia', 'Brett']
>>> n1.append("Sia")
>>> print(n1)
['Sam', 'Helen', 'George', 'Antonia', 'Brett', 'Sia']
>>>
```

TIP

How do I extend a list with items from an iterable other than a list?

Use the `extend()` method and specify the iterable as the argument. For example, say you type `list0 = [1, 3]` and press [Enter] to create a list, then type `tuple0 = (11, 17)` and press [Enter] to create a tuple. You can use `list0.extend(tuple0)` to extend `list0` with the items from `tuple0`. Typing `print(list0)` returns `[1, 3, 11, 17]`. Similarly, you can type `set0 = {7, 9, 13}` and press [Enter] to create a set, and then type `list0.extend(set0)` to add the set to `list0`. Python adds the tuple's items in the order you created them, but the order of the set's items varies.

Remove Items from a List

Python provides three methods for removing items from a list. When you need to remove a single item by specifying its index position, use the `pop()` method. When you need to remove the first item that matches the value you specify, use the `remove()` method; you may then need to check for other instances of the item in the list and remove them too if necessary. When you need to remove all the items from the list, use the `clear()` method.

Remove Items from a List

1 In Visual Studio Code, create a new script, and then save it.

2 Type the following statement, which creates a variable named `dx` and assigns to it a list of integers. Press **Enter**.

```
dx = [1, 3, 4, 4, 4, 5, 7, 4, 8, 4, 11]
```

3 Type the following statement, which uses the `print()` function to display a string giving the number of instances of 4 in the list. Press **Enter**.

```
print("The list contains " + str(dx.
count(4)) + " instances of 4.")
```

4 Type the following statement, which uses the `index()` method to return the position of the first 4 in the `dx` list and the `print()` function to display a string announcing its removal. Press **Enter**.

```
print("Removing the 4 at index position " +
str(dx.index(4)) + ".")
```

5 Type the following statement, which uses the `pop()` method of the `dx` list to remove the first 4 by specifying its index position. Press **Enter**.

```
dx.pop(dx.index(4))
```

6 Type the following statement, which starts a `while` loop that runs while the `count()` method returns more than one 4 in the `dx` list. Press **Enter**.

```
while dx.count(4) > 1:
```

7 Copy the step **4** statement and paste it onto the line after the `while` line, accepting the indent that Visual Studio Code automatically applies.

```
print("The list contains " + str(dx.
count(4)) + " instances of 4.")
```

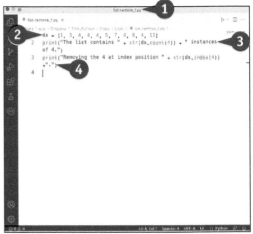

8 Type the following statement, which creates a variable called msg and assigns to it a string announcing the removal of the 4 at the index position it specifies. Press Enter.

```
msg = "Removing the 4 at index position
" + str(dx.index(4)) + "."
```

9 Type the following statement, which uses the remove() method to remove the first instance of 4 from dx. Press Enter.

```
dx.remove(4)
```

10 Type the following statement, which uses the print() function to display msg. Press Enter.

```
print(msg)
```

11 Press Backspace to remove the indent, ending the while block, and then type the following statement to display the contents of dx. Press Enter.

```
print(dx)
```

12 Type the following statement, which uses the clear() method to remove the contents of dx. Press Enter.

```
dx.clear()
```

13 Type the following statement to display the contents of dx — nothing.

```
print(dx)
```

14 Click **Run Python File in Terminal** (▷).

The Terminal pane appears.

Ⓐ The print() statements display the output as the while loop whittles down the instances of 4 until only one remains.

TIP

Is there an easy way to deduplicate a list?
Yes. You can *deduplicate* — remove duplicate values from — a list by creating a set from the list. For example, you could create a list containing duplicate values by typing myList = [1, 1, 2, 2, 3, 3] and pressing Enter. You could then type mySet = set(myList) and press Enter to create a set called mySet containing {1, 2, 3}. If you want to end up with a list rather than a set, convert the set to a list — for example, type myList = list(mySet) and press Enter to get a list called myList containing [1, 2, 3].

Locate Items and Access Data in a List

Often, you will need to determine whether a list contains a particular item and, if it does, where that item is. Python provides the count() method and the index() method to take care of this need. You use the count() method to return an integer value giving the number of elements in the list that match a specified value. If this number is greater than 0, you can use the index() method to return the index number of the first item in the list that matches your specified value.

Locate Items and Access Data in a List

1 Open a terminal window and launch Python.

A The Python prompt appears.

2 Type the following statement, which creates a variable named scores and assigns to it a list containing several integers. Press **Enter**.

```
scores = [20, 15, 40, 48, 15, 8]
```

3 Type the following statement, which uses the len() function to return the number of items in the scores list. Press **Enter**.

```
print(len(scores))
```

Python displays 6, the number of items.

4 Type the following statement, which uses the count() method to determine the number of instances of 15 in scores, and then press **Enter**:

```
scores.count(15)
```

Python returns 2, because the scores list contains two instances of 15.

5 Type the following statement, which uses the index() method to return the index position of the first instance of 15 in the list. Press **Enter**.

```
scores.index(15)
```

```
Command Prompt - python                                    —    □    ×

C:\Users\guy>python
Python 3.10.0 (tags/v3.10.0:b494f59, Oct  4 2021, 19:00:18)
[MSC v.1929 64 bit (AMD64)] on win32
Type "help", "copyright", "credits" or "license" for more i
nformation.
>>> scores = [20, 15, 40, 48, 15, 8]
>>> print(len(scores))
```

```
Command Prompt - python                                    —    □    ×

C:\Users\guy>python
Python 3.10.0 (tags/v3.10.0:b494f59, Oct  4 2021, 19:00:18)
[MSC v.1929 64 bit (AMD64)] on win32
Type "help", "copyright", "credits" or "license" for more i
nformation.
>>> scores = [20, 15, 40, 48, 15, 8]
>>> print(len(scores))
6
>>> scores.count(15)
2
>>> scores.index(15)
```

Python returns 1, indicating that the first instance of 15 is at index position 1 in the list — in other words, it is the second item.

6 Type the following statement, which uses the `count()` method to determine the number of instances of 36 in `scores`, and then press **Enter**:

`scores.count(36)`

Python displays 0, because the `scores` list contains no instances of 36.

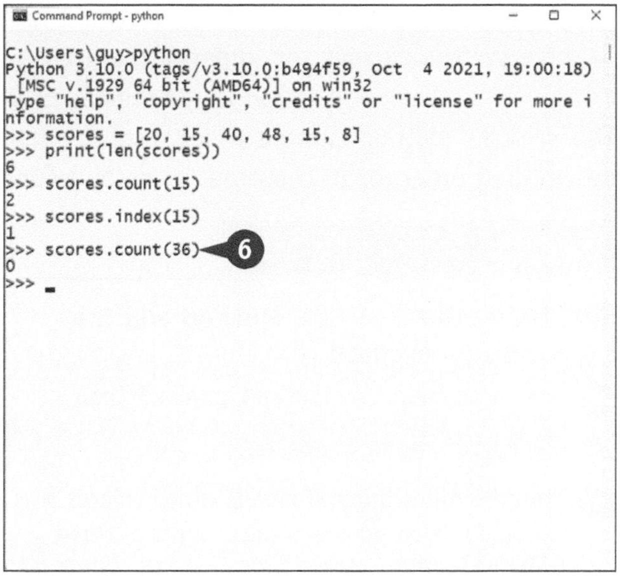

7 Type the following statement, which uses the `index()` method to return the index position of the first instance of 36 in the list. Press **Enter**.

`scores.index(36)`

B Python returns an error: `ValueError: 36 is not in list`.

TIP

How can I determine the number of unique values in a list?

Create a set containing the contents of the list, and then use the `len()` function to return the number of items in the set. For example, if you create the `scores` list as explained in the main text, you can type a statement such as `my_set = set(scores)` and press **Enter** to create a set name `my_set` containing the unique values from `scores`. You can then type `print(len(my_set))` to display the number of items in `my_set`.

Sort the Items in a List

Python provides two methods for sorting the items in a list. The `reverse()` method simply reverses the current sort order of the list, so if you have a list named `names1` that contains `["Alex", "Blake", "Cody")`, `names1.reverse()` returns `["Cody", "Blake", "Alex"]`. The `sort()` method is more widely useful, enabling you to sort a list in ascending order, in descending order, or in the order given by a function you specify.

Sort the Items in a List

Sort Using the `sort()` Method and the `reverse()` Method

1. Open a terminal window and launch Python.

A. The Python prompt appears.

2. Type the following statement, which creates a variable named `k7` and assigns a list of three fruits to it. Press **Enter**.

   `k7 = ["tomato", "avocado", "okra"]`

3. Type the following statement, which sorts the `k7` list into ascending order, and then press **Enter**:

   `k7.sort()`

4. Type the following statement, which displays the contents of `k7`, and then press **Enter**:

   `print(k7)`

   Python displays `['avocado', 'okra', 'tomato']`.

5. Type the following statement, which use the `reverse` argument to sort the `k7` list in descending order, and then press **Enter**:

   `k7.sort(reverse = True)`

6. Press ⬆ twice to repeat the `print(k7)` statement, and then press **Enter**:

   `print(k7)`

   Python displays `['tomato', 'okra', 'avocado']`.

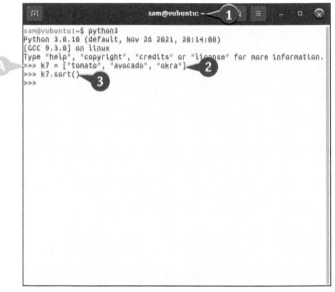

7 Type the following statement, which uses the
`reverse()` method to reverse the list's order, and
then press **Enter**:

```
k7.reverse()
```

8 Press ⬆ twice to repeat the `print(k7)`
statement again, and then press **Enter**.

```
print(k7)
```

Python displays `['avocado', 'okra',
'tomato']` again.

Sort Using a Function That Provides Sort Criteria

1 Type the following function, which implements a
crude sort by the last character of the input. Press
Enter at the end of each line, and then again to
end the function and create a blank line.

```
def sort_by_last(n):
    return n[-1]
```

Note: Indent the second line by four spaces.

2 Type the following statement, which creates a
variable named `animals` and assigns a list of
three animals to it. Press **Enter**.

```
animals = ["cat", "dog", "snake"]
```

3 Type the following statement, which uses the
`sort()` method to sort the `animals` list by the
`sort_by_last` function. Press **Enter**.

```
animals.sort(key=sort_by_last)
```

4 Type a `print()` statement to display the
contents of `animals`, and then press **Enter**:

```
print(animals)
```

Python displays `['snake', 'dog',
'cat']`, the terms sorted by their last letters.

TIP

Can the `sort()` method sort items of different types?

The `sort()` method can sort different types of numeric items successfully. For example, say you type `x15 = [0, -1, False, True, 1.2]` and press **Enter** to create a list named `x15`, you can then type `x15.sort()` to sort the list, even though it contains three types of values: `int`, `bool`, and `float`. Sorting the list in ascending order returns `[-1, 0, False, True, 1]`, because Boolean `False` has the value 0 and Boolean `True` has the value 1. However, if you add a string to the list, the `sort()` method returns a `TypeError` error, because Python cannot compare the string with the numeric values.

Understanding Dictionaries and Their Use

In Python, a *dictionary* is an object that enables you to store collections of data. The items in the dictionary consist of key/value pairs, in which a key enables you to access the corresponding value — similar in concept to a conventional dictionary, in which you look up a term to find its meaning.

Technically, a dictionary is an ordered, mutable sequence, so you can add items, remove specific items, or simply delete the entire contents of the dictionary.

Understanding What Python Dictionaries Are

In Python, a dictionary is an ordered, mutable collection that cannot have duplicates:

- **Ordered.** The items in a dictionary have a specific order, which Python maintains.
- **Mutable.** A dictionary is mutable, so you can change its contents. For example, you can add items to the dictionary or remove items from it.
- **No duplicates.** Each key in the dictionary must be unique so that you can identify each key unambiguously. However, the values assigned to the keys can contain duplicates.

Understanding the Layout of a Python Dictionary

To create a dictionary, you enter its key/value pairs within braces, `{ }`. Usually, you assign the entire dictionary to a variable so that you can refer to it easily. For example, the following statement creates a variable named `dog0` and assigns to it a dictionary consisting of a single key/value pair, the key being `name` and the value being `Spot`:

```
dog0 = {"name": "Spot"}
```

You can create a dictionary on a single line of code, as in the following example, which shows a single logical line wrapped to multiple physical lines by the constraints of the book.

Variable	Opening brace	Colon	Closing brace

```
dog0 = {"name": "Spot"}
```

Assignment operator	Key	Value

```
dog1 = {"name": "Minnie", "breed":
"Chihuahua", "weight": 5, "height": 6,
"age": 6}
```

Normally, however, it is more convenient to break the dictionary over multiple lines of code, using the kind of layout shown in the following example:

```
dog2 = {
    "name": "Max",
    "breed": "Newfoundland",
    "weight": 130,
    "height": 30,
    "age": 4
}
```

Here, each key — name, breed, and so on — appears on a separate line followed by a colon and its value, making the code easier to read quickly.

Variable   Opening brace

```
dog2 = {
        "name": "Max",
        "breed": "Newfoundland",
        "weight": 130,
        "height": 30,
        "age": 4
    }
```

Keys ——

—— Values

Closing brace

You Access Dictionary Items by Key

To access an item in a dictionary, you specify the item's key. For example, to access the value for the breed key in the dog2 dictionary, you specify dog2["breed"].

Dictionaries Are Ordered in Python 3.7 Onward

Python 3.7 changed dictionaries from unordered collections to ordered collections. If you are using Python 3.6 or an earlier version, your code's dictionaries will be unordered — that is, the items in a dictionary will be in an order, but that order will not be fixed.

As long as you access your dictionary items by key, it makes little difference whether the dictionary items are ordered or unordered. But if you access your dictionary items by index position — for example, by creating a list of the dictionary's keys and using that to determine a key's position — you should be aware of the difference, because in Python 3.6 or earlier the items' index positions are likely to change.

Create a Dictionary and Return Values

When you need to store data in a container that enables you to look up elements of the data quickly and easily, create a dictionary and assign it to a variable. You enter the entire dictionary within braces, { }, using a colon to connect each key to its value and a comma to separate each key/value pair from the next pair.

You can then either display the entire dictionary — for example, to verify its contents and completeness — or return individual values by specifying their keys.

Create a Dictionary and Return Values

1 Open a terminal window and launch Python.

Ⓐ The Python prompt appears.

2 Type the following statement, which creates a variable named `dog3` and assigns to it a dictionary containing several canine attributes. Press `Enter` at the end of each line.

```
dog3 = {
    "name": "Belle",
    "breed": "Rottweiler",
    "weight": 125,
    "height": 26,
    "age": 8
    }
```

3 Type the following statement, which uses the `print()` function to display the entire `dog3` dictionary. Press `Enter`.

```
print(dog3)
```

Python displays the dictionary's keys and values on a single logical line, wrapped here:

```
{'name': 'Belle', 'breed':
'Rottweiler', 'weight': 125,
'height': 26, 'age': 8}
```

4 Type the following statement, which uses the `print()` function to display the `breed` key from the `dog3` dictionary. Press `Enter`.

```
print(dog3["breed"])
```

Python displays `Rottweiler`.

Meet Python's Dictionary Methods

Python provides 11 methods for working with dictionaries. Five of these methods — `fromkeys()`, `get()`, `items()`, `keys()`, and `values()` — enable you to retrieve information from a dictionary. On the other side of the coin, three methods — `pop()`, `popitem()`, and `clear()` — enable you to remove one or more entries from the dictionary. One method, `update()`, lets you insert key/value pairs. One method, `setdefault()`, does double duty, returning information if it is there and adding it if it is not. Finally, the `copy()` method enables you to copy an entire dictionary.

Table 11-3 explains Python's methods for working with dictionaries.

Table 11-3:	Methods for Working with Dictionaries
Method	**Use This Method To**
`clear()`	Remove all the key/value pairs from the dictionary.
`copy()`	Create a copy of the entire dictionary.
`fromkeys()`	Return a dictionary containing the specified keys and their values from this dictionary.
`get()`	Return the value of the specified key.
`items()`	Return a list containing a tuple for each key/value pair in the dictionary.
`keys()`	Return a list of the dictionary's keys, without their values.
`pop()`	Remove the items whose key you have specified.
`popitem()`	Remove the last key/value pair inserted in the dictionary.
`setdefault()`	Return the value of the specified key, if it exists; if it does not exist, insert the key and assign it the specified value.
`update()`	Insert the specified key/value pairs in the dictionary.
`values()`	Return a list of all the dictionary's values.

The following list provides quick examples of using these methods. You will use the methods more extensively during the remainder of this chapter:

- Return the keys from the `dog3` dictionary:
  ```
  >>> dog3.keys
  dict_keys(['name', 'breed', 'weight', 'height', 'age'])
  ```
- Insert a key/value pair, with the key id_chip, in the `dog3` dictionary:
  ```
  >>> dog3.update({"id_chip": "yes"})
  ```
- Return the value of the key coat, if it exists, and assign the given value if the key does not exist. In the first instance, the key does not exist, so Python creates it and assigns the value provided. In the second instance, the key exists, so Python returns the current value.
  ```
  >>> dog3.setdefault("coat", "short")
  'short'
  >>> dog3.setdefault("coat", "long")
  'short'
  ```

Create a Dictionary from an Existing Iterable

Python's `fromkeys()` method enables you to create a dictionary whose keys come from an existing iterable, such as a list, a set, or another dictionary. This way of creating a dictionary is convenient when you have an iterable that contains the data required for the keys in a new dictionary you want to create. The `fromkeys()` method lets you either assign the same value to each of the key/value pairs or not assign a value, leaving the values blank until you populate them otherwise.

Create a Dictionary from an Existing Iterable

1 Open a terminal window and launch Python.

Ⓐ The Python prompt appears.

2 Type the following statement, which creates a variable named `pet_factor` and assigns to it a list of factors to consider when choosing a pet. Press **Enter**.

```
pet_factor = ["space",
"character", "cost",
"interactivity"]
```

3 Type the following statement, which creates a variable named `considerations` and assigns to it a dictionary whose keys are derived by using the `fromkeys()` method on the `pet_factor` list. Press **Enter**.

```
considerations = dict.
fromkeys(pet_factor)
```

4 Type the following statement, which uses the `print()` function to display the contents of `considerations`. Press **Enter**.

```
print(considerations)
```

Python displays `{'space': None, 'character': None, 'cost': None, 'interactivity': None}`.

Note: Each key contains the value `None` because the `fromkeys()` method in step **3** did not assign a value to the keys.

① **Command Prompt - python** — □ ×

```
C:\Users\guy>python
Python 3.10.0 (tags/v3.10.0:b494f59, Oct  4 2021, 19:00:18)
 [MSC v.1929 64 bit (AMD64)] on win32
Type "help", "copyright", "credits" or "license" for more i
nformation.
>>> pet_factor = ["space", "character", "cost", "interactiv
ity"]
>>> 
```

Ⓐ ②

Command Prompt - python — □ ×

```
C:\Users\guy>python
Python 3.10.0 (tags/v3.10.0:b494f59, Oct  4 2021, 19:00:18)
 [MSC v.1929 64 bit (AMD64)] on win32
Type "help", "copyright", "credits" or "license" for more i
nformation.
>>> pet_factor = ["space", "character", "cost", "interactiv
ity"]
>>> considerations = dict.fromkeys(pet_factor)
>>> print(considerations)
{'space': None, 'character': None, 'cost': None, 'interacti
vity': None}
>>> 
```

③ ④

5 Type the following statement, which creates a variable named `pet_pros` and assigns to it a list of benefits of having a pet. Press Enter.

```
pet_pros = ["companionship",
"affection", "exercise", "memory",
"schedule"]
```

6 Type the following statement, which creates a variable called `cat` and assigns to it a dictionary whose keys are derived by using the `fromkeys()` method on the `pet_pros` list. The statement assigns a default value of `True` to each key. Press Enter.

```
cat = dict.fromkeys(pet_pros, True)
```

7 Type the following `print()` statement to display the contents of `cat`, and then press Enter:

```
print(cat)
```

Python displays `{'companionship': True, 'affection': True, 'exercise': True, 'memory': True, 'schedule': True}`.

You can now change the values of the keys, as needed.

```
Command Prompt                                  —  □  ×

C:\Users\guy>python
Python 3.10.0 (tags/v3.10.0:b494f59, Oct  4 2021, 19:00:18)
 [MSC v.1929 64 bit (AMD64)] on win32
Type "help", "copyright", "credits" or "license" for more i
nformation.
>>> pet_factor = ["space", "character", "cost", "interactiv
ity"]
>>> considerations = dict.fromkeys(pet_factor)
>>> print(considerations)
{'space': None, 'character': None, 'cost': None, 'interacti
vity': None}
>>> pet_pros = ["companionship", "affection", "exercise", "
memory", "schedule"]
>>> cat = dict.fromkeys(pet_pros, True)
>>>
```

```
Command Prompt                                  —  □  ×

C:\Users\guy>python
Python 3.10.0 (tags/v3.10.0:b494f59, Oct  4 2021, 19:00:18)
 [MSC v.1929 64 bit (AMD64)] on win32
Type "help", "copyright", "credits" or "license" for more i
nformation.
>>> pet_factor = ["space", "character", "cost", "interactiv
ity"]
>>> considerations = dict.fromkeys(pet_factor)
>>> print(considerations)
{'space': None, 'character': None, 'cost': None, 'interacti
vity': None}
>>> pet_pros = ["companionship", "affection", "exercise", "
memory", "schedule"]
>>> cat = dict.fromkeys(pet_pros, True)
>>> print(cat)
{'companionship': True, 'affection': True, 'exercise': True
, 'memory': True, 'schedule': True}
>>>
```

TIP

How do I use the `copy()` method with a dictionary?
Create a variable, and then use the `copy()` method to assign a copy of the dictionary to it. For example, if the variable `myD` contains a dictionary, you can use a statement such as `newD = myD.copy()` to create a new variable and copy the dictionary to it. The copy contains copies of the references from the original dictionary. Changes you make to the copy do not affect the original dictionary.

You can also use the assignment operator to copy a dictionary — for example, `newD = myD`. This approach creates a new reference to the original dictionary. Changes you make to the new dictionary, such as clearing its contents, affect the original dictionary.

Add Key/Value Pairs to a Dictionary

When you need to add one or more key/value pairs to a dictionary, use the update() method. You can either add the key/value pairs by providing their information directly or add them from an iterable object — for example, from another dictionary. The update() method places the new key/value pairs at the end of the dictionary.

You can also add a key/value pair to a dictionary by using the setdefault() method. If the key/value pair already exists, this method returns the current value. If the key/value pair does not exist, this method creates the pair and assigns the value you provide.

Add a Key/Value Pair to a Dictionary

1 Open a terminal window and launch Python.

A The Python prompt appears.

2 Type the following statement, which creates a variable named dog4 and assigns to it a dictionary containing a single key/value pair. Press **Enter**.

```
dog4 = {"name": "Rex"}
```

3 Type the following statement, which uses the update() method to add one key/value pair to dog4, and then press **Enter**:

```
dog4.update({"breed": "Newfoundland"})
```

4 Type the following print() statement, and then press **Enter**:

```
print(dog4)
```

Python displays {'name': 'Rex', 'breed': 'Newfoundland'}.

5 Type the following update() statement, which adds two more key/value pairs, and then press **Enter**:

```
dog4.update({"age": 5, "color": "black"})
```

6 Press ⬆ twice to enter the print() statement again, and then press **Enter**:

```
print(dog4)
```

Python displays {'name': 'Rex', 'breed': 'Newfoundland' , 'age': 5, 'color': 'black'}}.

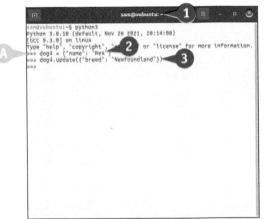

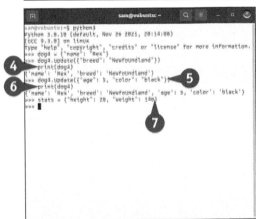

7 Type the following statement, which creates a variable named stats and assigns it a dictionary containing two key/value pairs. Press **Enter**.

```
stats = {"height": 28, "weight": 146}
```

⑧ Type the following statement, which uses the
update() method to insert the key/value pairs
from stats into dog4. Press Enter.

```
dog4.update(stats)
```

⑨ Press ↑ thrice to enter the print()
statement again, and then press Enter:

```
print(dog4)
```

Python displays {'name': 'Rex',
'breed': 'Newfoundland', 'age':
5, 'color': 'black', 'height':
28, 'weight': 146}.

⑩ Type the following statement, which uses the
setdefault() method to return the value
of the breed key, if it exists, and to create the
key/value pair if it does not. Press Enter.

```
dog4.setdefault("breed")
```

Python returns 'Newfoundland', because the
breed key does exist.

⑪ Type the following statement, which uses the
setdefault() method to return the value of
the temperament key, if it exists, and to create
the key/value pair if it does not. Press Enter.

```
dog4.setdefault("temperament",
"amiable")
```

Python returns 'amiable', which tells you that
the temperament key's value is amiable.

⑫ Type the following print() statement, which
displays the temperament key's value, and then
press Enter:

```
print(dog4["temperament"])
```

Python displays amiable.

TIP

What happens if I use the update() method for a key that exists?
If the key already exists, Python updates it with the new value you supplied.

Remove Key/Value Pairs from a Dictionary

Python provides three methods that enable you to remove key/value pairs from a dictionary. First, you can use the `pop()` method to remove an item by specifying its key. Second, you can use the `popitem()` method to remove the last key/value pair that was added to the dictionary; because Python places the newest key at the end of the dictionary, this method removes the last key and its value. Finally, you can use the `clear()` method to remove all keys and their values from the dictionary, leaving the dictionary empty.

Remove Key/Value Pairs from a Dictionary

1 Open a terminal window and launch Python.

Ⓐ The Python prompt appears.

2 Type the following statement, which creates a variable named `ocelot` and assigns to it a dictionary containing eight key/value pairs. Press Enter.

```
ocelot = {
... "Kingdom": "Animalia",
... "Phylum": "Chordata",
... "Class": "Mammalia",
... "Order": "Carnivora",
... "Suborder": "Feliformia",
... "Family": "Felidae",
... "Subfamily": "Felinae",
... "Genus": "Leopardus"
... }
```

3 Type the following statement, which uses the `popitem()` method to remove the last key/value pair. Press Enter.

```
ocelot.popitem()
```

Python displays `('Genus', 'Leopardus')` to indicate that it has removed the `Genus` key, whose value was `Leopardus`.

Note: In Python versions 3.6 and earlier, the `popitem()` method removes a random key/value pair from the dictionary rather than the last pair.

4 Type the following statement, which uses the `popitem()` method again but this time assigns the resulting tuple to a variable named `y`. Press Enter.

```
y = ocelot.popitem()
```

```
guy@Mac-Pro-2 ~ % python3
Python 3.10.0 (v3.10.0:b494f5935c, Oct  4 2021, 14:59:20) [Clang 1
2.0.5 (clang-1205.0.22.11)] on darwin
Type "help", "copyright", "credits" or "license" for more informat
ion.
>>> ocelot = {
... "Kingdom": "Animalia",
... "Phylum": "Chordata",
... "Class": "Mammalia",
... "Order": "Carnivora",
... "Suborder": "Feliformia",
... "Family": "Felidae",
... "Subfamily": "Felinae",
... "Genus": "Leopardus"
... }
>>>
```

```
guy@Mac-Pro-2 ~ % python3
Python 3.10.0 (v3.10.0:b494f5935c, Oct  4 2021, 14:59:20) [Clang 1
2.0.5 (clang-1205.0.22.11)] on darwin
Type "help", "copyright", "credits" or "license" for more informat
ion.
>>> ocelot = {
... "Kingdom": "Animalia",
... "Phylum": "Chordata",
... "Class": "Mammalia",
... "Order": "Carnivora",
... "Suborder": "Feliformia",
... "Family": "Felidae",
... "Subfamily": "Felinae",
... "Genus": "Leopardus"
... }
>>> ocelot.popitem()
('Genus', 'Leopardus')
>>> y = ocelot.popitem()
>>>
```

5 Type the following `print()` statement to display the contents of y. Press Enter.

`print(y)`

Python displays `('Subfamily', 'Felinae')`.

6 Type the following statement, which uses the `pop()` method to remove the `Class` key, and then press Enter:

`ocelot.pop("Class")`

Python displays `'Mammalia'` to indicate the value that was assigned to the key it has removed.

7 Type the following `print()` statement to display the contents of the `ocelot` dictionary as they now stand. Press Enter.

`print(ocelot)`

Python displays `{'Kingdom': 'Animalia', 'Phylum': 'Chordata', 'Order': 'Carnivora', 'Suborder': 'Feliformia', 'Family': 'Felidae'}`.

8 Type the following statement, which uses the `clear()` method to remove the dictionary's contents, and then press Enter:

`ocelot.clear()`

9 Press ⬆ twice to enter the `print()` statement again, and then press Enter:

`print(ocelot)`

Python displays `{}`, indicating that the dictionary is empty.

```
guy — Python — 66×29
guy@Mac-Pro-2 ~ % python3
Python 3.10.0 (v3.10.0:b494f5935c, Oct  4 2021, 14:59:20) [Clang 1
2.0.5 (clang-1205.0.22.11)] on darwin
Type "help", "copyright", "credits" or "license" for more informat
ion.
>>> ocelot = {
... "Kingdom": "Animalia",
... "Phylum": "Chordata",
... "Class": "Mammalia",
... "Order": "Carnivora",
... "Suborder": "Feliformia",
... "Family": "Felidae",
... "Subfamily": "Felinae",
... "Genus": "Leopardus"
... }
>>> ocelot.popitem()
('Genus', 'Leopardus')
>>> y = ocelot.popitem()
   print(y)
('Subfamily', 'Felinae')
>>> ocelot.pop("Class")
'Mammalia'
>>> print(ocelot)
```

```
guy — -zsh — 66×29
Python 3.10.0 (v3.10.0:b494f5935c, Oct  4 2021, 14:59:20) [Clang 1
2.0.5 (clang-1205.0.22.11)] on darwin
Type "help", "copyright", "credits" or "license" for more informat
ion.
>>> ocelot = {
... "Kingdom": "Animalia",
... "Phylum": "Chordata",
... "Class": "Mammalia",
... "Order": "Carnivora",
... "Suborder": "Feliformia",
... "Family": "Felidae",
... "Subfamily": "Felinae",
... "Genus": "Leopardus"
... }
>>> ocelot.popitem()
('Genus', 'Leopardus')
>>> y = ocelot.popitem()
>>> print(y)
('Subfamily', 'Felinae')
>>> ocelot.pop("Class")
'Mammalia'
>>> print(ocelot)
{'Kingdom': 'Animalia', 'Phylum': 'Chordata', 'Order': 'Carnivora'
, 'Suborder': 'Feliformia', 'Family': 'Felidae'}
>>> ocelot.clear()
>>> print(ocelot)
{}
>>>
```

TIP

What happens if I use the `pop()` method on a key that does not exist?
If the key does not exist, the `pop()` method causes Python to throw a `KeyError` error. The error includes the name of the missing key so you can easily identify the problem.

Return Keys and Values from a Dictionary

You can return a value from a dictionary by entering the corresponding key's name in brackets after the dictionary's name — for example, `dog1["breed"]` returns the value of the `breed` key in the dictionary called `dog1`. Alternatively, you can use the `get()` method to return the value for a specific key.

You can use the `keys()` method to return all of a dictionary's keys, use the `values()` method to return all its values, or use the `items()` method to return both the keys and the values. These three methods return views that update automatically when the dictionary's contents change.

Return Keys and Values from a Dictionary

1 Open a terminal window and launch Python.

A The Python prompt appears.

2 Type the following statement to create a variable called `dog5` and assign to it a dictionary containing a canine's key attributes. Press **Enter**.

```
dog5 = {
... "name": "Hondje",
... "breed": "Boerboel",
... "height": 24,
... "weight": 70
... }
```

3 Type the following statement, which uses the `get()` method to return the value of the `breed` key. Press **Enter**.

```
dog5.get("breed")
```

Python returns `'Boerboel'`.

4 Type the following statement, which uses the `keys()` method and displays all the keys in the `dog5` dictionary, and then press **Enter**:

```
print(dog5.keys())
```

Python displays `dict_keys(['name', 'breed', 'height', 'weight'])`.

Note: The `keys()` method returns a list containing the keys. Similarly, the `values()` method returns a list containing the values.

5 Type the following statement, which uses the `values()` method and displays all the values in the dog5 dictionary, and then press **Enter**:

`print(dog5.values())`

Python displays `dict_values(['Hondje', 'Boerboel', 24, 70])`.

6 Type the following statement, which creates a variable named q and assigns to it the result of using the `items()` method on the dog5 dictionary. Press **Enter**.

`q = dog5.items()`

Note: The `items()` method returns a list of tuples, each containing a key/value pair.

7 Type the following statement, which uses the `print()` function to display the contents of q. Press **Enter**.

`print(q)`

Python displays `dict_items([('name', 'Hondje'), ('breed', 'Boerboel'), ('height', 24), ('weight', 70)])`.

```
Command Prompt - python                                    —  □  ×
C:\Users\guy>python
Python 3.10.0 (tags/v3.10.0:b494f59, Oct  4 2021, 19:00:18)
 [MSC v.1929 64 bit (AMD64)] on win32
Type "help", "copyright", "credits" or "license" for more i
nformation.
>>> dog5 = {
...   "name": "Hondje",
...   "breed": "Boerboel",
...   "height": 24,
...   "weight": 70
... }
>>> dog5.get("breed")
'Boerboel'
>>> print(dog5.keys())
dict_keys(['name', 'breed', 'height', 'weight'])
>>> print(dog5.values())
dict_values(['Hondje', 'Boerboel', 24, 70])
>>> q = dog5.items()
>>>
```

```
Command Prompt                                             —  □  ×
C:\Users\guy>python
Python 3.10.0 (tags/v3.10.0:b494f59, Oct  4 2021, 19:00:18)
 [MSC v.1929 64 bit (AMD64)] on win32
Type "help", "copyright", "credits" or "license" for more i
nformation.
>>> dog5 = {
...   "name": "Hondje",
...   "breed": "Boerboel",
...   "height": 24,
...   "weight": 70
... }
>>> dog5.get("breed")
'Boerboel'
>>> print(dog5.keys())
dict_keys(['name', 'breed', 'height', 'weight'])
>>> print(dog5.values())
dict_values(['Hondje', 'Boerboel', 24, 70])
>>> q = dog5.items()
>>> print(q)
dict_items([('name', 'Hondje'), ('breed', 'Boerboel'), ('he
ight', 24), ('weight', 70)])
>>>
```

TIP

What does it mean that `keys()`, `values()`, and `items()` return view objects?
Using the `keys()` method, the `values()` method, or the `items()` method returns a view object, an object that gives you a view of the current data inside the dictionary. For example, say you execute the statement `dog6 = {"name": "Rover"}`, creating a dictionary named dog6 with one key/value pair. If you then execute the statement `n = dog6.items()`, n contains `dict_items([('name', 'Rover')])`. But if you then execute the statement `dog6["name"] = "Spot"`, changing the value of the name key in the dictionary, n now contains `dict_items([('name', 'Spot')])`, because the view gives you the current data from the dictionary.

## CHAPTER 12

Working with Classes

In this chapter, you work with Python's classes, which enable you to create custom objects in your scripts. You learn to create a class, create objects based on that class, and work with those objects. Because of the nature of classes, this chapter is set up as an extended example using Visual Studio Code rather than terminal windows, and we recommend you work through the chapter from start to end.

```python
class BranchOffice():
    company = "CheeseWheat Associates"
    sector = "food science"
    @classmethod
    def showClassInfo(self):
        ci = self.company + ", a "
        ci = ci + self.sector + " trendsetter"
        return ci
    def __init__(self, city, street, state, zip, manager):
        self.city = city
        self.street = street
        self.state = state
        self.zip = zip
        self.manager = manager
    def getInfo(self):
        br = (
            f"{self.city} Office\n\n"
            f"Manager: {self.manager}\n\n"
            f"{self.street}\n"
            f"{self.city}, {self.state}  {self.zip}"
        )
        return br
    @staticmethod
    def cm2cf(m3):

a = BranchOffice("Arcata", "442 Front", "CA", "95221-1111", "Aurora Smith")
```

Understanding Classes and Instances

In Python, a *class* is a template for creating objects of a particular type — a "class" of object, in computer terms. When you need to create standardized objects of the same type, you can declare a class for that type of object. You can then create what are called *instances* of the class — individual objects based on the class.

In this chapter, you create a class called `BranchOffice` to use for creating objects that store data on the individual branch offices of a notional company. After creating the class, you can create a separate instance for each branch office.

When Should You Create a Class?

Consider creating a class when you need to create consistent objects of a type that Python itself does not provide.

Classes are especially useful for *encapsulation*, using a single object both to store data and to provide functionality for manipulating that data. Creating a class makes encapsulation easy, as you can define attributes to store the data and construct methods to provide the necessary functionality.

How Do You Create a Class?

You create a class by using a class header statement. The class header begins with the `class` keyword. Next, it provides the name you want to give the class. Like other headers, the class header ends with a colon, after which the statements that belong to the class definition are indented by four spaces.

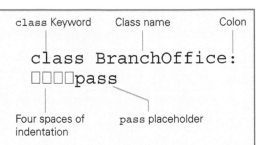

class Keyword   Class name   Colon

```
class BranchOffice:
    pass
```

Four spaces of indentation   pass placeholder

For example, the following class header creates the class called `BranchOffice`. The second statement, `pass`, is a placeholder indicating where code for the class will appear. As with other Python structures, the code for the class is indented by four spaces beyond the class header.

```
class BranchOffice:
    pass
```

How Are Python Class Names Usually Capitalized?

Python convention is to use a capital letter at the start of each word in the class — for example, `BranchOffice`. This capitalization style is sometimes called Pascal Case, named after the programming language Pascal, which in turn was named after the French mathematician and philosopher Blaise Pascal.

How Do You Create an Instance of a Class?

After creating a class, you can create an instance of the class, an object based on the class. Creating an instance is sometimes referred to as *instantiating* the instance.

To create an instance, you create a variable and assign an object based on the class. The following statement creates a variable named `a` and assigns to it an instance of the `BranchOffice` class:

`a = BranchOffice()`

The illustration shows the relationship between a class and instances of that class.

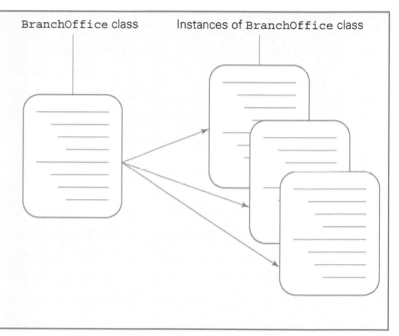

BranchOffice class   Instances of BranchOffice class

Create a Class and Instantiate Instances

In this section, you create the `BranchOffice` class, giving it the absolute minimum of code required for Python to run it without raising errors. You then create two instances of the `BranchOffice` class, verify their class type using the `type` function, and compare the two instances to prove that they are not the same object.

Because this chapter presents an extended example, we recommend you work in Visual Studio Code rather than in a terminal window. Using Visual Studio Code enables you to return easily to the code you have written so far and make changes to it without extensive retyping.

Create a Class and Instantiate Instances

1 Open Visual Studio Code and create a new Python script.

2 Type the following statement, which creates the `BranchOffice` class, and then press `Enter`:

```
class BranchOffice:
```

Visual Studio Code automatically indents the next line.

3 Type the following `pass` statement, which enables Python to run the class code without raising an error. Press `Enter` twice.

```
pass
```

4 Type the following statement, which creates a variable named `a` and assigns to it an instance of the `BranchOffice` class. Press `Enter`.

```
a = BranchOffice()
```

5 Type the following statement, which creates a variable named `b` and assigns to it another instance of the `BranchOffice` class. Press `Enter`.

```
b = BranchOffice()
```

6 Type the following statement, which uses the `type` function to retrieve the type of `a` and the `print()` function to display the result. Press `Enter`.

```
print(type(a))
```

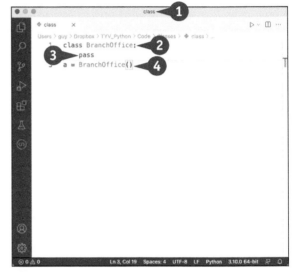

7 Type the following statement, which uses the `type` function to retrieve the type of b and the `print()` function to display the result. Press **Enter**.

```
print(type(b))
```

8 Type the following statement, which uses the `print()` statement to display the result of comparing a and b. Press **Enter**.

```
print(a == b)
```

9 Click **Run Python File in Terminal** (▷).

The Terminal pane appears.

Ⓐ Python displays the object types of a and b. Each object is of the following type:

```
<class '__main__.BranchOffice'>
```

Ⓑ Python displays `False` as the result of the a == b comparison. This indicates that a and b are not the same object, even though they are of the same object type. Similarly, if you have two quarters in your pocket, they are equal in that they have the same value, but they are separate coins, not the same coin.

TIP

What does comparing the a object and the b object prove?

Checking whether a `==` b — in other words, whether a is equal to b — enables you to see that these two objects created from the same class are not identical. If you compare a to itself — for example, `print(a == a)` — Python returns `True`; likewise if you compare b to itself.

Understanding Class and Instance Attributes

Once you have created a class, Python enables you to set two types of attributes related to it: class attributes and instance attributes. In this section, you learn the difference between class attributes and instance attributes and how to create both types. You also learn about the __init__() method of the class object, a special method that runs automatically when you create a new instance from a class, and the self keyword, which Python uses to refer in code to an object itself.

Given that a class is a template that defines an object type and that an instance of a class is an object that uses that class as its template, you can quickly grasp the difference between class attributes and instance attributes.

- **Class attribute.** A *class attribute* applies to the class as a whole, so every instance of the class has the same information for the attribute. Any changes you make to the attribute apply to the entire class. You can access a class attribute either through the class itself or through any instance of the class.

- **Instance attribute.** An *instance attribute* applies only to a particular instance of a class, not to the class as a whole. Any changes you make to an instance attribute are confined to that instance. You can access the attribute only through that instance.

Understanding How You Set Class Attributes

To set a class attribute, you place a statement in the class definition block. After the class header and indented by four spaces as usual, you create a variable for the attribute and then assign the appropriate data to it.

For example, the following statements show the BranchOffice class header followed by a statement that creates the variable company and assigns to it a company name.

```python
class BranchOffice:
    company = "CheeseWheat Associates"
```

Understanding How You Set Instance Attributes

To set an instance attribute, you use the __init__() method of the class object. After the class header, and indented by four spaces, place the header for the __init__() method. The header

Class header

```
class BranchOffice:
    def __init__(self, address, manager)
```

Four spaces of indentation   def keyword   __init__() method name   self keyword   Instance attributes

consists of the def keyword, the __init__() name, the self parameter, and the name of each instance attribute you want to set. For example, the following method header provides the names address and manager:

```
class BranchOffice:
    def __init__(self, address, manager):
```

The self parameter refers to the current instance of the class — the instance that is being initialized by the __init__() method. The word self is the default term for this parameter, and it is usually easiest to use self. However, you can use a different word instead of self if you prefer. No matter which word you use, you must supply it as the first parameter of any function you define in the class.

After specifying the names of the instance attributes in the __init__() method header, you can set the values for these attributes, as in the following example:

```
class BranchOffice:
    def __init__(self, address, manager):
        self.address = address
        self.manager = manager
```

Set Class and Instance Attributes

In this section, you extend the `BranchOffice` class by setting class attributes and instance attributes for it. To set the class attributes, you include statements in the class definition block. To set the instance attributes, you add code for the class's `__init__()` method. The method's name has two underscores before it and two after it.

The class attributes for the `BranchOffice` class are `company` and `sector`. The instance attributes for the instances of the `BranchOffice` class are `manager`, `street`, `city`, `state`, and `zip`.

Set Class and Instance Attributes

1 In Visual Studio Code, open the script you created earlier.

2 Double-click the `pass` statement in line 2 to select it, and then type over it the following statement, which creates the variable `company` and assigns to it the company name. Press Enter.

```
company = "CheeseWheat Associates"
```

Note: When you replace the `pass` statement, make sure you maintain the indentation for the `company` statement.

3 Type the following statement, which creates the variable `sector` and assigns a string to it. Press Enter.

```
sector = "food science"
```

4 Type the following statement, which uses the `def` keyword to create the `__init__()` method for the class. The statement gives `self` as the required first argument and adds five instance attributes: `city`, `street`, `state`, `zip`, and `manager`. Press Enter.

```
def __init__(self, city, street,
state, zip, manager):
```

Note: Type two underscores before `init` and two after it.

5 Type the following statement, which assigns to the `city` attribute of the `self` object the value passed by the `city` argument in the call to initialize the class. Press Enter.

```
self.city = city
```

6 Type the following four statements, which similarly populate the street, state, zip, and manager attributes of the self object. Press **Enter** at the end of each line.

```
self.street = street
self.state = state
self.zip = zip
self.manager = manager
```

7 Click inside the parentheses of the a = BranchOffice() statement, and then type in strings for the five instance attributes.

```
a = BranchOffice("Arcata", "442 Front",
"CA", "95521-1111", "Aurora Smith")
```

Note: You do not need to provide a value for the self attribute.

8 Repeat step **7** for the b = BranchOffice() statement:

```
b = BranchOffice("Blythe", "6 Lincoln",
"CA", "92225-1234", "Art Kimura")
```

9 Select the five print() statements, and then type over them the five following statements, pressing **Enter** at the end of each line:

```
print(a.manager)
print(a.street)
print(a.city)
print(a.state)
print(a.zip)
```

10 Click **Run Python File in Terminal** (▷).

The Terminal pane opens.

A Python displays the information from the instance attributes of the a object.

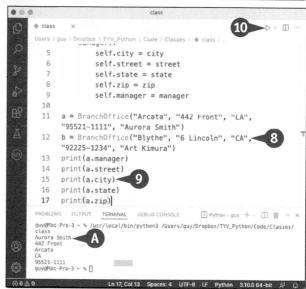

TIPS

Must I assign an initial value to a class attribute?
Yes, each class attribute must receive an initial value. But you can assign None as an initial value if you do not have an actual value to assign.

How do I return a class attribute?
Use the class name, a period, and the attribute name. For example, print(BranchOffice.company) displays the company attribute of the BranchOffice class.

Grasp Class, Instance, and Static Methods

A *method* is a unit of code that performs an action on an object. A method is similar to a function, but it is bound to a particular object rather than being globally available. Python enables you to create and use three different types of methods within a class: class methods, instance methods, and static methods. In this section, you learn how these three types of methods work and how they differ from each other. You also learn how and when to use each type of method.

A class can contain class methods, instance methods, and static methods. You create any methods needed when you define the class, including the methods' code as part of the class definition.

Class Methods

A *class method* belongs to the class object that declares it. A class method can access only data within the class itself, not data within any particular instance of the class. A class method can change the data in the class.

You would create a class method to take action in the class, such as changing the class's state.

Instance Methods

An *instance method* belongs to a particular instance created from the class object that declares the method. An instance method can access data within that instance, but it cannot access data within other instances created from the same class object. An instance method can also access data within the class itself by using the `self.__class__` attribute.

You would create an instance method to take action within a particular instance of the class, accessing data from within the class itself if necessary.

Static Methods

A *static method* is bound to the class that declares it but cannot change the data in the class; it also cannot access, let alone change, the data in an instance based on the class. A static method is similar to a function except that it belongs to the class's namespace and becomes available only when you create the class.

You would create a static method to add functionality that was needed only when the class or an instance of the class was active and that did not require access to the data of either the class or the instance.

Which Type of Method Should You Use in Your Classes?

Generally speaking, instance methods are the most widely useful of the three types of methods bound to classes, because an instance method can manipulate data either in its own instance or in the class on which the instance is based. By contrast, a class method can manipulate data only in its own class; and a static method cannot even access data within its own class, though it can perform other actions freely.

When you create a method inside a class definition, Python makes the method an instance method by default. You can change the method to a class method or an instance method if necessary.

The following sections show you how to create and call instance methods, class methods, and static methods.

Create an Instance Method

To create an instance method, you place code inside the class definition. The first line of the instance method is the method head, which consists of the def keyword, the method name, parentheses containing the required parameter self and any other parameters, and a colon. For example, the first of the following statements starts the class definition, the second is a comment, and the third contains the method header for an instance method called getManagerName:

```
class BranchOffice():
    # the def __init__ function appears here
    def getManagerName(self):
```

After the method header, you include the statements for the method, indented by four spaces. Here is an example:

```
class BranchOffice():
    # the def __init__ function appears here
    def getManagerName(self):
        mgr = f"{self.city} Office Manager: {self.manager}"
        return mgr
```

Call an Instance Method

You can call an instance method only from an instance of the class. For example, the first of the following statements creates a variable named c and assigns to it an instance of our BranchOffice class. The second statement calls the getManagerName() method and displays the resulting information.

```
c = BranchOffice("City of Industry", "1810 Elm", "CA", "91748-0019", "Ri Zhang")
print(c.getManagerName())
```

continued ▶

Grasp Class, Instance, and Static Methods (continued)

Python provides two different ways of creating class methods and static methods. The first way is to use the @classmethod decorator for a class method or the @staticmethod decorator for a static method. The second way is to use the classmethod() method or the staticmethod() method. Both ways work, and you should know how to use them, because you may encounter them in code. However, the classmethod() method and staticmethod() method are considered "un-Pythonic," and using the decorators is considered better practice.

Create a Class Method

To create a class method, you place code inside the class definition, as for an instance method. But before the method header for the class method, you place the @classmethod decorator. This decorator tells Python to turn the method into a class method.

For example, the first of the following statements starts the class definition, and the second is a comment, as before. The third statement supplies the @classmethod decorator. The fourth statement is the method header for the showClassInfo method. The fifth line is the method's only statement, setting it to return a string including self.company, the company attribute of the class object.

```
class BranchOffice():
    # the def __init__ function appears here
    @classmethod
    def showClassInfo(self):
        return "Company Name: " + self.company
```

You can also create a class method by using the classmethod() method to return a class method from an instance method. For example, if you have created an instance method called info() in the BranchOffice class, you can create a class method of info() like this:

```
BranchOffice.info = classmethod(BranchOffice.info)
```

You can then call the info() method through the BranchOffice class like this:

```
BranchOffice.info()
```

Call a Class Method

You can call a class method either from the class itself or from an instance of the class.

From the class, use the class name followed by a period and the method name, like this:

```
print(BranchOffice.showClassInfo())
```

From an instance of the class, use the instance name followed by a period and the method name. For example, if you have created an instance called c, you can call the class method like this:

```
print(c.showClassInfo())
```

Create a Static Method

You create a static method in a similar way to a class method: You place the method's code inside the class definition, but you precede it with the @staticmethod decorator, which tells Python to turn the method into a static method.

For example, the first statement shown in the following code block starts the class definition, the second contains a comment, and the third provides the @staticmethod decorator. The fourth statement is the method header for the cm2cf method, which returns the approximate number of cubic feet for the number of cubic meters specified by the m3 parameter. The fifth line is the method's only statement, setting it to return m3 multiplied by 35.3, the number of cubic feet in a cubic meter.

```
class BranchOffice():
    # the def __init__ function appears here
    @staticmethod
    def cm2cf(m3):
        return m3 * 35.3
```

As with a class method, you can create a static method by using the staticmethod() method to return a static method from an instance method. For example, if you have created an instance method called convert() in the BranchOffice class, you can create a static method of convert() like this:

```
BranchOffice.convert = staticmethod(BranchOffice.convert)
```

Call a Static Method

To call a static method, you call it either via the class name and the method name or via the object name and the method name.

For example, say you have instantiated an object called office1 of the BranchOffice class. The class includes the static method jp. You can call the static method via the class like this:

```
BranchOffice.jp()
```

Or you can call the static method via the object like this:

```
office1.jp()
```

Create an Instance Method

In this section, you create an instance method called `getInfo()` in the `BranchOffice` class. This instance method pulls information from the instance's attributes, such as the `city` attribute and the `manager` attribute, so that it can return an f-string containing information about the branch office the instance represents.

In an instance method, the first parameter refers to the instance itself. The default term for this parameter is `self`; it is generally easiest and clearest to use `self`, but you can use a different term instead if you prefer.

Create an Instance Method

1 In Visual Studio Code, open the Python script for your class.

2 Click the line after the end of the `__init__()` method, press `Tab` to apply a four-space indent, and type the following statement, which declares the `getInfo()` method and gives it the required `self` parameter. Press `Enter`.

```
def getInfo(self):
```

Python automatically indents the next line one step further.

3 Type the following statement, which creates the variable `br` and begins assigning to it a group of f-strings that pull information from the instance attributes and combine it with static text. Press `Enter` at the end of each line.

```
br = (
    f"{self.city} Office\n\n"
```

4 Type the following three statements, which add to the group of f-strings:

```
    f"Manager: {self.manager}\n\n"
    f"{self.street}\n"
    f"{self.city}, {self.state} {self.zip}"
)
```

5 Press `Backspace` to unindent one step, and then type the following return statement, which returns `br`:

```
return br
```

6 Select the five `print()` statements, and type the following `print()` statement over them:

```
print(a.getInfo())
```

7 Click **Run Python File in Terminal** (▷).

The Terminal pane opens.

Ⓐ Python displays the branch office information.

274

Create a Class Method

In this section, you create a class method called `showClassInfo()` in the `BranchOffice` class. This class method returns the class's `company` attribute and `sector` attribute and places them in an f-string that it returns to the code that called it.

To create the class method, this section uses the `@classmethod` decorator rather than the `classmethod()` method. The first parameter in the class header refers to the class itself. This section uses the default term for this parameter, `self`, but you can use a different term if you like.

Create a Class Method

1 In Visual Studio Code, open the Python script for your class.

2 Click after the `sector = "food science"` line, and then press Enter to create a new line.

3 Type the following `@classmethod` decorator, and then press Enter:

`@classmethod`

4 Type the following method header, and then press Enter:

`def showClassInfo(self):`

Visual Studio Code indents the next line automatically.

5 Type the following two statements, which create a variable named `ci` and assign to it the class's `company` attribute and `sector` attribute plus some linking text. Press Enter.

```
ci = self.company + ", a "
ci = ci + self.sector + " trendsetter"
```

6 Type the following statement, which ends the method and returns `ci`. Press Enter.

`return ci`

7 At the end of the script, edit the `print()` statement to the following:

`print(BranchOffice.showClassInfo())`

8 Click **Run Python File in Terminal** (▷).

The Terminal pane opens.

Ⓐ The class method displays the class information.

Create a Static Method

In this section, you create a static method in the `BranchOffice` class. The method is called `cm2cf()` and converts cubic meters to cubic feet. The method takes a single argument, `m3`, which gives the number of cubic meters, and returns the corresponding number of cubic feet. Because a static method accesses neither the class nor any instance of it, it does not use the `self` parameter.

This section uses the `@staticmethod` decorator rather than the `staticmethod()` method to tell Python to create the static method.

Create a Static Method

1 In Visual Studio Code, open the Python script for your class.

2 Click on the blank line following the `return br` statement at the end of the `getInfo()` method, and then press `Tab` to indent the line by one step.

3 Type the following `@staticmethod` decorator, and then press `Enter`:

```
@staticmethod
```

4 Type the following method header, and then press `Enter`:

```
def cm2cf(m3):
```

Python indents the next line by another step.

5 Type the following `return` statement, which returns a string including the `m3` value multiplied by `35.3` and lightly rounded. Press `Enter` twice.

```
return str(round(m3 * 35.3, 1)) + " cubic feet"
```

6 At the end of the script, change the `print()` statement to the following, which prompts the user to enter the number of cubic meters, converts the resulting string to a float, passes it to the `cm2cf` method, and displays the result.

```
print(BranchOffice.cm2cf(float(input
("Enter the number of cubic meters: "))))
```

7 Click **Run Python File in Terminal** (▷).

The Terminal pane opens.

8 Type the input number and press `Enter`.

A The result appears.

Review the Class's Code

This section presents the code for the class you have created in this chapter. The class starts with the class definition (A), followed by statements defining the class attributes `company` (B) and `sector` (C). The `@classmethod` decorator (D) precedes the `showClassInfo()` class method. The `__init__()` method (E) declares and populates variables for each new instance of the class. The `getInfo()` instance method (F) displays information about a particular instance. The `@staticmethod` decorator (G) introduces the `cm2cf()` static method, which converts cubic meters to cubic feet. The code then instantiates two instances (H) of the class, and the `print()` statement (I) displays information.

```python
class BranchOffice:
    company = "CheeseWheat Associates"
    sector = "food science"
    @classmethod
    def showClassInfo(self):
        ci = self.company + ", a "
        ci = ci + self.sector + " trendsetter"
        return ci
    def __init__(self, city, street, state, zip, manager):
        self.city = city
        self.street = street
        self.state = state
        self.zip = zip
        self.manager = manager
    def getInfo(self):
        br = (
            f"{self.city} Office\n\n"
            f"Manager: {self.manager}\n\n"
            f"{self.street}\n"
            f"{self.city}, {self.state}  {self.zip}"
        )
        return br
    @staticmethod
    def cm2cf(m3):
        return str(round(m3 * 35.3, 1)) + " cubic feet"
a = BranchOffice("Arcata", "442 Front", "CA", "95221-1111",
"Aurora Smith")
b = BranchOffice("Blythe", "6 Lincoln", "CA", "92225-1234",
"Art Kimura")
print(BranchOffice.cm2cf(float(input("Enter the number of
cubic meters: "))))
```

Index

A

B

C

Index